About Island Press

Island Press is the only nonprofit organization in the United States whose principal purpose is the publication of books on environmental issues and natural resource management. We provide solutions-oriented information to professionals, public officials, business and community leaders, and concerned citizens who are shaping responses to environmental problems.

In 1994, Island Press celebrated its tenth anniversary as the leading provider of timely and practical books that take a multidisciplinary approach to critical environmental concerns. Our growing list of titles reflects our commitment to bringing the best of an expanding body of literature to the environmental community throughout North America and the world.

Support for Island Press is provided by Apple Computer, Inc., The Bullitt Foundation, The Geraldine R. Dodge Foundation, The Energy Foundation, The Ford Foundation, The W. Alton Jones Foundation, The Lyndhurst Foundation, The John D. and Catherine T. MacArthur Foundation, The Andrew W. Mellon Foundation, The Joyce Mertz-Gilmore Foundation, The National Fish and Wildlife Foundation, The Pew Charitable Trusts, The Pew Global Stewardship Initiative, The Rockefeller Philanthropic Collaborative, and individual donors.

Lost Landscapes and Failed Economies

Lost Landscapes and Failed Economies

The Search for a Value of Place

Thomas Michael Power

ISLAND PRESS
Washington, D.C.
Covelo, California

© 1996 Island Press

Island Press is a trademark of The Center for Resource Economics.

Library of Congress Cataloging-in-Publication Data

Power, Thomas M.
   Lost landscapes and failed economies : the search for a value of place / by Thomas Michael Power.
      p.   cm.
   Includes bibliographical references and index.
   ISBN 1-55963-368-9 (cloth : acid-free paper)
   1. Mineral industries—United States.   2. Environmental protection—Economic aspects—United States.   3. Sustainable development—United States.   I. Title.
HD9506.U62P69   1996
333.8—dc20   95-32365
                                                   CIP

Printed on recycled, acid-free paper ∞ ✿

Manufactured in the United States of America

10   9   8   7   6   5   4   3

To the two young people who have brought challenge, diversity, inspiration, and confusion into my life, to my children, Kate Marias Shore and Donovan Spear Power, this book is gratefully dedicated. They have kept me young and taken years off of my life. May we act now to see that they, their children, and all future generations continue to be supported by nature's beauty, challenge, and complexity.

Contents

Preface

This book seeks to persuade readers that there is something counter-productive, even dangerous, about the way we usually think and talk about our local economies. In the eyes of some, especially fellow academicians, my purpose may not fit with the role of the disinterested observer that university researchers are often expected to play. Advocacy is frowned on in most academic circles; one should pursue the facts and let them speak for themselves.

To the charge of advocacy, I plead guilty. To the claim that advocacy undermines the pursuit of useful knowledge, I take strong exception.

The focus here is on how people think about the local economy. There are competing modes of thought: the one, a popular folk economics shared by most noneconomists and the other, an approach built around the research of academic economists. This book seeks to convince people that folk economics is incomplete, distracting, and seriously misleading. Not surprisingly, it often supports certain political and economic interests. That having been said, it should be added that folk economics also expresses important elements of economic truth.

Though this book responds to the bias embodied in folk economics, it is not simply an exercise in ideological argument. It is, however, quite consciously rhetorical. Economic science is necessarily rhetorical in the sense that it aims to persuade people that a particular way of looking at the world is more useful, more satisfying, more aesthetically appealing, or better contributes to our overall understanding of the world around us (McCloskey, 1985). Science cannot be limited to statements of fact, logical or mathematical proofs, or reports on carefully controlled laboratory experiments. Ideally, science strives to help people see things and make connections that were not visible before. This book endeavors to do just that.

To the extent that this book succeeds, it does so by drawing upon the theoretical and empirical literature of conventional academic economics to show that folk economics not only misleads the public; it distorts local economic policy. Most academic economists will find nothing new here, although the focus and application may strike them as interesting. Because today's professional economists tend to focus on issues of regional, national, or international importance, they have largely withdrawn from the parochial fray of local economic development policy. It is in the void created by this withdrawal that folk economics has developed and come to dominate. As the pages that follow confront the folk economic vision, what may seem heretical to many noneconomists will be old hat to economists. For this reason, I ask that economists bear with me in my attempt to present a more informed view of the local economy than has prevailed recently in popular economic dialogue. Carrying the fruits of economic research into the economic debates within our local communities can only improve the quality of the decisions made there and, with that, the qualify of life.

Some, notably leaders of Montana's extractive industries, will be surprised that this book was produced by an employee of the Montana State Government, albeit a professor at the state's flagship university. At most public universities in the West professors whose research carries them into controversial areas are informed, officially or by less explicit means, that they are risking their own and other researchers' funds. The pressure of this threat in the field of economics has the effect of diluting the very technical expertise that public universities should be providing their communities to enable a smoother adjustment to a changing economy. Knowledge is diverted to less relevant but safer topics.

It is impressive that the University of Montana and the citizens of Montana have had a more independent view of the mission of higher education. Citizens, after bitter experience with the political pressure that mining companies were bringing to bear on the university system, rewrote their state constitution to guarantee the autonomy of Montana's institutions of higher learning. Before that happened, the University of Montana had begun to develop a strong commitment to academic freedom. By the time I arrived in 1968, there was a passionate commitment to critical inquiry on the campus and a somewhat bemused acceptance by the citizenry of all that that entailed.

And so I would like to take this opportunity to thank the citizens of Montana for their commitment to freedom of inquiry. I would also like to thank the University administration for shielding me from the vocal complaints and political pressure that many powerful interests in the state brought to bear on the University of Montana. No administrator ever hinted that I should change the focus of my research, or my conclusions, or the way I was presenting my results. University administrators handled the emotional and politically charged arguments leveled at them and at the faculty, explaining that critical analysis, even if disconcerting, is one of the primary functions of a university.

Without the University of Montana's Wilderness and Civilization program this book could not have been written. The program, run by the Wilderness Institute of the School of Forestry for almost two decades, has given me the opportunity to teach a long-standing course on the economics of wildland preservation. The eager and critical students in that program contributed significantly to the development of the analysis in these pages.

I would also like to acknowledge the support of colleagues both on campus and off. In the Economics Department, Becky Hanway helped enormously with the organization and graphics. Richard Barret played the role of watchdog, protecting the English language and alerting me to conceptual errors. Doug Dalenberg helped save me from statistical distortion. Off campus, Jeff Olson of the Ford Foundation was supportive and critical, both in a productive way. Ray Rasker in the Bozeman office of the Wilderness Society gave me the gift of his long experience. And the support and assistance of George Darrow, an advocate of economic sanity and forward thinking in the State of Montana, is much appreciated.

Finally, my thanks to Sophie Engelhard Craighead, the Engelhard Foundation, and the Craighead Wildlands and Wildlife Institute for providing the financial support that ultimately allowed me to bring this book to a successful conclusion. For close to half a century, the Craighead family has been a strong voice for environmental sense not just in Montana but worldwide. They have consistently provided inspirational examples of good science devoted to the public interest.

Of course, none of these people or institutions can be blamed for any error or confusion that might remain in the pages that follow. I ask for advice, but I do not always take it!

Lost Landscapes and Failed Economies

Introduction

Conflict over environmental issues continues to build across the United States. In our nonmetropolitan areas, politics is still personal and natural resources still play an important economic role, so that at times the conflict resembles a civil war. Combatants see a lot at stake. On the environmental side, animal species that once symbolized huge ecosystems—the grizzly bear, the salmon, and the wolf—are on the verge of extinction, and mountain rivers, deserts, and prairies face the threat of irreparable modification. On the resource-industry side, ways of life that have supported generations of families are threatened: logging, mining, and farming, and the manufacturing activities built around them.

With so much permanently at stake, it is not surprising that emotions run strong. Both sides have been mobilizing resources for a struggle to the end. Consider the magnitude of some conflicts:

- The survival of the northern spotted owl and many other species depends on the protection of a significant portion of the remnants of the temperate rain forest that once covered the Pacific Northwest. But these ancient forests also contain the raw material for what was once the dominant industry in the region, timber. Industry spokespersons have argued that over a hundred thousand jobs are at stake. So is the economic stability of a tristate area, western Washington, Oregon, and northern California. Environmentalists point out that most of this unique rain-forest ecosystem has already been destroyed and that the rest is about to go.[1]

- The complex set of dams on the Columbia River has virtually halted the successful migration and reproduction of once-abundant stocks of wild salmon. What was formerly the dominant food supply for the indigenous people of the area, an important commercial industry, and a major recreational resource has virtually been wiped out. Salmon recovery probably depends on a major change in the Columbia's hydroelectric, irrigation, and shipping systems. Some dams may need to be removed or radically modified. To those who work in the electric-energy-intensive-metals, and chemical industries, or who make their living using cheap electricity to pump river water to crops growing in the high deserts of the area, proposals to protect salmon are like news of impending layoffs. To environmentalists, it is a matter of saving the river from biological death.[2]

- Cattle grazing in the arid West has led to the degradation of plant cover, soil, and most important, streams, so that public lands cannot support fisheries, wildlife, and recreation. Environmentalists want to stop the damage by restricting grazing in public areas. In addition, they support the recovery of endangered wildlife that are seen as directly or indirectly threatening domestic livestock: the wolf, grizzly bear, eagle, and black-footed ferret. Ranchers interpret this as a direct assault on their way of life and on their traditional right to use public land for livestock production as they see fit.

- An increase in gold prices during the 1970s and new extraction technologies have made feasible the mining of ores that contain only hundredths of a percent of precious metal. To extract useful ores, mountains have to be completely dismantled and valleys filled with waste. Yawning open pits and ravaged landscapes are the result. Mining interests insist that national security, low wages, and high unemployment make such mining crucial to the well-being of rural areas. Environmentalists point to the toxic legacy from mining, which has left Superfund sites stretching along hundreds of miles of rivers and streams and done irreparable damage to the landscape.

These are just a few of the dramatic conflicts between natural resource industries and environmental advocates in our rural areas. Rural economies often rely upon industries that extract from the earth the basic raw materials they use. Those industries, referred to as extractive in this book, include agriculture, minerals, forest products, and fishing. Because, on the surface, environmental protection appears to restrict such economic activity, an energetic antienvironmental movement has sprung up to battle it. "Wise use" and "grass roots for multiple use" groups, with ample funding from natural resource industries, have launched campaigns across the country to "take back" control over public land from federal agencies and from the environmental interests they see as having undue influence. Some of these groups have convinced local and state governments to try and open public land to extractive economic activity, and they have pushed through local and county ordinances requiring federal authorities to manage the land in a manner consistent with local "custom and culture," that is, with past extractive activity. In addition, efforts have been made requiring that any private citizen whose economic activities have been harmed by government regulation be fully compensated. Drawing on the constitutional protection against government taking of property without just compensation, wise-use groups argue that environmental restrictions limiting grazing or mining or logging or irrigation amount to a "taking" of peoples' livelihoods. The hope is that the government will not be able to afford environmental regulations.

Grassroots organizations on both sides—those that seek to preserve the landscape, and those that seek its continued exploitation—are locked in an increasingly acrimonious struggle that has promoted violence or threats of violence from the anti-environmental side.[3] The "militia" movement is one manifestation of this. Communities, local organizations, and local governments are splitting into hostile camps. Extractive industries have a vested interest in convincing communities that their economic future is tied exclusively to extractive activities. Even if most of a community would like to protect the natural landscape, when they are told that doing so would mean job loss and foreclosed homes, only a few self-sacrificing environmental heros are likely to support protection measures.

If we could lay to rest the fear that environmental protection will cause the imminent economic collapse of communities, the acrimony would subside and it would be much easier to engage in civil discourse over the real choices communities face. For that reason, it is important to examine two issues: first, the role actually played by extractive industry in local communities, and second, the impact that protected landscapes are likely to have on local economies. In fact, extractive industry does not play as central a role in local economies as many assume. In addition, to the extent that protected landscapes actually support local economic vitality, the choices "extractive-dependent" communities face, as well as their likely futures, are drastically altered. Neither the present nor the future are quite so grim.

A popular folk economics teaches us that the extraction and

processing of natural resources are the heart of economic development, that "all wealth springs from the earth." That view is incomplete and misleading. It assumes that people can afford to live in a particular area only because of the income brought into the local economy by the extraction and exportation of local raw materials or products manufactured from them. Two economic assumptions underpinning this model we know to be false: first, that people do not care where they live (or, at least, not very much), and second, that businesses do not care about the available labor supply.

The massive shifts in America's population and economic activity since World War II challenge both of these assumptions. People seeking higher-quality residential environments (suburbs, the Sunbelt, nonmetropolitan areas) and businesses seeking lower-cost labor have transformed the nation's economic geography. It should be possible, then, to construct an "environmental model" of local economic development in which people's preferences for certain surroundings lead to a redistribution of economic activity. From this perspective, protected landscape is a central part of the local economic base. People do care where they live. Because of this, and because businesses care where labor supplies and markets are located, desirable environments are likely to have an economic worth of their own unrelated to the extractive potential of the landscape. In fact, their economic worth may depend on restricting the environmental havoc wreaked by extraction.

This should prompt a fundamental shift in the economic role we envision for our natural landscapes. Increasingly, nature should be viewed not as a warehouse of raw materials but rather as the precious backdrop that makes an area's living environment desirable. Over the past three decades, the resettlement of many of America's nonmetropolitan areas—the West, the South, parts of New England and Appalachia—has been motivated by precisely this attitude.

Meanwhile, familiar arguments about local prosperity depending almost exclusively on ongoing extraction are increasingly dubious. First, despite the high wages often associated with mining, lumber, and farming, few towns devoted to these industries are prosperous. In fact, the more dependent a community is on one such industry, the more depressed it tends to be. Specialization rarely leads to the prosperity communities are promised. Second, over the last decade and a half, extractive industries have been in relative decline, providing a smaller and smaller percentage of both jobs and income. Yet during this same period of decline, many "extractive-dependent" communities experienced rapid economic expansion in nonextractive sectors. This calls for some explanation.

Empirical analysis shows that mining, timber, and agriculture make a much more modest contribution to local economies than is usually assumed. The ongoing transformation of local economies, including technological and market changes, has drastically reduced the relative importance of such industries. As a result, rather than being a source of economic vitality they are likely to play a declining and destabilizing role in local economies in the future.

Once the preservation of natural landscapes is seen as an economic act enhancing the local economic base rather than only an ethical or aesthetic act, the polemics of extraction versus environment should change. The issue is not sacrificing economic health to protect some obscure bird, fish, or plant, but rather ensuring economic health by avoiding needless damage to the natural—and therefore human—environment. Environmental protection and extractive industry are both economic activities that can contribute to local economic well-being. Both generate needed jobs and income. To the extent that the two unavoidably conflict, a choice needs to be made as to which should be partially sacrificed in the pursuit of the community's long-run interests.

The long-run economic health of the community may, at times, require that the natural landscape, part of the community's permanent economic base, not be sacrificed to stopgap measures to maintain extractive employment at past levels. Such a decision may actually result in a net gain in employment. In many cases it is quite possible that job losses on the extractive side are more than compensated for by employment gains resulting from protecting the attractiveness of our communities and the landscapes in which they are embedded. In this situation, we face not a choice between protecting jobs and protecting the environment but rather, a choice about how best to protect the community's long-run economic vitality.

Thinking About the Local Economy

Most of us remember the maps in our geography books that associated regions with particular types of economic activity. On a map of the United States there would be an icon of a blast furnace at Pittsburgh, an automobile at Detroit, corn in Iowa, beer at Milwaukee, and cotton in the Deep South. Geographically specialized economic activities presumably explained why people settled and lived where they did.

The theory behind this view, the economic base model, argues that for people to inhabit an area they need money to purchase from the larger, external economy those things that cannot easily be produced locally. And to earn money, they must successfully market some exportable product. Exports give them the money to pay for the imports that make life in a particular location viable. Spending on locally oriented economic activities such as child care, restaurants, and grocery stores depends on income earned in export sectors. Export-oriented economic activity is basic or primary, while locally oriented activity is derivative or secondary.[1] This causal relationship is often described in terms of an income or employment multiplier: export activity has an amplified effect on the rest of the economy, triggering cycle after cycle of local spending that puts people to work in locally oriented economic activities. For each dollar injected into the local economy, three or four dollars may be earned by local residents as those dollars move from one locally oriented business to another. In a circular flow, exports inject income into the local economy, which then gets spent and respent until it slowly leaks out of the economy to finance imports (figure 1-1). By the time expansionary forces come to an end, local income and employment have grown as

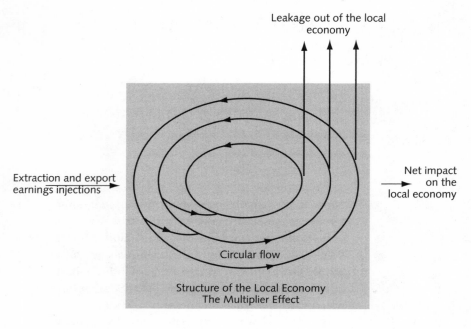

FIGURE 1-1.   The circular flow view of the local economy. Income injection from the export sector stimulates the rest of the economy through a multiplier process.

much as four times the income and employment associated with export activity.

This familiar view of the local economy carries a political message: all economic activities are not equal in importance. Primary activity, a subset of all economic activity, either directly or indirectly "butters our bread." This primary economic activity must be nurtured and supported, for without it the community will fade into a ghost town.

As we shall see, this simple economic base approach to local economies has proven to be misleading for several reasons, including (1) confusion about what the model actually depicts, (2) an incomplete picture of the actual economic base, and (3) specific empirically false assumptions. With such a range of shortcomings it might seem reasonable to conclude that the model is unlikely to be useful or reliable. However, despite its flaws, it must be noted that like any good model it still offers one distinct advantage: it provides a readily comprehensible vision of the overall local economy, which accounts for its success as a part of folk economics. Because the economic base model will persist for some time to come, this and the following chapter seek to employ the model more accurately and usefully—to rehabilitate it, in other words—rather than reject it outright as useless and hopelessly distorting.

The View through the Rearview Mirror

In most nonmetropolitan areas, the most visible exportable goods come from the natural environment: agricultural products, forest products, minerals, and their processed derivatives. Because these goods have their source in the natural environment, the industries associated with them are often labeled extractive. An extractive industry tends to be seen as the economic engine energizing the local economy and making ongoing settlement of that particular area possible.

Many extractive activities are historically entrenched, being associated with European settlement a century or more earlier. They create a shared community vision of what the population does for a living. When the pattern of economic activity begins to change, the vision is slow to adjust. In that sense, conventional wisdom about the local economy is the view through the rearview mirror, focused on the past rather than the present and dismissing all economic alternatives as unreliable or inferior. What could replace mining or ranching or timber in the Old West? What could replace steel and automobiles in Pittsburgh and Detroit?

The rearview mirror, of course, is an important safety device, especially when traveling in congested traffic or changing lanes. But it would be terribly unsafe to negotiate through congestion relying on nothing but a rearview mirror. The driver's eyes should concentrate on the traffic ahead. Similarly, a historically bound economic view can be dangerous to the economic health of a local community.

Misreading the Economic Base Model

A standard interpretation of the economic base model is that exports and the income they inject into the local economy are all that really

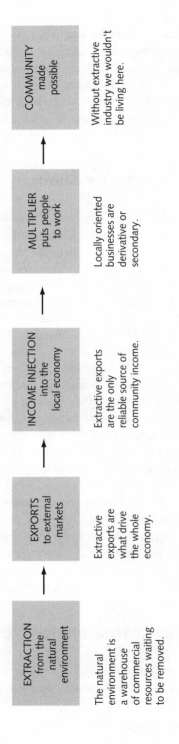

FIGURE 1-2. The extractive view of the local economy. Income from extraction and export makes local habitation possible.

matter—they cause or enable all other economic activities (figure 1-2). Income earned in export-oriented activities circulates through the local economy, putting people to work in locally oriented economic activities that provide the vast majority of jobs. Fluctuations in export income cause fluctuations in nonexport sectors in a relationship summarized by a more or less constant multiplier.

But this is not the only or most appropriate interpretation of the economic base model. It ignores that which determines the multiplier: the character and structure of the local economy. The more quickly injected income leaks out of the local economy, the smaller the multiplier. The multiplier is inversely related to the fraction of local spending that goes to importing goods. The more self-sufficient a local economy is, the longer injected income circulates within and the larger the overall multiplier impact.

In that sense, the impact of export earnings is determined by the structure of the local economy and the range of locally produced goods and services, and not just by the volume of export earnings. The character of the local economy is crucial too. The standard interpretation of the economic base model would dismiss a restaurant or recreational facility as derivative or secondary, passively relying on export earnings to survive. The alternative interpretation would say that such local economic activity absorbs and holds dollars longer in the local economy, increasing jobs and income. Local economic activity directly generates jobs too. In fact, it is the strength and diversity of local sectors that determine the size of the multiplier.

This can be put slightly differently: leakage from the local economy to finance outside goods and services limits the impact of export earnings. Local economic activities that slow or stop leakage generate jobs and income. This is often referred to as "import substitution" activity, but the concept is more encompassing.[2] If an area offers abundant recreational opportunities, for example, residents will travel away less than if it offers few. An attractive environment leaks fewer dollars and therefore generates more jobs and income.

Consider, for example, an Arctic outpost where minerals are being extracted. Despite the huge volume of export activity and income being generated, the forbidding site of the extraction is unlikely to experience economic development. Workers will be temporarily imported along with all of the goods and services to support them, travel away from the site every opportunity they get, send their income elsewhere to support families, and leave as soon as the job is done.

The economic base model should not be interpreted as meaning that only exports matter. Rather, export earnings interact with a particular local economy to determine the overall level of local economic activity. Both export earnings and local economic structure matter. The internal logic of the economic base model has simply been misinterpreted.

Economic Dependence versus Economic Development

An even stronger statement can be made about the role of export earnings in local economic development. "More of the same"—expansion of an already specialized export industry—can hardly be called economic development. Economic development occurs when a complex web of locally oriented economic activities is spun, making an area increasingly less dependent on imports and, as a result, not as dependent on export earnings. Successful local activities often lead in turn to new exports and economic diversification.

Intensified specialization in a few exports is not economic development but rather a prescription for dependence and instability. It is through export industries that fluctuations in national and international markets are imported into the local economy. Commodity-price cycles, general business cycles, and long-term declines tied to technological change all threaten an economy that specializes in the export of a few products. The instability of specialization explains the malaise that afflicts most U.S. mining, mill, and agricultural towns and the reluctance of individuals and businesses to reinvest in them,[3] even when local wages are high.

The economic base model, because it takes a single snapshot of a local economy at a particular time, tends to ignore the dynamics of a local economy over time, concentrating on isolated economic impacts at the expense of economic development. It also tends to overlook sources of local income that are substantial but not tied directly to the export of a product. Consider, for instance, the income brought to an area when a retiree decides to settle there.[4] Retirement income circulates within the local economy, but nothing has been exported. Such "footloose" income sources can be considerable—as much as 30 to 60 percent of a local area's personal income may be associated with factors like retirement income, investment earnings (dividends, rent, and interest), and government income-support payments. Whatever attracts or holds income of this sort is a major part of the local economic base.

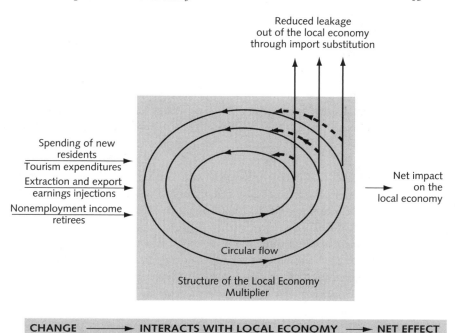

FIGURE 1-3. Modified-circular-flow model of the local economy. This includes the role of import substitution and other nonexport sources of income.

Or consider the income from small businesses, which can be relatively easily located depending on the preferences of their owners. People relocating are likely to spend savings getting established. And then there are the expenditures of visitors who come to a place because of its natural or cultural endowment.

In thinking about a local economy from the perspective of its economic base, such nonexport sources of income have to be taken into account (figure 1-3). Extraction and export are only some of the forces shaping the local economy. The analyst should make sure that all of a community's significant income sources are being taken into account.

A House Built on Sand: The Economic Base Model

The economic base model rests on assumptions that are familiar enough to seem quite plausible and unremarkable: people have to move to where jobs are located, and job location is dictated by such facts of economic geography as the location of natural resources and markets, and transportation costs. But too often these assumptions are contradicted by economic reality.

That some people go looking for work and as a result get distributed in a particular way across the landscape is certainly true. That some local economic-development policies seek to recruit new businesses is also true. But as generalities these are not simple, intuitively obvious principles. Stated differently, they say that one, people do not care where they live, and two, firms do not concern themselves about labor supply. There is nothing in economic theory or fact to support such assumptions. Quite the contrary, both of these assumptions, in general, are wrong.

The economic geography of the United States has been transformed during the second half of the twentieth century as a result not of people passively relocating for work but, rather, actively seeking particular residential environments. How else is one to explain the suburbanization of U.S. metropolitan areas after World War II? For several decades suburbanization represented a move away from both employment and commercial centers. Certainly the negative aspects of living in the city—congestion, pollution, crime, ethnic conflict—spurred relocation, as did the positive aspects of suburban and exurban living: lower density, parklike settings, less social conflict.

Similar motives lay behind the settlement of the desert Southwest and the Sunbelt in general. In fact, the term amenity was coined as an economic concept by an economic geographer in southern California to explain the postwar population boom in that area.[5] During the 1980s, while most of nonmetropolitan America suffered a depression, the economies of many rural counties with attractive landscape features experienced ongoing growth, testimony to the powerful draw of desirable living environments.[6] During the first half of the 1990s, recreation and retirement communities continued to lead both metropolitan and nonmetropolitan areas in economic vitality.[7]

And what about the notion that firms do not concern themselves about the labor supply because, it is assumed, workers will eagerly follow employment opportunities and thus there will always be an adequate supply wherever a firm chooses to relocate? History as well as contemporary experience contradicts this view. Industry often relocated in the pursuit of a cheaper labor force. The textile industry's move from New England to the rural South earlier in this century, the more recent shift of the Midwestern meat-packing industry from large cities to small towns and rural areas,[8] and current migration of businesses from the Frostbelt to the Sunbelt and across the border into Mexico are all dramatic examples of industries relocating in pursuit of a relatively inexpensive labor supply. Other industries seek a relatively well-educated, skilled, and disciplined work force and locate at least partially with that in mind. Overall, labor supply is a powerful force in determining the geographic distribution of economic activity. Some economists have gone so far as to argue that labor supply is the primary factor in determining the location activity in an economy where resources are mobile.[9] At the very least, the size, quality, and cost of the local labor supply have a significant impact on an area's economic development.

It would seem as appropriate, then, to reverse the basic causal connections of the economic base model: people choose a location and economic activity follows, rather than the other way around. For this reason people specializing in regional economics have been urging for years that the economic base model be "buried . . . without prospects for resurrection."[10] Economists since the late nineteenth century have seen economic results as issuing from the interaction of supply *and* demand. The economic base model tends to ignore the important role played by labor supply in influencing the location of economic activity. In that sense it is incomplete.

An Environmental View of the Local Economy

The economic base model often degenerates into the claim that site-specific natural resources which industry can extract and process are directly or indirectly responsible for almost all jobs and, therefore, for the ongoing survival of a local economy. The alternative "environmental" view recognizes that people are attracted to certain desirable social and natural environments, creating, by virtue of numbers, an available supply of labor at relatively low cost (figure 1-4). Labor supply not only attracts economic activity but also injects income into the local economy as individuals spend and invest. And retirees bring in retirement income. The net effect on the local economy is expansionary. Entrepreneurs will explore every opportunity to replace imported goods or to capture dollars that would otherwise flow out by

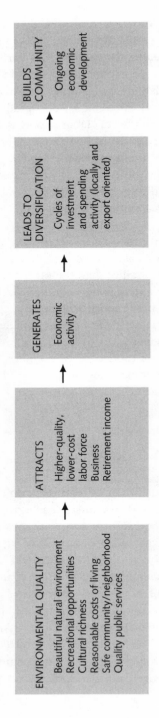

FIGURE 1-4. An environmental view of the economy. The pursuit of high-quality living environments causes a shift in the location of economic activity and stimulates local economic vitality.

ENVIRONMENTAL QUALITY

Beautiful natural environment
Recreational opportunities
Cultural richness
Reasonable costs of living
Safe community/neighborhood
Quality public services

ATTRACTS

Higher-quality,
lower-cost
labor force
Business
Retirement income

GENERATES

Economic
activity

LEADS TO
DIVERSIFICATION

Cycles of
investment
and spending
activity (locally and
export oriented)

BUILDS
COMMUNITY

Ongoing
economic
development

developing a wider array of locally available goods and services. Businesses that are most successful at displacing imports and serving local needs may build on their record and begin exporting to the larger economy. All of this raises the number of residents that the local economy can support, increasing its "critical mass." The community becomes less isolated and the cost of inputs comes down, attracting more economic activity to the area. Cycles of expansion continue as long as the area remains a relatively attractive place to live, work, and do business.

The environmental view of the local economy focuses on individual preferences and how they affect economic activity. In conventional economic analysis, the idea of preference guiding resource use is common. Consumer preferences interact with the range of goods and services it would be possible to produce to determine what, in fact, gets produced, where resources are used, and what gets sold. The environmental view of the local economy simple extends that approach: Preferences for various residential environments interact with the available range of environments to determine a broad set of economic activities, which, in turn, influence both preferences and the range of available residential environments (figure 1-5).

The population has diverse preferences when it comes to residential environments. People consider a host of factors in various combinations: the diversity and sophistication of the commercial environment, the natural environment, including climate, landscape, water and air quality, and recreational opportunities, and the social environment. The diversity of relevant environmental factors, the subjectivity of people's judgments about them, and the lack of unanimity in those judgments do not create a serious problem here or anywhere else in the economy. Diversity of preferences is an economic fact of life that market economies are particularly good at serving. People vote with their feet just as they do with their dollars.

Broadening Our Economic Vision: The Value of a Thing of Beauty

One reason that environmental qualities tend to be regarded as non- or anti-economic (in the sense of undermining economic well-being) is that, in common usage, *economic* and *economy* have come to be synonymous with commercial activities that satisfy our material needs.

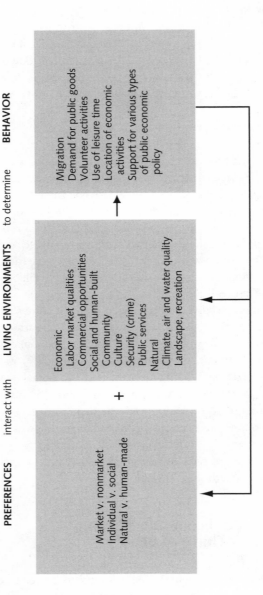

PREFERENCES interact with **LIVING ENVIRONMENTS** to determine **BEHAVIOR**

Market v. nonmarket
Individual v. social
Natural v. human-made

+

Economic
  Labor market qualities
  Commercial opportunities
Social and human-built
  Community
  Culture
  Security (crime)
  Public services
Natural
  Climate, air and water quality
  Landscape, recreation

Migration
Demand for public goods
Volunteer activities
Use of leisure time
Location of economic
  activities
Support for various types
  of public economic
  policy

FIGURE 1-5. Preferences for living environments. These cause changes in the location of economic activity. Preferences and environments also change as a result of the new economic activity.

Environmental qualities appear to lie outside the realm of economics both because they are largely noncommercial and because, except in extreme circumstances, they do not appear necessary to our biological survival.

This folk economic view conflicts with the conventional notion that the economy is the part of human social organization that develops and uses scarce resources to produce and distribute goods and services to satisfy needs and desires. The conventional definition says nothing about commercial business activity, money value, or financial flows. Instead, it focuses on scarcity and the satisfaction of needs and desires. Because not all scarce resources are privately owned and bought and sold in commercial markets, because it is not only commercial businesses that transform resources into useful goods and services, because we have preferences for goods and services that commercial businesses do not provide, and finally, because the distribution of goods and services is not always through commercial channels, we have to broaden our vision to include much more than the world of commercial business, money value, and financial flows if we are to paint a complete picture of the economy (figure 1-6).

The social and natural environments should figure prominently in our economic view because they are the only sources of economic raw material. Natural resources flow from the natural environment and labor productivity flows from the social environment. Noncommercial institutions such as family, schools, not-for-profit organizations, and government should figure prominently because they are the institutional framework of our commercial economy as well as the source of considerable economic production in their own right. Moreover, the social and natural environments make life more meaningful, satisfying, and diverse. It is only in this larger context that fully informed rational decisions can be made about how resource use affects human well-being.

In the large economic context, conflicts between commercial and environmental interests should not be described in terms of sacrificing "economic value" for "aesthetic value" but rather in terms of typical economic tradeoffs, where scarce resources can be used to produce alternative "bundles" of goods and services. Some of those goods and services are provided directly by the natural and social environment; others are produced by commercial business. When both seek to make use of the same scarce resource base, a straightforward economic

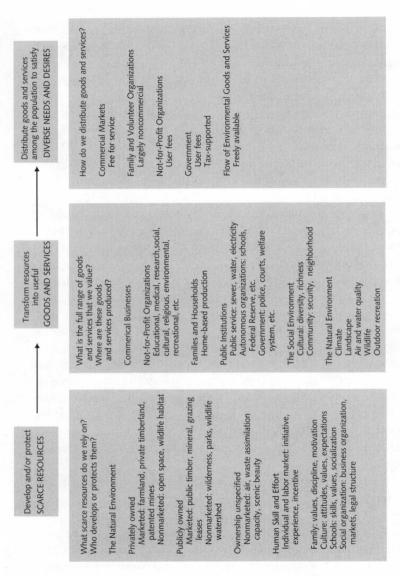

FIGURE 1-6. The total economy, including the noncommercial sources of important resources, goods, and services. An exclusive focus on the commercial business sector ignores resources, goods, and services that contribute significantly to economic well-being.

choice has to be made, no different than the choice between using farmland to produce wheat rather than barley. In the face of scarcity, each decision to use a resource in one way involves sacrifice. The same is true with the use of resources to protect or enhance the natural environment: one set of valued goods and services is chosen at the expense of another. Such choices are not economically irrational. Tradeoffs are typical of any economic choice.

The concept of economic choice has significant implications for how we evaluate local economic well-being. If people strongly prefer a certain type of living environment, one would expect them to make sacrifices in order to obtain access to it, for instance, paying a higher price for a home with access to a park, lake, or scenic vista. Such familiar economic choices are the bread and butter of the real-estate profession. But one can "purchase" access to natural or social environments by making other sacrifices, for example, moving to a high-amenity area despite the fact that real wages are lower, employment opportunities are scarcer, and/or cost of living is higher. In fact, an attractive area is likely to be afflicted by one or more of these circumstances. Because it draws people, it may well have a surplus labor supply, which puts downward pressure on wages and upward pressure on unemployment rates. If land is limited, a larger population will also raise the price of houses, the primary determinant of local cost of living. Such disadvantages of living in a high-amenity area, along with the deterioration of the surroundings caused by ongoing growth, ultimately operate to control the number of people who seek to live there. Meanwhile, lower real wages or a higher unemployment rate is not a sign of economic malaise, but the opposite, of how attractive a high-amenity area is to people. It is a measure of the value residents place on the services they receive from the natural or social environment.[11]

This suggests that we should not be using per capita income or money wages alone to measure local prosperity. We have to adjust for the local cost of living and add the value of goods and services residents receive from the environment:

$$\text{Local economic well-being} = \frac{\text{Local money income}}{\text{Local cost of living}} + \text{Value of local noncommercial environmental qualities}$$

Economists label such wage differences "compensating wage differentials" because they offset the value of site-specific amenities, leaving residents about as well-off in one location as they would be at another.

This type of analysis has two important policy implications. First, lower average incomes are not necessarily a sign of economic distress, and therefore may not need to be addressed by local economic policy. Second, some lower average incomes, fixed by a feature of the local area, namely its attractiveness, cannot be eliminated by stimulating the local economy. The wage differential can be eliminated only by eliminating the area's attractive features. That would hardly seem rational.

Lower real income or higher unemployment in a desirable area is *not* the result of high environmental standards "strangling" economic development. Rather, the phenomenon can be explained by an excess labor force being drawn to the area and depressing wages. There is little evidence to support the idea that vigorous protection of environmental quality limits economic opportunity. If one ranks states by their efforts to protect environmental quality and then compares that list with one measuring states' economic growth, environmental protection appears to be associated with economic development. A state's gross product, total employment, and labor productivity are all positively correlated with the vigor of state environmental regulation.[12]

Alternatively, one can analyze the Environmental Protection Agency's Toxic Release Inventory data base to study the relationship between the level of toxic waste allowed and the level of prosperity in each state. Indeed, high levels of permissable toxic release are associated with higher unemployment, greater poverty, and lower disposable per capita income.[13] These correlations do not establish causality. Rather than environmental quality stimulating economic development, it may be that poorer areas are more willing to sacrifice environmental quality in the pursuit of jobs and income. The feasibility of that strategy, however, is certainly challenged by the increasing demand on the part of both residents and businesses for environmental quality. Many towns show surprising vitality after a mine or mill closes and local environmental quality improves. Examples of areas that have prospered in the midst of environmental deterioration are much more difficult to come by.

Beyond Bread and Butter: From the Necessary toward the Discretionary

Another reason qualities associated with the living environment are often treated as non- or anti-economic is the emphasis on necessity in folk economics. The economy is usually characterized as primarily providing us with the "material means of life." Economic issues are "bread and butter" issues. People work to "bring home the bacon" and keep a "roof over our heads." Environmental concerns are often dismissed on the grounds that "you cannot eat the scenery." Prevailing economic rhetoric tells us that biological necessity ought to take precedence over social or cultural or aesthetic concerns.

There is little in the modern economy to support this emphasis on biological necessity. Consider what is offered for sale in our premiere commercial institutions, shopping malls and supermarkets. In the typical mall one would be hard-pressed to find anything that was necessary for biological survival. The emphasis is on fashionable clothing, home decoration, and entertainment centers. And the eighth-mile-long aisles at our supermarkets, packed with junk food, sacrifice little space for nutritious staples. Or consider our homes: they aren't just shelters. We hire residential developers, architects, interior decorators, and landscape architects to help create our dream environment. A good part of the cost of housing goes to nonessential features. Not even our medicine is aimed primarily at survival. Much of it simply makes us "feel better" when we have minor "dis-ease." We seek to change our appearance with orthodontics and cosmetic surgery, to feel better about ourselves with the help of mental health specialists, to live beyond our years on sophisticated machines and potent drugs.

All in all, not much more than 10 percent of our economic activity provides us with those things that are necessary for biological survival.[14] The rest of our economic activity is devoted to attractive but discretionary phenomena.

Although folk economics suggests that material inputs are the source of our economic productivity, nothing could be further from the truth. If this were so, countries with the largest populations and the most raw materials—China, India, Zaire, and Mexico—would have the richest and most productive economies. They do not. Quite the contrary, much of their population is mired in poverty. Empirical analysis of what it is that determines productivity in various economies identifies primarily nonmaterial inputs such as the quality (not the quantity) of the work force, education levels, entrepreneurial spirit, work ethic, and legal–political institutions.[15]

This emphasis on discretionary-quality is not new in economics (figure 1-7). It is the way that economists look analytically at the world, and it reflects the world more accurately than does the materials-necessity view. The latter ignores the focus and purpose of most economic activity as well as the sources of productivity, and it mischaracterizes many of the choices people face in a way that prejudices

Folk Economic View	Analytical Economic View
Basic inputs	**Basic inputs**
Amount of raw material processed	Quality of the labor force Work ethic Entrepreneurial spirit Skill, training, experience
Number of workers	Quality of organization Effective cooperation Motivation
Quantity of capital	Quality of technology Organization State of applied knowledge
	Quality of the legal structure Property rights Contracts Control of predatory behavior
Basic outputs	**Basic outputs**
Necessities Basic food Shelter Medical care	Discretionary, subjective qualities Tasteful food Attractive clothes Appealing home environment Supportive medicine Satisfying services

FIGURE 1-7. Folk economics versus the analytical economic view.

the outcome of those choices. To regard discretionary qualities as the trivial interest of the leisure class and to focus public economic policy on a quantitative expansion in the volume of material input and output is to systematically ignore what we really want from our economy and the most productive ways of obtaining it. Discretionary qualities are not the frosting on the economic cake, they *are* the cake. But you would never know that from listening to current discussions of public economic policy.

The discretionary-quality perspective helps us see a way out of what would otherwise appear to be a nearly hopeless conflict between economic improvement and environmental quality. A material view of the economy makes the future of Western affluence appear doubtful. After all, the affluent nations have only about two-thirds of a billion of the earth's 5 billion–plus aspiring souls. If, over the next two generations, the consumption level of the rest of the earth's population succeeds in approaching that in the industrial world, and if industrial countries modestly expand their economies—say, at a rate of 2 percent per year—the planet will face a fourteen-fold increase in the material demands placed upon it.[16] That certainly poses a catch-22: either the rest of the world's population must not be allowed to improve, or we must surrender our affluence. Fortunately, the catch-22 derives from a false perception of the economy as depending on nothing but material production and consumption. In fact, neither the basic inputs into the economy nor the basic outputs are primarily material.

If both primary inputs and primary outputs are qualitative, then economic improvement at least appears possible over the long run. While the extraction of materials from the earth and their return to the biosphere as waste are always disruptive, improving quality of life does not have to be. Because "qualities" are not primarily material, they can be limitlessly improved without burdening the natural world. A more beautiful song, a more graceful athletic performance, a better designed home, greater knowledge, or honed professional skills do not necessarily require expanded material flows out of and into the natural world. A dynamic and efficient economy could increase access to valuable qualities while decreasing the material throughput of resources and goods. We need to focus on the material efficiency with which we pursue the things that are important to us. At least conceptually, we would continue to improve our well-being without having to threaten our communities and the natural world.

This is not meant as a description of how our economy currently operates. Ongoing quantitative growth is constantly increasing pressure on the natural and social environments. The point is, we could continue to improve our well-being while reducing the material pressure on the environment if we were to abandon the emphasis on quantitative expansion of material production.

Job Loss: Catastrophe or Transition?

One of the most emotionally powerful arguments to mobilize in support of particular public economic policy is that of job loss or job creation. Socially respected, useful employment is central to any adult's self-esteem and the income generated by that employment is crucial for the individual's and family's full participation in their community.

"Jobs" is one of the first issues raised whenever public policy is discussed.

In a healthy economy, some industries and businesses are always expanding while others are contracting. As a result, some industries are always laying off workers while others are hiring workers. Layoffs in some sectors are a sign of a dynamic, not an unhealthy, economy. If workers and other resources were not being released by some sectors, expanding sectors would find it difficult and costly to expand. Economic development requires that workers and other resources be released in less productive sectors and shifted to more productive sectors.

If over the years workers had not been released from such sectors as agriculture, horse-drawn transportation, wood-fuel production and leather manufacturing, the U.S. economy could not have modernized. In general, laid-off workers are relatively quickly absorbed into other sectors of the economy (figure 1-8). During the 1980s, almost all American workers who lost their jobs found new jobs within a year, and half of those laid off found new work in less than two months.[17]

When a mill or mine or factory lays off some of its workers, analysts often react as if those workers have been permanently lost to the economy. This is not the way the labor market works. The U.S. Bureau of Labor Statistics estimates that during the 1980s over 19 million adult Americans were displaced from their jobs owing to layoffs, plant closings, and business failures.[18] If the assumption about permanent unemployment were correct, the total number of unemployed in the nation should have risen by about 19 million. Instead, during the 1980s the total number of unemployed *declined* by about 700,000. Not only were most of these 19 million displaced workers put back to work, but there were an additional 18 million new entrants into the labor force.[19] American workers and labor markets are much more resilient than many analysts suggest.

Consider another measure of the American labor market. The average term of job tenure in America is about 4.5 years.[20] That is, in the last five years half of all American workers changed their jobs. Even those in their fifties and sixties regularly change jobs, roughly every ten years. Americans successfully change employment many times. Leaving a job most certainly does not represent permanent unemployment.

Another popular concern is the loss of good jobs and their replacement with inferior jobs, each change representing a steady downward slide. We will see later that for most workers this is not the case. The U.S. economy continues to create high-paying, skilled jobs. It continues to demand skilled workers and to reward them well for those skills.

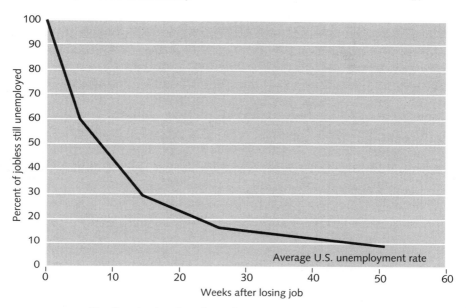

FIGURE 1-8. Decline in the duration of unemployment, 1980–87. The unemployed are steadily absorbed back into the labor force. (*Source:* "Labor Force Statistics Derived from the Current Population Survey, 1948–87," *Bureau of Labor Statistics Bulletin* 2307, August 1988.)

This is not to suggest that layoffs and unemployment are not painful and disruptive to individuals, families, and communities. They are. But they are also inevitable in a dynamic economy. Public policy needs to smooth the transition of workers from one employment opportunity to another rather than treating each job change as a personal and social catastrophe that is to be avoided at all costs. Individuals and communities have proven themselves to be incredibly adaptable. It would be bad economic policy to keep the work force in the same jobs permanently by directly or indirectly subsidizing businesses that have ceased to be sustainable.

The Total Economy

If we are going to have a useful conception of the local economy, we have to move beyond the folk economics that most of us have been taught since grade school. Folk economics is not flat out wrong,

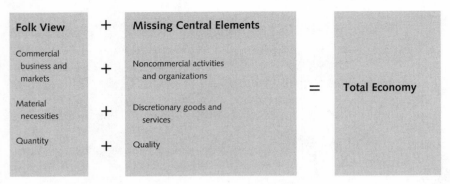

FIGURE 1-9. Completing the economy. The conventional economic emphasis on business, material necessities, and quantity needs to be supplemented with the noncommercial, discretionary, and qualitative.

but it is incomplete. To the almost exclusive focus on commercial business activity we have to add the contributions to our economic well-being flowing from noncommercial sectors and the natural and social environments. (figure 1-9). To free ourselves from the obsession with biological necessities, we need to realize that most of what we produce and purchase is discretionary goods and services that make our lives interesting and satisfying. Finally, while admitting the material and quantitative characteristics of our economy, we need to recognize the qualitative character of what we fundamentally seek and of our primary economic resources. Only with this more comprehensive view can effective public economic policy be crafted. In this broader context, the dynamism and diversity of opportunity that we seek in our local economies is better described by the qualitative term *vitality* rather than the quantitative term growth.

Seeking Greener Pastures: Residential Choice and Local Economic Vitality

The most familiar approach to analyzing a local economy is implicit in the types of questions that the noneconomist is likely to ask when first introduced to a particular area. What do people do for a living here? Who are the major employers that create jobs which allow people to live here? Actually, these are the same questions, stated in less technical terms, that regional economists would also tend to ask. These familiar questions make two important assumptions about the economy. First, they assume that people do not work for themselves, but rather some special set of economic actors make a living for them by offering employment opportunities. The second assumption is that jobs are created locally, principally as a result of the export of specialized products. Although there is an obvious element of truth embodied in both of these assumptions, they also significantly distort our conception of the local economy in such a way that local economic policy can become unproductive or counterproductive. These assumptions depict communities as passive and helpless, with residents largely relying on outside markets, corporations, and government organizations to create jobs. The community's economic future is seen as tied to the external demand for whatever local specialized products can be produced. Thus residents are considered doubly dependent, on nonresident corporations and on external demands. Such community passivity and helplessness is rarely a productive basis for local economic development efforts.

29

Exports in the Local Economy

If one shifts focus from a particular local economy to a larger economy, the logic behind this "double economic dependency" view is considerably weakened. The development of the American economy, for instance, did not primarily consist of people waiting around passively for foreign investors to create jobs for them. Immigrants to America created jobs for themselves by looking at their own and their neighbors' needs and desires. They didn't primarily depend on foreign demand for their products.[1] Indeed, the American economy was largely self-sufficient well into the second half of the twentieth century. Or consider the world economy. Few inhabitants of the planet are waiting for extraterrestrials to start new firms or create an export market for earth's output. In general, economic development on a global or continental scale has been possible even when we have only our fellow residents with whom to trade. What changes as one moves from this aggregate scale to a local economy that seems to dramatically increase the importance of exports and outside investors, which, in turn, makes us less self-sufficient?

As we've seen, the economic base model pictures local economic activity as being funded by the money that export activity injects into the local economy. Export-injected dollars circulate and recirculate, putting people to work in locally oriented businesses such as retail trade and services. This view of the economy, at least three or four hundred years old, is largely a "mercantile" vision in which the export of local specialty goods in return for foreign gold is the dominant objective of public economic policy. Exports are all that matter.

This is a perverse, anti-economic perspective. It suggests that local well-being is tied to sending away valuables in return for colorful pieces of paper or shiny metal called money, without which local economic activity would not be possible. This is not a defensible description of the determinants of local economic activity and well-being.

Consider locally oriented economic activity such as schooling, repair services, day care, and medical treatment. The sale of these services primarily consists of local residents exchanging their specialty for the specialty their neighbor provides. This activity could take place without national currency, through actual barter or a local currency.[2] That is what the individual nations of Europe have been doing for as long as they have existed. Exports are not needed to stimulate or facilitate much local economic activity. It takes place because of diverse productive capacities within the local economy.

The role of export-injected income is not to stimulate and facilitate local economic activity but rather to fund the import of goods and services that the local economy cannot easily produce. That is, the direct economic function of exports is solely to fund imports. Imports that we need and want are what directly contribute to our well-being, not exports. Because almost all of us have needs and desires that cannot be satisfied from production within the local economy, the convenience and satisfaction of living in the local area depends on a certain level of imported goods and services. In that sense, imports, and the exports that fund them, are crucial to ongoing local economic activity. But it is important to keep the focus on the direct reasons for this: the current inability of the local economy to provide certain types of goods and services.

When the function of export-oriented activity is spelled out in this manner, it is clear why, with economic development, the role of export activity and even the visibility of the "export base" begins to decline. Services and goods that were previously imported are produced locally, reducing the need for exports or increasing the size of the population that a given level of export activity can support. The more self-sufficient the local economy becomes, the smaller the role of imports and therefore exports. With a shift toward more locally produced services and fewer imported goods, the community becomes more self-sufficient and can expand despite a static or shrinking export base. This is not to say that export activity ceases. Firms that successfully produce for local consumption are likely to start competing for outside markets too. A few specialized export industries, however, probably won't dominate the local area's economic base.

The Sources of Local Economic Activity

Cataloguing the different reasons economic activity might take place within a particular local economy gives a complete overview of the possible source of local economic vitality, a critical adjustment of the rearview mirror vision that focuses on economic activities that were important in the past but may be of little relevance to future economic vitality. Indirectly, that cataloguing of economic forces puts into context the competing extractive and environmental views of a local economy, that is, allows us to compare the role played by extractive-industry exports with the decision to relocate made by residents and businesses on the basis of the area's social and natural features.

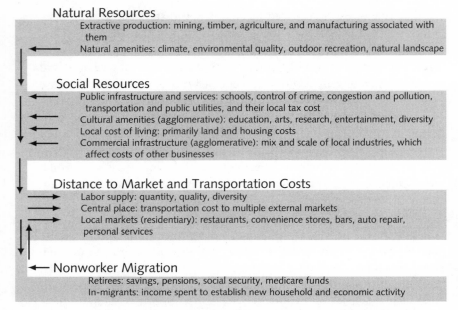

Natural Resources
 Extractive production: mining, timber, agriculture, and manufacturing associated with them
 Natural amenities: climate, environmental quality, outdoor recreation, natural landscape

Social Resources
 Public infrastructure and services: schools, control of crime, congestion and pollution, transportation and public utilities, and their local tax cost
 Cultural amenities (agglomerative): education, arts, research, entertainment, diversity
 Local cost of living: primarily land and housing costs
 Commercial infrastructure (agglomerative): mix and scale of local industries, which affect costs of other businesses

Distance to Market and Transportation Costs
 Labor supply: quantity, quality, diversity
 Central place: transportation cost to multiple external markets
 Local markets (residentiary): restaurants, convenience stores, bars, auto repair, personal services

Nonworker Migration
 Retirees: savings, pensions, social security, medicare funds
 In-migrants: income spent to establish new household and economic activity

FIGURE 2-1. Local factors that determine the geographic distribution of economic activity.

Economists talk of three general forces that determine the location of economic activity: site-specific, nontransportable, resources; proximity to input and product markets and transportation costs; and "agglomerative" advantages associated with the scale or mix of local economic activities.[3] These categories break down into diverse economic forces influencing the location of economic activity (figure 2-1). Consider site-specific, nontransportable resources. These include not just natural resource–based economic activities (mining or timber harvest) but also nonextractive natural resources (recreational opportunities, climate, and scenic beauty) and "social resources" (security from crime, schools, and cultural amenities).

The line between categories is not always clear. Consider agglomerative forces. As a local economy develops, a more diverse mix of economic activities becomes feasible because of the growing local market. In addition, as more similar businesses come into being, firms serving their special needs emerge. This local market–related activity is generated by the cost advantages to firms of being close to their markets. But because it involves a mix of firms, it is included under the agglomerative category. Agglomerative forces lead to cities of increasing size and complexity serving broader regional markets. Agglomerative forces also expand the public and nonprofit sectors. Larger communities can support more sophisticated educational, research, and cultural institutions, site-specific resources that may attract both people and businesses. Of course growth may be accompanied by crime, congestion, pollution, and the higher cost of living, agglomerative "disamenities" that discourage potential newcomers.

Another factor that doesn't fit easily into one of the three categories is local labor supply. Firms move in pursuit of relatively cheap, high-quality labor, and workers commute or move toward relatively well-paying jobs. In this context, labor supply is associated with all three categories: "distance to market" (labor market), specific amenities (which may draw or hold a surplus work force), and, depending on the diversity and sophistication of the work force, an agglomerative force that supplies firms with a large open pool from which to hire. In any case, the quality and quantity of the available labor force is an important determinant of the location of economic activity.

Making Less Living from the Land

America's first European settlers had to be largely self-sufficient, so they made heavy use of local natural resources. Each area was characterized by site-specific natural resources and activities: farming, ranching, mining, fishing, timber, food processing, smelting, refining, milling. Because the United States is such a young country, areas are still commonly characterized by this early economic activity, but the tendency is misleading. Local history has forged a set of cultural beliefs about what it is people do for a living. Outside of large metropolitan areas, this is invariably a natural resource–based (extractive) view.

One way to get a feeling for the relative importance of natural resource–based activity is to look at the percentage of the U.S. work force employed in it and the percentage of total national output derived from it. Similarly, some indication of the likely future contribution of natural resource industries to local economic vitality can be had by looking at long-term trends in employment and in income. In 1992, agriculture, mineral extraction, and forest products together were responsible for generating only about 3 percent of the personal income of Americans—a modest role. And this role has been declining for most of U.S. economic history, with fewer and fewer people making a living on the farm, in the mine, or in the forest. In the early 1800s extractive activities provided 85 percent of all jobs (figure 2-2). Over the last two decades, the contribution of natural resource industries to total income fell by almost half, from 6 percent to 3 percent (figure 2-3). In addition, income from these industries has been unstable, rising at times by 50 to 100 percent in just a few years only to plummet by a half or two-thirds (figure 2-4). If communities are concerned about their current and future economic vitality, this record should serve as a warning. The long-term trend in natural resource industries as a source of jobs and income is downward and has been for 200 years.

Industrial Location: On the Heels of the Work Force

Businesses that face substantial transportation costs, either in obtaining raw materials or delivering product, have to pay close attention to their

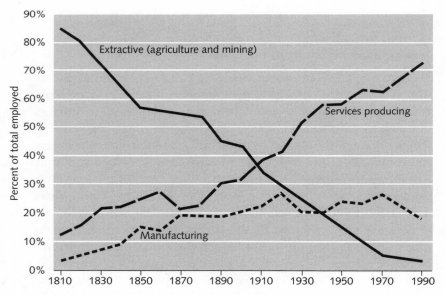

FIGURE 2-2. Changes in the relative economic importance of extraction, manufacturing, and services in the U.S. economy since 1810. The rise of services and the decline of extractive activity is not new. (*Data sources:* Historical Statistics of the United States [Bureau of the Census] and Bureau of Economic Analysis Regional Economic Information System [BEA REIS].)

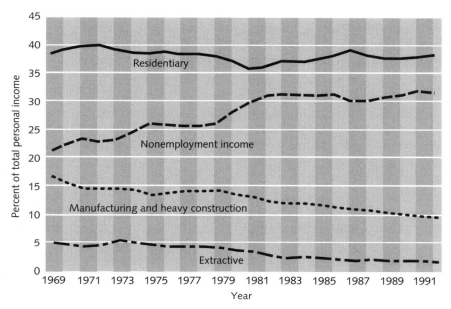

FIGURE 2-3. Sources of income in the American economy. (*Data sources:* BEA REIS deflated by the CPI.)

choice of location. To minimize transportation costs, industrial operations will at least partially choose their location on the basis of where markets are. Transportation costs tend to dictate a general optimal location, and businesses may have to shift location as population and markets shift. During the second half of the twentieth century, American manufacturing shifted its location from the industrial manufacturing belt in the North and Northeast to the South and West. The driving force behind this shift was the relocation of the American population. Manufacturing followed the population, not the other way around.[4]

This contradicts the folk economic view that people move to where manufacturing jobs are—to Michigan to produce automobiles, to Pennsylvania to produce steel, to California to produce computer components. Of course, large manufacturing operations are not constantly shifting location. Their investments keep them attached to particular locations for fairly long periods. Only by looking at the pattern of industrial shifts over time does one see clearly that heavy industry follows population.

The fact that the population can shift independently of heavy industry tells us something important. During the late nineteenth and

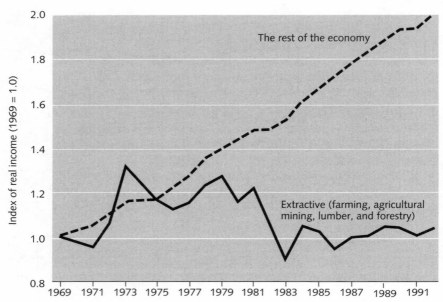

FIGURE 2-4. The instability of income from extractive industries compared with the rest of the economy. (*Date sources:* BEA REIS deflated by the CPI.)

the first half of the twentieth centuries, when much of the nation's economic development was fueled by the shift of the labor force from relatively low-productivity agriculture to higher-productivity manufacturing, the labor force was indeed moving toward manufacturing centers. During the last half century, however, improvements in transportation and communications and the change in manufactured products have allowed manufacturing to decentralize.

Manufacturing, especially heavy manufacturing, besides shifting location, has been declining in importance. Since 1969 the share of U.S. jobs and income provided by manufacturing has dropped 30 to 40 percent (see figure 2-3). Individual communities may have little influence over the location of such firms because transportation costs and markets dominate location decisions. Those communities that do rely on manufacturers have to be concerned about their long-term reliability as sources of income, given the declining role of manufacturing in the overall economy, the instability associated with international competition, and the trend of manufacturers shifting locations in the pursuit of lower costs. At the very least, local economic vitality will depend on other sources of jobs and income.

Taking In Each Other's Wash

About 60 percent of U.S. economic activity is local and provides residents with the goods and services that make their lives comfortable. This includes retail activities; personal, repair, medical, educational, and professional services; construction; public utilities; local transportation; financial institutions; real estate; and government services. Thus almost all local economies are dominated by residents taking in each other's wash (figures 2-3 and 2-5). (Of course, the smaller the community, the less likely it is that such "residentiary" services will be provided in the immediate area. Residents may have to travel to local trade centers or even regional trade centers.)

There is a distinct pattern to the type of economic activity found in communities of particular sizes. Convenience stores, bars, restaurants, and minimal government services (post office, road crew) are found in almost all communities, even tiny crossroads. Slightly larger towns will have a more diverse set of businesses, including automotive repair, personal services, and supermarkets. The economic functions of a community grow more complex as its size increases.

This pattern should not be interpreted as completely deterministic. A population of a given size in a particular area does not dictate exactly what set or number of businesses will come into existence there.[5] In communities of like size there is considerable variation in the range of businesses. One study of just three regions found that small trade centers with a population of 10,000 could differ by as much as 60 percent in the types of businesses present and by as much as fourfold in the total number of businesses. Statistical estimates indicate that for a local population of a given size, the locally oriented sector can vary in size by 50 to 100 percent.[6] Some of this variation is explained by location-specific factors. If a city is isolated from other trade centers, it may have a much broader range of businesses than a similarly sized city that is close to a larger trade center. Cities of 100,000 in Montana are likely to have a more sophisticated mix of businesses than cities of similar size in western Washington or southern California simply because of the isolation of Montana's cities from larger trade centers.

Whatever explanation is offered for such variation, some role has to be assigned to entrepreneurial energy. If a city is a stable trade center with a traditional way of doing business, new entrepreneurial activity may be discouraged by the inertia of the city's commercial culture as well as by cautious financial institutions. Alternatively, pressure on the community from either a decline in traditional economic activity or in-migration may lead to creative exploration of ways to exploit markets

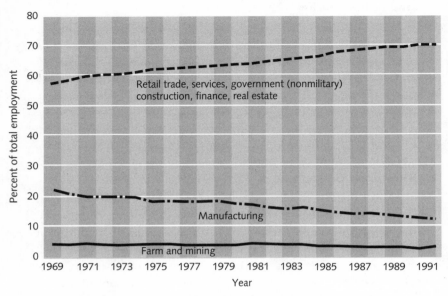

FIGURE 2-5. Sources of employment in the U.S. economy. (*Data sources:* BEA REIS.)

previously ignored or left to out-of-town business. The degree of entrepreneurial energy has a significant impact on the number of markets explored and developed. Inmigration plays a dual role here. The growth in population increases market size and therefore the range of economic activity that may be feasible at that locale, and it may also provide the entrepreneurial spirit to exploit markets previously filled by other trade centers.

The point is that a sizable part of total economic activity consists of delivering services to local households. This opens up a whole menu of possibilities for local businesses to maintain local economic vitality independently of what is happening to the traditional economic base.

Footloose Nonemployment Income

Not all income derives from current employment. Retirees receive income from Social Security and other pension programs. Others receive income from savings and investments. Such income sources along with unemployment insurance and government welfare will be called non-employment income here, as opposed to employment-earned income.

On average, over a third of all dollars received by Americans comes in the form of nonemployment income. For communities with higher concentrations of retirees or those receiving income maintenance support, 40 to 50 percent of all income received is nonemployment. Moreover, nonemployment income is growing in importance while both manufacturing and extractive activity are declining as sources of income. Statistical analysis of the impact of nonemployment income flow on local economic activity indicates that it can have an impact as great as or greater than income from basic industry.[7]

However, not all nonemployment dollars have the same impact on the local economy. Many investors keep their money in financial institutions rather than spending it on consumer goods or real investments within the community. Thus some property income (dividends, interest, and rent) never really touches the local economy. Only nonemployment income expended within the local economy has an impact on employment and income. Retirees' expenditures tend to be on services and labor-intensive goods as opposed to those of younger families; that is, a larger share of elderly purchases are for local rather than imported goods. In this sense, the nonemployment income of retirees may have a larger impact on the local economy than the same number of payroll dollars. In addition, because retirees do not fill most of the jobs their expenditures create, their net impact on the demand for labor is also greater.[8] Finally, inmigrating retirees do not place disproportionate, expensive demands on local services—they tend not to use schools and not to take up space in prisons.[9] As one analyst put it: "When rural counties float on a cushion of social security, pensions, annuities, and asset income, local economic conditions improve, particularly in the service sector."[10] During the 1980s and the first part of the 1990s, retirement areas were identified as among the fastest-growing nonmetropolitan counties.[11]

Stirring Things Up: An Enhanced Labor Supply

For most businesses, payroll is the largest expense by far. And for that reason the productivity of the work force and the wages it is paid are crucial in determining the overall profitability of the firm's operations. In addition, there is considerable cost associated with personnel operations: employment turnover is costly in terms of both dollars and

reduced productivity. For all of these reasons, the availability of a relatively high quality labor supply at a relatively low price is an important
consideration for almost every business. Firms primarily concerned
with the location of a good labor supply and a market for their products
will follow population for the simple reason that with migration goes
both labor supply and markets.[12]

Do jobs follow people or do people follow jobs? It is a chicken-or-egg
matter: both forces are usually operating simultaneously. Inmigration
generates jobs, and job creation supports inmigration. The point here is
to underline the role that an available supply of labor plays in stimulating the local economy, continuing the economic emphasis on both
supply and demand.

Inmigration can stimulate local economic activity in a way that is
self-reinforcing. It expands job creation without the threat of labor
scarcity and rising wages. At the same time, inmigration heightens
demand for locally produced goods and services, which also creates
new jobs. Inmigrants also invest in new homes and businesses. Meanwhile public investment tends to follow newcomers. The empirical evidence is that each employment-aged inmigrant has a direct effect on
local employment equal to at least one job.[13] New residents trigger
changes in the local economy that help create the jobs necessary to support them.

The local labor supply plays a positive role in attracting economic
activity. The supply, however, should not be thought of only in terms of
the number of "available" workers and the wages they have to be paid.
Of course, some firms do relocate primarily in the pursuit of low-
priced labor. Some of the shifts in manufacturing within the United
States (textiles from New England to the rural South) and out of the
country (Mexico) have been driven by the pursuit of lower wages. But
the pursuit of an appropriate labor supply is far more complex than a
search for the cheapest work force. For most firms, minimum-wage day
laborers are not an adequate work force. Reliability, skill levels, work
ethic, and job performance are crucial for many productive operations.
It is costly to screen potential employees, train them, and then allow
them on-the-job experience. Employee turnover can be costly in terms
of both the firm's investment in its workers and disrupted work. Most
firms, then, are interested in not only local wage levels but also the
quality of the work force. And if workers that firms seek to hire have
preferences for where they would like to live, firms may have to respect
those preferences or face higher labor costs or lower productivity.[14]

The size of the local labor supply also has to be thought of as flexible. It would be a mistake to characterize employment as an all-or-nothing situation. Workers may be partially employed or employed in something other than the situation they would prefer. There are many opportunities outside of the formal market economy to engage in productive economic activity, including housework and other subsistence activities.[15] In addition, there is a substantial underground economy built around self-employment and barter.

If an area is attractive, inmigrants may be willing to make short- and long-term sacrifices to stay, for example, accepting part-time work or jobs that do not make full use of their skills. Widespread underemployment represents a local labor surplus that allows new employers to hire better workers at less cost. Over time, an area with a substantial skilled surplus-labor supply is likely to attract economic activity, either through local entrepreneurs putting people to work or outside firms coming in.

Fashionable Watering Holes

Amenities, in economic terms, refer to local nontransportable goods or services. These include a broad range of natural, cultural, institutional, commercial, and economic features (see figure 2-1). There is nothing new or unusual about the economic role of amenities in changing the geographic distribution of economic activity. As early as 1811, British observers commented on the economic growth in "fashionable watering-places" such as Bath and Brighton.[16] That phenomenon, of course, continues today at locations with specific recreational resources such as Jackson, Wyoming, and Aspen, Colorado. But recreational communities are only extreme examples of a much broader phenomenon.

Twenty years ago David Bell was characterizing the postindustrial society as one where economic well-being was determined by quality of life as measured by services and amenities rather than quantity of goods.[17] (The word *amenities* was first used in the context of economic development in explaining post–World War II growth in southern California.)[18] The role that research universities in such places as Boston, Chapel Hill, and Palo Alto played in the relocation of high-tech firms and population is familiar.[19] New York City certainly gains significant economic advantages from its role as the nation's premiere cultural center. Its theater, ballet, opera, symphony orchestras, publishing, and art are big business as well as cultural assets. The role of disamenities such as crime, racial tension, congestion, and pollution in shifting population and economic activity from center city to suburbs or attractive nonmetropolitan communities is equally familiar.

For forty years economists have also been explaining people's choices of residential sites in different political jurisdictions in terms of packages of public goods and amenities (schools, parks, clean streets) and accompanying tax burdens. It has now become standard practice in regional economic analysis to measure local amenities and public goods (including such factors as low crime rate and abundant sunshine) when trying to explain the dynamics of economic change.[20] One estimate of the difference in amenity values between the top- and bottom-ranked American metropolitan areas (Pueblo, Colorado, and St. Louis, respectively) came to almost $10,000 per year per household in 1994 dollars.[21] Other studies indicate that, when city-specific traits such as public services and taxes are included, the difference between high- and low-amenity areas might be closer to $15,000 per year.[22] Economic differences of this size certainly affect residential location directly and business location indirectly.

It is not just the attractiveness of certain areas that defines residential choice. People want to avoid toxic waste sites, nuclear and coal-fired power plants, high-voltage power lines, and congested shopping centers. Economists and geographers have documented and quantified such "geographic discounting."[23]

Estimates have thus far been limited to those aspects of local areas that are easily quantified. One can measure sulfur-oxide pollution, how cold the climate is, what the crime rate is, and how often the sun shines. But many local features that are important to people, not so easily measured, have been omitted from analyses: scenic beauty, recreational opportunities, cultural richness, friendliness, sense of community, quality of schools and public services, biodiversity and ecosystem stability, and so forth. In fact, economists have only just begun to analyze the economic importance of the full range of location-specific features that people value. These empirical estimates are crude. Nonetheless, when one steps back and surveys broad population movements in the second half of the twentieth century, from city to suburb, from Frostbelt to Sunbelt, from large metropolitan to smaller urban centers, it is clear that local amenities have played an important role.

Take two examples. During the early and mid-1980s, U.S. nonmetropolitan areas suffered simultaneous decline in almost all traditional natural-resource industries—energy minerals, forest products, metal mining, and agriculture. This had a depressing effect on many rural areas and small towns. But during that same period the non-metropolitan counties that prospered were those with "locational assets"—lakes, mountains, shorelines—that made them attractive residential locations. They experienced nearly 85 percent of the population growth that took place in nonmetropolitan areas.[24] During the early 1990s this trend continued, with recreation and retirement counties growing at twice the nonmetropolitan average and a third faster than metropolitan areas.[25] Or consider the impact of attractive natural landscapes on the location of small businesses. A Montana State University study of small businesses in the northern portion of the Greater Yellowstone region revealed that firms decided to locate or remain in this rather remote but rapidly growing area mainly for such reasons as scenic amenities, the rural character of towns, the low crime rate, and proximity to wildlife-based recreation. Traditional "economic" reasons ranked very low.[26]

What Do You Do Here for a Living?

Studying how the residents of nonmetropolitan areas make their living should paint a picture of the extent of local specialization and reliance on exports. Surprisingly, the structure of local economic activity in nonmetropolitan areas is similar to the structure for the entire nation. The vast majority (over 88 percent) of residents in nonmetropolitan areas are employed in the same types of economic activity as workers elsewhere in the nation, and in almost identical proportions. Metropolitan areas do specialize more in financial and business services, while nonmetropolitan areas specialize more in extractive activities, agriculture, forestry, mining, and manufacturing. But these are relatively small differentials. Only about 8 percent more of the work force in nonmetropolitan areas was employed in extractive activities and 4 percent more in manufacturing. This is almost offset by a similar degree of metropolitan specialization in financial and business services.

What is impressive is the lack of difference between the type of work performed in nonmetropolitan and urban areas.[27] It suggests the increasing importance of residentiary or locally oriented economic activity. One reason jobs tend to follow people is that a rising proportion of economic activity serves local economic needs locally. Local economic vitality is not primarily tied to an export-oriented economic base.

Bootstrap Economic Development

We have challenged the familiar folk economic view that people passively traipse after businesses when they move. In addition, we have
challenged the proposition that it is only the export of goods to the
larger national or international economy that energizes a local economy
and creates all other employment. In this section we stress the choices
of people in relocating and how those choices quantitatively affect the
location of economic activity.

As discussed above, the empirical evidence covering the period from
1950 to 1990 indicates that inmigration directly creates at least one new
job for each working-aged newcomer. Job creation and inmigration re-
inforce one another in a way that can be summarized with an employment multiplier of approximately 3.[28] Indeed, a local economy and the
people who choose to live there can "pull themselves up by their boot-
straps" even when there is no expansion in export-oriented economic
activity.

Different residential locations offer people different "packages" of
nonmarketed goods and services.[29] Each package offers people a
unique set of economic opportunities. It takes only a minority of the
population (those acting "at the margin") to change their economic activities in response to these opportunities to have a significant impact
on the geographic pattern of national economic activity (figure 2-6).

An area receiving inmigrants experiences a variety of economic impacts. Newcomers bring income and savings or borrowed money that
they intend to use in getting themselves established, for example,
buying homes or starting up businesses. Their presence adds to the
available labor supply and puts downward pressure on wages. This attracts yet more business activity. New residents expand local markets,
increasing the range of viable commercial businesses. Larger markets
as well as the entrepreneurial energy contributed by new residents help
the local economy capture and hold the dollars circulating within it.
This, too, increases local employment opportunity. A certain amount
of state and federal spending and investment is based on population
size. So an expanding population brings with it more public spending
and investment. The overall expansion in local economic activity feeds
yet more expansion and attracts still more inmigrants. That is the dynamic we wish to explore here in greater detail.

It should be pointed out that the forces described here do not operate solely in rapidly growing areas. A residential decision to *continue*

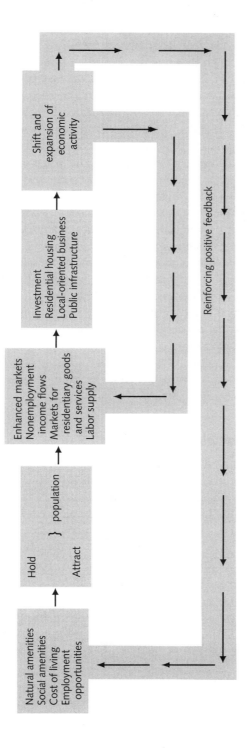

FIGURE 2-6. Bootstrap economic development. Attractive living environments attract and hold economic activity, which stimulates additional economic activity.

living in a location because of its amenities often has the same economic impact as a decision to inmigrate. Nor does inmigration necessarily imply ongoing population growth. All areas lose population to out-migration and death. Newcomers may simply be keeping the population stable, and if they arrive when traditional local industries are in decline, it may provide resiliency that the community would otherwise lack. Local economic vitality depends not necessarily on population growth but rather on protecting or expanding the range of economic options open to the local population. When options narrow, the costs of continued residence at a given location rise.

The discussion here may be misinterpreted as describing a situation where once population growth starts, it continues indefinitely until the natural and social environment deteriorates sufficiently to discourage further inmigration. Of course, there are large metropolitan areas such as southern California where that appears to be happening. But in considering the set of economic forces outlined here, it is important to keep in mind that there are other local economic forces, including those emphasized in the traditional economic-base approach, operating to constrain local economic expansion.

With the above road map and warnings in mind, we now turn to a more detailed analysis of the way residential location decisions stimulate supporting local economic activity.

The Impact of Nonemployment Income

On average, a third of total personal income is not associated with current participation in the work force.[30] Because nonemployment income (investment returns and government support of all types) is income injected into the local economy, one should treat it as part of the local economic base, but the tendency is to emphasize only "productive" economic activity such as participation in the labor force and production of exports that generate earnings.[31] Nonemployment income flow is large, in 1992 averaging about $6,600 per person nationwide. If a typical economic-base income multiplier of 2.5 or 3 applied to this income as it circulates within the local economy, it would boost local income by $16,000 to $20,000. This is the equivalent of the average income of an individual in 1992. That is, if the crude arithmetic of the economic base is applied to nonemployment income flow, this flow itself would seem sufficient to generate the economic activity to support the average person in his or her residential choice.

To a certain extent, this is supported by empirical analysis. Several studies have shown that nonemployment income flow has at least as large an impact on the local economy as traditional economic-base activity. Analysis of nonemployment income flow into Michigan counties showed multipliers in the 3 to 4 range for nonemployment income in the aggregate as well as for transfer payments and investment income separately. Earnings in traditional basic industry had much lower multiplier values.[32] An analysis of the impact of public transfer payments (primarily social security and medicare, but including unemployment compensation and welfare) on small Arizona communities estimated income multipliers for this category of nonemployment income of about 2, while basic industry earnings had a multiplier of about 1.5.[33] Because these communities were quite small (1,000 to 30,000), and the general belief is that income leaks more quickly from local economies, one would expect a smaller income multiplier.[34]

Given that nonemployment income flow is dominated by retirement income, there is additional evidence to support the idea that this income will have a significant positive impact on the local economy. Studies of the expenditure patterns of individuals at different stages in their lives indicate that local spending (for example, on medical services) rises with age and decreases with the distance traveled to work.[35] For both of these reasons, retired individuals are more likely to spend income locally.

There are, however, reasons to be hesitant about treating all nonemployment income just like earnings in export-oriented industry. A small part of total nonemployment income is not actual cash flow. To ensure that housing is treated the same in national economic accounts whether it is owned or rented, estimates of local personal income are increased to include an imputed rent from owner-occupied homes. Although the housing service the owner receives are real, the imputed income is not cash that actually circulates in the local economy. Another difference between nonlabor income and earnings is that, as mentioned above, some substantial part of the investment income that residents receive is immediately reinvested outside of the local economy. This is especially true of investment income flowing to those who have not retired. Finally, some retired individuals travel extensively. Northern "snowbirds" who winter in the South are the most dramatic examples: a considerable portion of their retirement income is spent outside the local economy.

Because nonemployment income flow is more dispersed geographically than economic activity as a whole, it tends to narrow the differences between income and income growth in metropolitan and nonmetropolitan areas. In addition, because the retirement component of transfer payments does not fluctuate with the business cycle, it tends to stabilize local income during cyclical fluctuations. When earned income in export-oriented economic activities collapses during national recessions, stable transfer payments help maintain local income and employment.[36]

As mentioned above, a significant part of nonemployment income is that which flows to retirees. In 1992 white senior citizen households (65 years and older) had a mean income of about $25,000. In addition to this money income, senior citizens also generated income in the form of medicare reimbursements averaging about $3,200 per person, or $5,600 per household.[37] Thus the total income of an average senior household was about $31,000, or about $17,500 per senior citizen. If an income multiplier of 3 were applied to this, each senior citizen's spending would be responsible for $52,500 in income, $35,000 more than their direct contribution. If the average earning per job is $26,500, the impact of this income would support 1.32 new jobs. At the national average of 1.8 people supported by each job, 3.4 people (including the senior citizen) could be supported as a result of senior spending. If retirees represent a sixth of the total stream of newcomers, the income associated with retirees would be sufficient to support over half (57 percent) of the total inmigrants.[38]

The impact of retirees has been especially significant in recent years. The rate of growth of the elderly population from 1950 to 1987 was 2.5 percent per year. For the 1990–2010 period, the rate of growth is projected to be less than half of that.[39] Thus growth in retirement income may provide less of a stimulus to the local economy than it has in the past. Keep in mind the savings, public and private, that go to support retirees. The social security tax, for instance, reduces the disposable income of all working households. Spending by retirees is not a "free lunch." Nonetheless, some analysts have pointed out that the inmigration of retirees can be expected to have a larger impact on local development than the inmigration of job seekers because retirees will not fill jobs themselves.[40]

The Rise of Local Self-Sufficiency

The degree to which local economic activity can be supported by the income flow into an area depends on how self-sufficient the local economy is, how successful residents are at taking in each other's wash.

An area that imports almost all of what it needs from elsewhere will have almost no local economic activity, regardless of how many dollars flow into it. The degree of self-sufficiency can be measured by the tendency of residents and businesses to purchase locally. In a primitive economic base model, the income multiplier is simply the reciprocal of the tendency to spend income externally, or the reciprocal of 1 minus the tendency to purchase locally. For instance, in a small town located within commuting distance of a much larger trade center, 90 percent of local expenditure may flow out of the community without first circulating there. With such limited self-sufficiency, the crude income multiplier would be the reciprocal of 90 percent, or the equivalent, the reciprocal of 1 minus 10 percent, 1.11. If, on the other hand, the town was more self-sufficient and a third of its residents' expenditures circulated within the local economy initially, the multiplier would be the reciprocal of two-thirds, or 1.5. A largely self-sufficient community, where three-quarters of expenditures first moved through the local economy, would have a multiplier equal to the reciprocal of a quarter, or 4.0.

Several forces determined the extent of reliance on external suppliers of goods and services. Over time, communities with populations over 5,000 have tended to become more self-sufficient. A larger and larger share of expenditures go to locally produced goods and services. With the shift from goods production to the provision of services, the locus of production shifts toward the local economy.[41] Over the last two decades, for instance, the aggregate of retail and wholesale sales, services, financial and real estate, and state and local government has made up a larger and larger percentage of total earnings, rising from 52 to 60 percent, a growth rate of 0.6 percent per year.[42] If one uses minimum requirements to define locally oriented production, the percentage has systematically increased since 1940, from 42 to 52 percent by 1980, or 0.5 to 0.6 percent per year for cities of 200,000.[43] For cities with populations greater than 1 million, the annual rate of growth of the share of locally oriented economic activity from 1969 to 1989 was 0.7 percent. From 1979 to 1989, the rate accelerated to over 0.8 percent per year as economic activity shifted still further toward locally produced services. Locally oriented manufacturing's share increased at a rate of almost 2 percent per year during this period.[44] Such increases allow local economies to expand without any increase in the number of dollars flowing into them. The rate of expansion is the same as the rate of increase in the income multiplier. This is determined by the growth in local spending. If it increases at 0.6 percent per year and the initial percentage of income spent locally is 60 percent, it would be sufficient to support a 1 percent annual expansion in the local economy.[45] The increasing range of locally supplied goods and services appears to have allowed growth in the economies of relatively small towns and cities even when their economic status in the hierarchy of urban trade centers has not changed.[46]

Inmigration into certain areas may be systematically changing the degree of self-sufficiency too. As population rises, the range of feasible locally oriented production increases too. In addition, considerable entrepreneurial energy is likely to be pumped into the local economy as new migrants search for opportunities to tap markets previously ignored or served by the external economy. inmigration tends to boost self-sufficiency. If, to use the same arithmetic as above, inmigration raised the fraction of income spent locally from 60 to 64 percent over a ten-year period, this change alone would allow the local economy to expand by 1 percent per year.[47] If the change is added to the long-run national trend toward local self-sufficiency, a community could grow by 1 to 2 percent annually with no increase in the flow of outside income into the local economy from export or other sources. Although only relatively diverse local trade centers that are in the midst of being discovered are likely to feel the full impact of these nonexport forces, relatively small towns and cities (population 2,500 and above) may well experience some growth as a result.

Such calculations are crude, ignoring such factors as the impact of net savings, nonlocal taxes, and the potential for expansion of locally oriented economic activity in communities of different size. Expansion of locally oriented economic activity through increased self-sufficiency and inmigration, however, is a reality in many U.S. communities despite lack of growth or decline in their traditional economic bases. Such resiliency has been an important buffer against depression and shrinking traditional export bases.

Inmigrant Investment and Spending

Setting up a new residence and/or business requires money. Inmigrants have to support themselves while they get re-established. Funds may come from savings from economic activities elsewhere or be borrowed from outside the local economy. Local businesses providing goods and services to new residents expand their operations. Ultimately, population growth triggers additional public infrastructure in the form of schools, roads, government offices, and so forth.

One could argue that none or little of this investment will take place if the inmigrants fail to establish themselves, or that without expansion in the economic base, attempts at resettlement will probably fail. Rational individuals, believing that inmigrants are only temporary, will not invest. But this ignores the dynamic process that inmigration can trigger. To the extent that the investment associated with inmigrants reinforces other positive effects of population growth, investment may well support expansion even though a particular investment, by itself, might not be viable. When other expansionary forces are operating, investment activity significantly bolsters expansion. Real investment will take place, though the stability of the resulting expansion may be in question. Investment, by its very nature, can exaggerate swings in one direction or the other. When expansion occurs, investment accelerates it. When expansion slows, investment declines and can create forces that actually lead to contraction. But the point here is that investment associated with residential relocation does support it.

To get a feeling for the potential size of this impact, consider a situation where an average of one half of per capita income is expended in support of each inmigrant, partly to cover expenses getting established and partly as investments in housing, business expansion, and public infrastructure. If per capita income was $20,000, this would represent an expenditure of $10,000 per new resident by new residents, by businesses serving them, and by various government agencies. Even if only one in ten new residents constructed a new $100,000 home, this level of investment would be achieved. Actual gross private investment in new construction comes to about 12 percent or the equivalent of one-eighth of personal consumption expenditure. Newcomers, however, can be expected to be responsible for a significantly higher level of investment as they get established, and there is also business and government investment as well as dis-savings supporting living expenses. If households consumed a quarter of their annual income getting established *and* investment was at the average level of private construction investment, the level of dis-savings supporting local economic activity would come to $7,500 per inmigrant. If an income multiplier of 2.5 or 3.0 were applied to these investments, the total impact would be $19,000 to $23,000—about the average income for one year. At least temporarily, economic activity triggered by inmigrant-related investment would support the inmigrant.

One might argue that such temporary income flow cannot support a sustainable local economy. That may not be true. Ongoing inmigration will create ongoing investment that will sustain a certain amount of economic activity from year to year. Even those who do not succeed in establishing themselves will have expended significant resources in the attempt. In an attractive area, there could be a substantial flow of individuals trying to reside there, only a fraction of whom succeed. In some growing areas, four or five migrants try to set up residence for every one that permanently succeeds.[48] Given the mobility of the American population and its size, it is possible that the phenomenon of migrants coming and going injects a considerable and continuing flow of income into attractive communities. If, for instance, for each four people who spend one month trying to establish themselves in an area, one succeeds and an income multiplier of 3.0 applies, it would represent a flow of income sufficient to support one resident permanently.

Or consider this example: the *total* investment level associated with permanent inmigrants is no larger than the average rate of private construction investment, 12 percent of personal outlays, that two individuals attempt to reside in an area for each who succeeds, and that those who fail leave after a month. With an income multiplier of 2.5, the income generated by such efforts would amount to seven-eighths of average income for each inmigrant who succeeds. Initially, the effort almost entirely supports relocation.

It is important to note that this type of stimulus by itself cannot *maintain* growth. Although initial investment and spending by inmigrants can generate employment and income, investment and spending have to continue indefinitely if they are going to provide ongoing support. That means that future inmigrants primarily *maintain* income and employment levels established initially, they don't add to expansion. Thus inmigrant dis-saving, spending, and investment represent a substantial initial boost to the local economy, and then only a modest continuing stimulus. In a more complex context where these factors interact with other growth stimulants, however, they can be expected to fuel overall growth.

The Falling Costs of Residential Choice

As population grows, an area's local characteristics change. Some of the original amenities that attracted inmigrants may deteriorate, while others, especially social, cultural, and commercial may develop. Inmigration may be so extensive that congestion, pollution, and crime begin to discourage additional newcomers. Some would argue that that is what happened as a result of ongoing growth in southern California. The out-migration from California to more attractive locations in the West during the first half of the 1990s has been attributed to the environmental and social "gridlock" generated by rapid growth. But most areas, at least in the intermediate run, do not reach physical and social limits to expansion. Although existing residents may see their quality of life decline as a result of changes brought on by inmigration, potential newcomers are still likely to see the advantages of the area.

As population grows, the availability of goods and services will expand, and transportation and communication infrastructures will likely improve along with government services. These changes are viewed as positive by most potential inmigrants.[49] What may discourage them is the isolation and sacrifice required of many migrants: limited commercial opportunity, limited medical services, limited educational opportunities, cultural isolation, distance from family, and so on. Initially, only pioneers who are strongly attracted by an area's endowments will consider settling there, because the sacrifices are too great. As development continues, the sacrifices diminish, and if the area's amenities remain intact they will draw more newcomers. This is a dynamic process: inmigration stimulates further inmigration by reducing the costs associated with it.

The Impact of Residential Relocation

The crude estimates of how residential relocation can stimulate local economic activity seek to quantify the economic dynamic behind the environmental model of local economic vitality (table 2-1). Even if these estimates are reduced by 50 percent, the economic activity created by individuals' relocation efforts is enough to support those efforts. This phenomenon, consistent with both regional economic theory and with empirical economic research, should not be startling. Neither the world's population nor America's citizens are clustered around coal mines, steel mills, or automobile assembly plants. Quite the contrary, extractive activities have shrunk in absolute and relative importance, and manufacturing activities have dispersed in the pursuit of markets and work force. Meanwhile, it is locally oriented economic activity that has been systematically increasing in importance as U.S.

TABLE 2-1

The Impact on the Local Economy of Attracting/Holding Residents

Type of Impact	Percent Expansion of the Local Economy from Ten Percent Net Immigration
1. Retirement Impact	
a. Nonemployment Income[50]	
(33% of total income)	6.7%
b. Number of Retirees[51]	
(1 in 6 age 60+)	5.6%
2. Increase Self-Sufficiency[52]	
(Local share grows 0.6%/yr)	6.2%
3. Enhanced Labor Supply[53]	
(1 in 6 inmigrants added	
to local labor supply)	5.0%
4. Dis-savings/Investment of	
New Migrants[54]	6.7%
Cumulative Impact	*23.5%*

Source: Author's calculations; see text above and endnotes.

communities become more self-sufficient. America's local economies have diversified with the decline of extractive and export activities. This is what economic development is all about—not extracting, producing, and exporting more and more of the same products. Specialization is a prescription for instability and decline, not economic vitality. It is when economies begin to take care of their own needs and desires that development takes off.

As mentioned earlier, most of the effects of residential relocation are felt even if the local economy is not gaining population. A retiree who decides to remain in place keeps his or her nonemployment income within the local economy. A job is opened by the retirement, while an alternative income stream supports the retiree's spending. At the very least, the decision to remain prevents a decline in local spending. Rapid out-migration because residents have lost their jobs or their interest in an area shrinks the local labor supply as well as local markets, discouraging new business. Instability associated with external markets that export-oriented firms serve also discourages investment in the local economy. Clearly, commitment to place kindles local economic vitality.

The phenomenon of economic activity following and supporting people as they relocate is not necessarily positive change. At the extreme, it represents the Daniel Boone syndrome: people abandon the decaying urban areas of the Northeast for the fresh environments of California, which they proceed to "trash" before fleeing to the Pacific Northwest and from there, to the small towns of the inland West. One can interpret such shifts as a collective shunning of the social problems associated with modern urban living. Rather than confronting and solving problems, people move on and spread them.

Hypnotized by the Rearview Mirror

Why do almost none of us think of the local economy in terms of this environmental model? Why do we tend to adopt the view of the local economy embodied in the economic base model? Despite empirical and theoretical support for the environmental model, our economic vision continues to be dominated by the extractive view. Part of the answer is historical and cultural. Though local economies are constantly changing, we learn about the communities in which we live from parents, grandparents, teachers, and local opinion leaders. They tell us stories based on their own experiences, which become part of local lore whose truth is taken for granted. Meanwhile, the economy continues to change. This is understandable cultural and intellectual inertia. Of course, the "lords of yesterday" will enthusiastically proselytize on behalf of their way of looking at the local economy.[55] Because they represent established economic interests and can contribute handsomely to political campaigns, they will also shape how our politicians look at local economic reality.

In addition, the economic insecurity endemic in our economy necessarily draws our attention to highly visible short-run impacts. Rarely do we attempt to track what happened to the laid-off worker or to analyze why it is that the new firm chose to locate where it did. Our understanding of the local economy is formed by current events, not by the long-term changes that are actually shaping the local economy. Most of us have no job tenure. We could be laid off tomorrow. National business cycles, new technologies, shifting patterns of economic geography, competition in national and international markets, government policies—all these can force disruptive and costly changes on us. The rearview mirror vision is reinforced by our feelings of general helplessness—the forces at work are usually well beyond our control. We appear to be passive victims of decisions made elsewhere, beggars who cannot afford to be choosers. This is the economic base vision.

By contrast, the alternative environmental economic view spotlights what has really been happening in America's local and regional economies, independent of local lore. The economic trends that have transformed the economic geography of the United States in the last half of the twentieth century are not interesting sidebars to the main story—they *are* the main story. The failure of the economic base model to depict accurately what has been going on is suggested by the virtual absence of ghost towns in America, despite the nearly complete demise or relocation of entire industries upon which communities once depended. Communities, once they reach a certain "critical mass," don't vanish when they lose their traditional economic base. Only small towns exclusively devoted to mining or agriculture, located in areas where people would prefer not to live, degenerate into the ghost towns that support the economic base vision.

To avert our gaze from the distracting rearview mirror, we need to take a longer view than the three-month to three-year time frame in which almost all public economic dialogue is conducted. As some economic opportunities die, others are born. Few people are permanently unemployed. Rather, they shift from one less productive undertaking to other more productive activities. The actors initiating new economic activity are not primarily national corporations or government agencies but ourselves, with the skills, commitment, and energy we bring to our communities. In a dynamic, changing economy like ours, there will be good times and there will be bad. We have to have the confidence that we and our communities can competently cope with both. We have to know that those very things that draw us to a particular area will ultimately be the primary forces that allow it to survive and prosper: they are the community's real economic base. Although there may be times when the community is undergoing economic dislocation, we do not have to make a desperate pact with the devils of the past in order to make the transition. Confidence in the endowments of our communities, and commitment to nurture those endowments, will ultimately assure the community's survival and prosperity.

3 Demystifying Local Economic Change

The shift toward a more diverse economy in which services and locally oriented activities play an expanding role has been particularly dramatic in America's nonmetropolitan areas, where extractive, natural resource industries have declined significantly in relative importance, but a similar shift has taken place in the nation's manufacturing belts. This trend has generally been deplored as undermining our prosperity and threatening the middle-class life-style.[1] Whatever might be said about the transformation away from heavy and extractive industry reducing stress on the natural environment, the impact on the social environment is usually assumed to be negative. Even though jobs have opened up in new sectors, they are considered low wage, dead-end, and unreliable, turning skilled craftspeople into unskilled drones. Full-time jobs are replaced with part-time jobs. We are all destined to become burger flippers. The proof, we are told, is clearly seen in the lower income levels in most of our nonmetropolitan areas and many center-city neighborhoods. Our communities dwindle along with our wallets. So the argument goes.

From a historical point of view, the shift from extractive and heavy-manufacturing industries toward services does not appear to be either a new or a disturbing change. The transition has been under way for almost the entire history of the United States, and if it is true that Americans' economic well-being has improved since the early 1800s, then the shift is not necessarily impoverishing. It is possible, however, that the form this economic transition has taken in the second half of the twentieth century has been more negative.

Depressed Wages

Before examining the characteristics of service jobs, it is important to survey the overall economy and trends that are operating independently of the shift toward services. Since 1970, if we adjust for inflation, average real hourly earnings have declined in goods-producing industries and increased in service industries. Between 1970 and 1992 the decline in manufacturing was about 4 percent in constant dollars, in construction, 24 percent. Between 1980 and 1992 real wages in mining declined by about 5 percent. From 1970 to 1992, wages in service industries increased about 6 percent in real terms.[2] Clearly, there are forces afoot that are depressing wages in goods production. Even if there were no shift of employment from goods to services, our wages would be falling. It would be incorrect to blame the overall decline in real average earnings (7.5 percent between 1970 and 1992) primarily on increased employment in services. If no such shift had taken place, most (83 percent) of the downward drift in real wages would have occurred anyway. Put slightly differently, the shift to services has been responsible for only a sixth of the decline in average real wages.[3]

The U.S. economy emerged from World War II as the only developed economy that was not seriously damaged, the war effort having enabled the United States to employ all its resources after a decade of depression. The demand for American goods and services to help rebuild the global economy was enormous, and for almost two decades there were no serious economic competitors abroad. The labor unions, which had secured federal support during the Great Depression, made sure now that the benefits of economic expansion were shared with workers. The full employment, high aggregate demand, strong labor unions, and scant foreign competition of that period were unusual circumstances. During the 1960s the United States began to confront competition from the recovering economic giants of Europe and Asia, Germany and Japan, and by the 1970s it had to face the fact that developing countries were no longer simply suppliers of raw materials but also manufacturing centers that competed directly with American industries. Some poorer countries, desperate for employment and foreign exchange, dumped raw materials on the world market and depressed commodity prices worldwide.

Like most other nations, the United States responded by erecting trade barriers to protect domestic producers from foreign competition. Eventually, however, the United States committed itself to free trade, working actively to reduce barriers around the world, including those in the United States. As a result, American businesses now operate with much less protection from foreign competition than at any other time in U.S. history. Competition has limited the real wages paid to American workers by threatening high-cost producers and sending some operations overseas. It is questionable to what extent the wage depression of the last two decades can be explained by increased competition from imports, but the *perception* of businesses that they face intensified competition and have to cut costs, especially labor costs, to survive has been strong.[4]

Integration into a global economy has been accompanied by other changes in the American economy. "High wage" jobs today usually refer to manufacturing, construction, or mining jobs. Historically these jobs were not high wage. It was American institutions (government protected labor unions), laws (minimum wage, restrictions on child labor and immigration), and government intervention in the economy that worked to raise the pay of relatively unskilled blue collar workers leading to the creation of a "blue-collar middle class."[5]

Blue-collar progress began to unravel in the 1980s. Labor unions were weakened by government action and the migration of firms to nonunion states. By not adjusting it for inflation, the minimum wage was allowed to fall by more than a dollar an hour in real terms. Immigration surged again, reaching levels in the 1980s three to ten times (depending on whether one counts all or only legal immigration) what they were in the 1950s. These recent immigrants, unlike their predecessors, were relatively unskilled and competed for jobs at the low end of the employment spectrum. Meanwhile, the end of the cold war had weakened the easiest justification Americans found for direct government involvement in the economy, national defense. Such changes were supported by a new conservative political mood that was probusiness, antiunion, and in favor of deregulation, free trade, and free markets.

During the last quarter of the twentieth century, then, the economic, legal, and institutional arrangements developed during the first half of the century that had helped boost wages for a number of relatively unskilled workers began to disintegrate. Entire factories shut down. Others shifted to nonunion states. Unilateral wage and benefit "takebacks" were imposed. Strikes turned into lockouts. High-wage, unionized jobs began to disappear. This was not a new phenomenon. Earlier in the century the textile industry had shifted form northeastern cities to southern rural areas. At mid-century other manufacturing shifted to the nonmetropolitan Midwest. The shift in the 1970s and 1980s to the Sunbelt was just a continuation of this general shift toward lower wages and benefits in manufacturing.

This summary of events is not meant as a criticism of free trade or immigration, of government regulation or military spending. Strong arguments can be made that in the long run an open world economy with limited government involvement will lead to higher employment, economic growth, and increased efficiency. In the short term, however, globalization and deregulation have caused disruption, instability, and depressed wages. In thinking about such changes, it is important to distinguish between negative global pressure, the change in political climate and public institutions, and the consequences associated with the shift toward services. Global pressure is largely beyond the control of state or local government or even, in the context of free trade, the federal government. It is part of the unstable economic environment in which we have to operate. As for political and institutional changes that are affecting real earnings, they are often presented as necessary adjustments to the competitive global economy. More accurately, they are tied to an ascendant laissez-faire ideology, not to actual changes in the world economy.

We might wish that the federal government had a different policy on free trade or that it were more involved in trying to guide and assist the economy as it develops and is transformed, but those are separate public policy issues largely unrelated to the decisions we make about how to use the environment. To blame local environmental protection for depressed wages or unemployment that is caused by international competitive pressure is not only unproductive; it seriously misrepresents the actual economic choices we face. Unfortunately, misrepresentation may be a useful political strategy for those who would milk economic fear to mobilize support for intensified natural resource extraction and toxic waste disposal.

The point here is simple: all or most of the economic pressure on local economies derives from something other than efforts to protect the environment, environmental protection did not *cause* the competitive pressure flowing from the globalization of the economy, and it was not environmentalists who led the attack on minimum wages and unions. There is little or no evidence that efforts at protecting communities and landscapes are what depressed real wages and caused the massive layoffs in goods-producing industries in the 1980s and 1990s.

All this has to be kept in mind as we consider further efforts to protect our local environments.

Solid Goods, Flimsy Services?

To many, there is something insubstantial and unreliable about employment in services. During the nineteenth century, conventional economic theory confirmed this view. Extractive activity was seen as primary and manufacturing activity secondary, while services were tertiary. Some economists went so far as to argue that no value at all was added in services. Because they helped realize the value associated with goods production, they were parasitic and even consumed some of that value. That view has lingered; consider the negative characterization of service-providing middlemen between farmer and consumer. It is important to realize, however, that such prejudice is an expression of cultural beliefs, not of economic facts.

Almost any shift in the structure of the economy leads to hand-wringing and expressions of impending collapse. Two centuries ago, Thomas Jefferson saw urbanization and the rise of manufacturing as threatening the survival of American democracy. To him, only a rural, agriculturally based self-sufficient homestead lifestyle provided the independence and equality needed to make democracy work. As industrialization and urbanization continued throughout the nineteenth and twentieth centuries, the increasing reliance of the majority on a small minority of food producers led many to predict certain poverty and famine. They urged that the United States adopt a national policy to keep a larger percentage of the population on the farm.

What used to be is almost always seen as more reliable and productive than what will be. To many people the current shift of employment and income from goods to services is ominous. It doesn't matter how many new jobs are being generated or what those jobs pay: newfangled jobs are inferior to those we used to have and the changes are certain to send us shuffling off to the poorhouse.

As common as this view is, its economic logic is hard to discern. Economic well-being is enhanced by stretching the productivity of scarce resources available so that more and more of our needs and desires can be satisfied. If what we most desire is a continuously expanding flow of material goods, then that should be one target of our economic effort. The other should be boosting the productivity of our scarce resources.

But it is certainly possible that some of the things that we most desire are not material goods but higher-quality services. It is possible that rather than more cars, we want higher-quality cars. It is possible that rather than larger houses, we want more attractive and convenient living environments. It is possible that rather than more calories of food energy, we want more tastefully prepared or healthier foods. It is possible that rather than more things to stuff into our houses, we want better care for our children, better health care, or more inspiring entertainment. It would be difficult to argue convincingly that now and forever what we want above all is more material goods.

Or consider the other determinant of economic well-being: improved productivity in the use of scarce resources. Since at least the time of Adam Smith, higher productivity has been interpreted as synonymous with the wealth of nations, as the primary source of economic progress. But achieving more efficient production involves science, technology, management, and improved skills. Importantly, all of these are service-sector related.

The truth is that, increasingly, both what we want most from our economy and the inputs most capable of boosting its productivity originate in the services sector. It is not true that producing more bushels of wheat will contribute more to our well-being than improved health care. Nor is it true that the best way to produce more wheat is to commit more "things"—land, people, tractors, gasoline—to the enterprise. Agronomists, biologists, and management specialists are far more likely to make a contribution. It also is not true that mining and smelting more copper will contribute more to our economic well-being than a computer designer or a software writer. Clear-cutting more trees will not contribute more to our well-being than the design of houses that are more efficient in their use of raw materials or the design of a recycling program that keeps us from wasting most of the wood fiber we produce.

There is nothing insubstantial or unproductive about services. They are what energize the productive side of our economy. They are also what we increasingly want from the economy to make our lives more satisfying. It is goods production that ultimately threatens us and our communities: a constantly increased flow of raw material from the natural landscape and a constantly increased flow of material waste back into the landscape. That pattern is not sustainable. The shift to services offers us a way out of this dilemma: it allows us to continue pursuing improvements in how well our needs and desires are met while reducing the demands we make on the environment. Perhaps we should stop complaining and start celebrating the transformation that is already well under way.

Some will still not be convinced. Because, in a service economy, almost none of us "work the land" to harvest the "bounty of nature," it is suggested that we have lost our human dignity, our connection with the earth, our link with the past. We have become rootless creatures, restless shadows whose work lacks meaning.

Though they ring a responsive chord in us, it is not clear how to make sense out of these concerns. How many of us really want to be underground miners or loggers wielding chainsaws or ranchers rounding up cattle in isolated scrubland? Many of us or our parents performed such work at one time and then decisively abandoned it. Miners don't encourage their children to go into the mines. Scores of loggers and mill workers leave their jobs when the opportunity presents itself. Ranchers and farmers, since the dawn of the modern era, have found it impossible to "keep the kids on the farm." The lure of the modern diverse economy is too great.

If most of us lack the stomach for traditional extractive and manufacturing activities and discourage our kids from such careers, why do we decry the economy and culture that emerge as other people make the same choices we have? Why do we attach near-religious significance to the occupations that happened historically to precede those that we have chosen? Working the land is not more "moral" than working with people to improve their lives—which is what much of the service sector is about. Teachers, healers, spiritual counselors, artists, and scientists are not temporary occupations of minor significance. Those who work with their heads and hearts are not less productive or less reliable in their contribution to the community than those who sweat, working with their muscles. Moreover, commercial exploitation of the earth is not the only way to understand and appreciate nature.

The "Lousy" Service Job

What are service jobs? Broadly speaking, service-producing jobs are any that are not identified as goods producing. Because extractive industries (such as agriculture, forestry, mining, and fishing), construction, and manufacturing produce tangible products for sale in markets, the goods classification may appear to be clear-cut. Service-producing jobs cover all residual economic activities, including medical and personal services, retail and wholesale trade, government, finance, transportation, communications, public utilities, and so forth. A more narrowly defined subset of service-producing jobs are labeled simply "services" and refer to work that is done at the behest of a customer, for example, dental work, advertising, repairs, and that cannot be stored or resold (in these pages, "services" refers to this narrower definition).

Services provided about 30 percent of total employment in 1992, while the broader service-producing category provided almost 80 percent of employment. Over the last two decades, services increased their employment role from 18 to 29 percent, while service-producing industries in general increased their employment role from 67 to 78 percent. All of the shift in the relative importance of the service-producing category was due to an increase in the importance of narrowly defined services. If one subtracts services from service-producing industries, the relative importance of the latter remains constant at 49 percent.[6] Thus the driving force in America's economic transformation comes from more narrowly defined services.

That is good reason to focus on services, but service-producing is what most people have in mind when discussing the *quality* of employment. The typical characterization of service industries is "flipping burgers at a fast-food joint." This can be misleading. Flipping burgers is a retail trade activity, not a narrow service activity. Retail trade is the lowest-paid major industry in the U.S. economy, but it is not rapidly expanding: over the last two decades its share of total employment has only risen from 15 to 16.5 percent. The popular lament that to make ends meet more and more American workers are resorting to jobs as hamburger flippers is misinformed.

Another important distinction to make when discussing services is the division between goods-producing and service-producing industries. This was dramatized during the debate over health-insurance reform in the early 1990s when automobile executives made the point that besides wages the largest single expense that goes into automobiles is not steel or plastics or rubber, but worker health care, a service. Health care is just one example of the services that go into automobile production. Consider design and engineering, both services, the financial services that automotive producers provide to automobile purchasers and dealers through such business arms as the General Motors Acceptance Corporation and Chrysler Credit Corporation. Then there are major expenditures on advertising and marketing. In truth, services are a major part of the "goods-producing" automobile industry.

This is not an extreme example. Consider another "manufacturing" activity, printing and publishing. Only a small part of the work force in a publishing house is engaged in the actual printing of books. Most of the staff is gathering information, writing, and editing. These, of course, are all service activities, and most of the value of a published book is tied to them, not to goods. What about the huge computer industry? Increasingly, actual manufacturing and assembly are relatively low-paid activities, responsible for only a small part of the total value of a computer. Its value begins to accumulate with the research and development that go into the design of new chips and components. Even this hardware is of limited value without accessible software to harness its capabilities. Software design and development represent the greatest value of computers. Almost all computers come with software inside. Indeed, the manufactured "good" begins to look more and more like a bundle of "services." The increasingly important role of services is not limited to service firms that directly receive our expenditures. Services are also an increasingly important component of the goods we purchase.

Demonizing Service Jobs

Service jobs have been criticized on the basis of many inaccurate characterizations, most notably the following:

- Low pay: the earnings associated with service jobs maintain families just above the line;
- Dead-end: service jobs offer no future in the form of increased earnings with increased experience;
- Unskilled: service jobs are entry-level jobs requiring little education or skill;
- Unstable: such jobs are unreliable because service businesses fail regularly and lay off workers; and
- Part-time: service jobs force workers into underemployment.

The Pay in Services

A casual look at the earnings data on service jobs, both narrowly and broadly defined, appears to support the widely held opinion that service jobs are significantly lower paid. Take, for instance, annual earnings per job. In both the broad and narrow sectors, annual earnings are roughly a third less than the annual earnings in manufacturing and nonfarm goods-producing industries. The difference represents $10,000 to $12,000 per year in 1992, not insignificant (table 3-1). Alternatively, one could compare the hourly wages paid in narrow services with those in manufacturing, skill level by skill level. This would also reveal significantly lower wages in services. Hourly wages are 15 to 25 percent lower in services for similar skilled jobs (table 3-2).

TABLE 3-1.

Annual Earnings per Job, 1992

	Dollars/yr.	% of Manufacturing
Farm	$16,485	45%
Nonfarm	26,754	72%
Private	26,477	72%
Agricultural services, forestry, fisheries, and other	16,114	44%
Mining	36,480	99%
Construction	29,171	79%
Manufacturing	36,923	100%
Transportation and public utilities	37,270	101%
Wholesale trade	35,379	96%
Retail trade	15,354	42%
Finance, insurance, and real estate	25,277	68%
Services	24,771	67%
Government and government enterprises	28,238	76%
Federal, civilian	38,789	105%
Military	19,761	54%
State and local	27,517	75%
Weighted goods-producing	32,218	87%
Weighted nonagricultural goods producing	34,954	95%
Weighted services producing	24,918	67%
Narrow services	24,771	67%

Note: Total earnings divided by employment.

Source: U.S. Department of Commerce, Bureau of Economic Analysis, Regional Economic Information System (BEA REIS), CD-ROM, 1969–92.

TABLE 3-2.

Hourly Wages by Occupation in Manufacturing and Narrow Services Industries, 1987

Occupation	Manufacturing Industries				Service Industries			
	Male Wage	Male % Distribution	Female Wage	Female % Distribution	Male Wage	Male % Distribution	Female Wage	Female % Distribution
Executive, Administrative, Management	$16.26	11	$11.76	8	$13.98	19	$10.57	11
Professional and specialists	16.38	10	12.30	5	13.20	40	10.96	41
Technical and related	12.94	4	10.49	3	11.15	8	9.28	9
Sales	13.55	4	9.89	3	9.85	3	6.48	3
Administrative Support and Clerical	10.04	5	8.09	26	7.75	7	7.09	33
Production, Craft, and Repair	11.03	25	7.66	9	8.80	14	7.51	1
Machine Oper and Assembly	8.89	29	6.20	41	6.79	4	5.18	2
Transportation and Material Movers	8.98	6	9.40	1	7.47	3	7.15	1
Handlers and Equip Cleaners	7.64	7	6.26	5	5.72	3	4.60	0
Weighted Average	$11.27		$7.83		$11.45		$9.19	
Average Male and Female		$10.07				$9.97		

Source: Current Population Surveys (1987) reported in R. W. Eberts and E. L. Groshen, "Service Jobs versus Manufacturing Jobs," *Economic Development Commentary* 14 (2): 4–10, p. 7, table 2.

These comparisons may seem convincing. However, there are several aspects of service jobs that the statistics obscure and that change the conclusions dramatically. First, women are more concentrated in services than in goods and are regularly paid less than men, no matter what type of job they hold. Second, the distribution of skill levels within services is skewed toward the higher end, in contrast to the manufacturing sector. Third, service jobs tend to involve fewer hours of work which may account for the lower annual salaries.

If women are disproportionately represented in services and they receive lower pay in all sectors, the lower earnings in services may be attributable to the fact that women get shabby treatment no matter where they work (table 3-3). The gap reported on an hourly basis for full-time workers is narrower, but service jobs still pay about 10 percent less than nonfarm goods-producing jobs. Even when one adjusts for skill level (occupation), women get paid significantly less in both manufacturing and services and in all occupations (see table 3-3). What is interesting, however, is that when one takes sex into account, the difference between service and goods employment vanishes or reverses itself: women's wages are *higher* in narrow services than in goods production and are almost identical in broad services and goods production. For women, service jobs are not low paid compared with manufacturing or goods jobs.[7]

If we look at the wages paid for similar skill or occupational levels in manufacturing and narrow services, there is also more than meets the eye. Although it is true that for each occupational level and for men and women separately, the wages paid in services are lower, and the distribution of jobs among occupational levels is also dramatically different (see table 3-3 and figure 3-1). Jobs in manufacturing are concentrated at the lower levels. While almost 45 percent of manufacturing jobs are lower end, only about 5 percent of narrow service jobs are. Put another way, less than a quarter of manufacturing jobs are upper-level professional-technical jobs, while almost two-thirds of narrow service jobs are upper level. As a result of this dramatically different skill distribution, the weighted average wage (by sex) in narrow service jobs is higher than in manufacturing, even though at each occupational level the wages are lower. In that sense, there is nothing "low paid" about service jobs overall. If one ignores the male–female distinction, wages in narrow services are slightly (1 percent) lower.

The positive side of these results is that services do provide a sub-

TABLE 3-3.

Industry	Average Hourly Earnings			Hourly Wage as a Percent of Nonfarm Goods-Producing Hourly Wage		
	Male	Female	Total	Male	Female	Total
Agriculture	$6.43	$5.61	$6.29	52%	67%	56%
Mining	14.26	11.40	13.85	115	136	122
Construction	10.89	8.31	10.70	88	99	95
Manufacturing	13.01	8.37	11.44	105	99	101
Transportation, Communications, Public Utilities	13.50	10.92	12.81	109	130	113
Trade	9.75	6.44	8.36	79	77	74
Firefighting	15.88	9.69	12.28	128	115	108
Public Administration	12.86	10.38	11.94	104	123	105
Services	12.47	8.87	10.40	101	105	92
Broad Services	11.99	8.48	10.18	97	101	90
Nonagricultural Goods Production	12.37	8.41	11.32	100	100	100

Source: Current Population Survey Tapes, 1988–91.

stantial number of well-paid jobs and, on average, the shift to services is not depressing wages. The negative side is that service jobs pay less than equivalent-level goods-production jobs. Put slightly differently, a worker shifting from goods-production to services would have to move into a higher-skilled service job to make the same money.[8] Fortunately, there are many more higher-skill jobs in services than in goods, though workers displaced from goods-production may not automatically qualify for them.

If one looks at what has happened to the distribution of wages among higher- and lower-paying jobs over the last two decades, the picture is not as bleak as is usually assumed. For women there has been a definite shift in employment toward higher-paying jobs. The percentage of employment in low-wage jobs has declined as the percentage in higher-paying jobs has risen.[9] For men the overall impact of the transition has been more complex. The percentage of lower-paying jobs

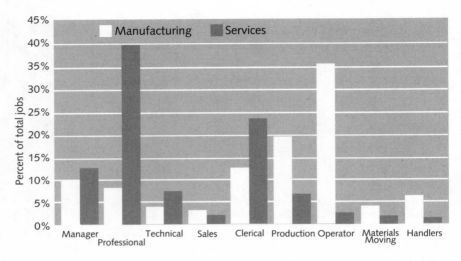

FIGURE 3-1. The distribution of skills in manufacturing and services. Service jobs tend to be higher skilled. (*Data sources:* Wage and Salary Workers 18-54, Current Population Survey, 1987.)

has increased, but there is also evidence that the percentage of higher-paying jobs has increased—the "squeezed middle" phenomenon.[10] In any case, the pattern is not a systematic downward slide as employment shifts from goods to services.

The other consideration in evaluating the low annual wages in services is the prevalence of a shorter work week. If one compares the hourly wage of full-time workers (35 hours per week or more) with annual wages, the importance of this factor becomes obvious. While the annual earnings in all services are only 66 percent of those in manufacturing, the hourly wages paid to full-time employees in services is about 90 percent of those in manufacturing. That is, when one takes into account shorter work weeks, the gap between services and manufacturing narrows considerably. (As discussed above, if gender is accounted for, the gap closes entirely or reverses.)

Some may object that it is annual pay that matters, not hourly, because people want full-time, not part-time work. That is not true. Most people hold part-time jobs through choice.[11] These include high-school and college students, farmers and their families, women with young children at home, and workers seeking to supplement the income from another job. There are also those who value their leisure time more than additional income. The U.S. economy provides a diversity of employment opportunities. Over half of American families would find farming far less viable financially if the labor market did not provide them with part-time outside employment opportunities.[12] Families with young children would be far more stressed financially and emotionally if there were not part-time employment opportunities. Many students cannot afford school unless they work their way through. To the extent that people filling part-time jobs do so voluntarily, part-time jobs are a positive, not negative, feature of the economy. However, it is also important to recognize that the percentage of part-time women workers who report that they would prefer full-time jobs has been rising, from about 20 percent in the late 1970s to about 25 percent by the early 1990s.[13]

A broad look at all of the jobs in both services and goods gives a better picture of what each sector offers in the way of pay. The fact is there are "lousy" jobs in both goods and services. Manufacturing, for instance, is not entirely unionized, high-pay employment. As we have seen, over the last half century much manufacturing shifted from the metropolitan Northeast to metropolitan areas throughout the nation, where some manufacturing wages are as low as the minimum wage. At the same time, many service jobs are relatively high paid technical and professional positions. The overall distribution of jobs in both broad sectors reveals not the significant differences in wages but their similarity (figure 3-2). Indeed, they are almost identical. In the lower-paid categories, service sectors have a slightly higher percentage of jobs. As a result, the median-wage job in goods production offers a few more dollars per week (about twenty dollars, or less than 4 percent in 1992). At the same time, many of the highest-paying opportunities are found in the service sector. If one judges the quality of employment in terms of pay level, goods and services offer similar opportunities, some of them excellent, some of them "lousy."

Career Opportunities in Services

Another disturbing claim often made about service jobs is that whatever the initial pay, they lead nowhere. Unlike manufacturing or construction, where pay and possible position increase with tenure, service jobs are like permanent entry-level positions. To evaluate this claim, we need data that tracks individuals over their working life in, say, both narrow services and manufacturing. Unfortunately, that information is not

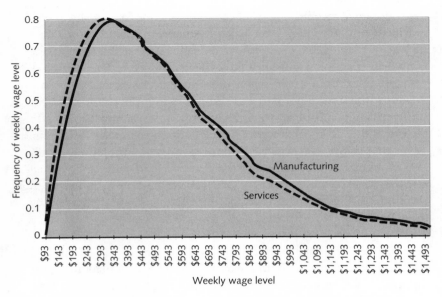

FIGURE 3-2. The distribution of weekly wages in manufacturing and services, 1992. (*Data sources:* M. Dupuy and M. E. Schweitzer, "Are Service-Sector Jobs Inferior?" *Economic Commentary,* Federal Reserve Bank of Cleveland, Feb. 1, 1994, figure 1.)

available. But we do have data on how workers of different ages are paid in these two industries. From that we can estimate an age-wage profile to see how earning potential changes with age. The data indicates that in narrow services, as in manufacturing, there is a significant increase in earnings with age. This is especially true for men: 1987 data indicates that wages rose 335 percent between ages 18 and 50 for both narrow services and manufacturing. Wages for younger employees were lower in services, but by the time workers were in their early thirties, wages were almost equal. This means that the chances for economic improvement were higher, not lower, in narrow services. For women there is a similar pattern, except that wages in neither narrow services nor manufacturing increase much past the age of thirty. For women, wages in services also begin lower than in manufacturing by almost a dollar an hour, but by the mid-twenties service wages exceed manufacturing wages and stay higher. Again, the range for improvement with age is greater in services than in manufacturing (figure 3-3). It should be clear that at least within narrow services, the potential for economic improvement with age is as great as the opportunity in manufacturing.

The Skill Level of Service Jobs

Some critics maintain that service jobs fail to make use of the skills and education of the work force. They are "kids' jobs" that ask little of employees. As we have seen (see table 3-3), however, narrow-service employment is largely professional-technical, more skill oriented, by far, than manufacturing. The educational makeup of the two work forces reflects this. Narrow-service workers tend to have more formal schooling. The higher level of education might be dismissed simply as a sign of the underemployment of skills in services, but the economic return of education is higher for service workers than for manufacturing workers. A one-year increase in education in services increases wages by 8.1 percent, while the same increase in education raises the wages of manufacturing workers by only 4.5 percent.[14]

Contrary to the characterization of service workers as burger flippers, narrowly defined services hire some of the most technically sophisticated workers in the economy. Consider some relevant industries: business services (including accounting, advertising, computers, and information technology); legal, educational (including universities),

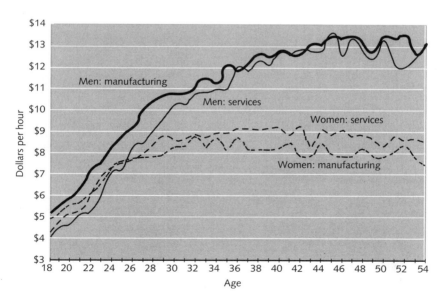

FIGURE 3-3. The change in earning potential with age in manufacturing and services. (*Data sources:* R. W. Eberts and E. L. Groshen, "Service Jobs versus Manufacturing Jobs," *Economic Development Commentary*, Summer 1990, figure 1.)

and health services; engineering and management services; and repair services. The same can be said of workers in the broader services, such as banking, insurance, real estate, government, justice, law enforcement, human resource programs, and national security.

Growth in the broad service sector is concentrated in relatively higher paid, more skilled industries such as business and health services (figure 3-4). From 1980 to 1992, low-wage hotel and restaurant establishments (for example, those employing "burger flippers") represented only about one-eighth of the total employment gain, clearly overwhelmed by other service-industry gains. Higher-wage service industries provided almost six times as many new jobs as lower-wage service industries.

The Reliability of Service Jobs

Finally, there is the belief that service jobs are unreliable. The general idea is that they provide intangible things that people do not need. We always need food, clothing, shelter, energy, and transportation; we do

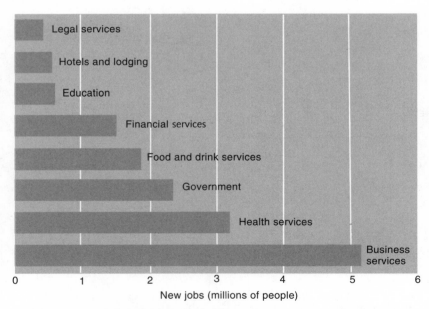

FIGURE 3-4. The sources of job growth, 1980–92. Higher-paying services were the dominant source of growth. (*Data sources:* BEA REIS, Wage and Salary Employment.)

not always need entertainment, advertising, and tourism. Moreover, there is assumed to be a weaker tie between employer and employee in service industries: workers are laid off more readily when it is a profitable business choice.

One way to test this last claim is to look at unemployment rates in services and compare them to those in manufacturing.[15] Throughout the last two decades the unemployment rate for narrow-service workers has been significantly lower than that for manufacturing workers. In addition, the unemployment rate in goods-producing industries has been 77 percent above that in service-producing industries (table 3-4). Work in goods production is more uncertain. However, although unemployment rates are higher in manufacturing, the length of unemployment is shorter than in narrow services. When the higher unemployment rate and shorter period of unemployment are combined, the expected number of weeks of unemployment is still about 8 percent higher in manufacturing than in services.[16]

Nonwage Benefits

One area where service-producing jobs are definitely inferior is in nonwage or fringe benefits, primarily health insurance, retirement contributions, and paid vacation. In 1992, the average insurance, retirement, and paid-leave benefits in goods production came to $3.68 per hour, while those in service production were only $2.34 per hour.[17] With today's increasing pressure on manufacturing, construction, and mining firms this gap may narrow, not because benefits will become more widely available to workers but because firms that now offer large benefits will seek to reduce costs by cutting benefits.

Do We Need More Burger-Flipping Jobs?

Having rebutted the claim that service jobs are inferior to jobs in goods production, we should nevertheless acknowledge that there is a serious problem associated with the current transformation of the economy. The economic fortunes of less educated men have fallen drastically since the mid-1970s. All of us are familiar with the closure of manufacturing plants that has pitched middle-aged men out of well-paid blue-collar jobs. Because most of these men had no education beyond high school, and many had less, their opportunities shrank drastically. Only

TABLE 3-4.

Unemployment Rates by Industry (percent)

Industry	Unemployment Rate				Average 1975–90
	1975	1980	1985	1990	
Agriculture	10.4	11.0	13.2	9.7	11.1
Mining	4.1	6.4	9.5	4.8	6.2
Construction	18.0	14.1	13.1	11.1	14.1
Manufacturing	10.9	8.5	7.7	5.8	8.2
Transportation and Public Utilities	5.6	4.9	5.1	3.8	4.9
Wholesale and Retail Trade	8.7	7.4	7.6	6.4	7.5
Finance, Insurance and Real Estate	4.9	3.4	3.5	3.0	3.7
Services	7.1	5.9	6.2	5.0	6.1
Government	4.1	4.1	3.9	2.6	3.7
Goods Producing (weighted)	12.2	9.9	9.5	7.3	9.7
Services Producing (weighted)	6.5	5.6	5.7	4.6	5.6
Ratio of Goods to Services	1.86	1.77	1.65	1.60	1.73

Source: Statistical Abstract of the United States, 1992, tables 655, 647, 648.

the least skilled, lowest paid jobs were open to them. This is the situation that created the general impression of the "de-skilling" of the American work force and the inferior quality of service jobs. There is a serious problem here. But a misinterpretation of the problem would be dangerous.

It is important to recognize that the growing gap in earnings is not primarily tied to the shift of employment from goods to services. Increased inequality within each industrial sector has had far greater impact on earnings inequality than the shift of workers from goods to services.[18] Within each sector, manufacturing and services, the "middle" has eroded as workers at the upper end of the pay scale have seen their wages protected or enhanced while those at the lower end have seen theirs drop.[19] This unfortunate phenomenon cannot be blamed on the shift to services.

Thus more of the economy's total income is flowing to the upper end and less to the lower end. If the economy were producing too many unskilled jobs and too few skilled jobs, the demand for less skilled workers would rise, hiking their wages, while the demand for skilled workers would be slack and their pay would drop. Just the opposite has been happening. One way to narrow the gap between the upper and lower ends of the wage scale would be to create more, not fewer, unskilled jobs boosting the demand for less educated workers. Alternatively, we could try to upgrade the skills of some workers so that they could fill more jobs at the upper end. What would make matters worse is effort focused only on reducing the number of low-skilled jobs and boosting the number of skilled jobs.[20]

The declining fortunes of less educated male workers has been cited as the cause of the shrinking middle class. Almost any way the middle class is measured, it appears during the 1980s to have grown smaller. But male blue-collar misfortune has less to do with this trend than does the "yuppie" phenomenon of dramatic increases in income for highly skilled service professionals. That is, the middle class shrank because of increased inequality associated with movement out of it at both the upper and lower ends.[21] Of course, having more folks in the upper middle class does not make up for having more people living close to poverty. The point is, much of the problem is the high pay associated with some service jobs, rather than the low pay in services.

There is no inevitable "economic law" that "forced" increased inequality on the American economy. Nor did "technology" force it on us. One cannot adequately explain the collapse in lower-skilled-male wages over the last two decades by focusing exclusively on technological shifts. Institutional and policy changes that set wage norms have a lot to do with the phenomenon.[22] Market economies in other developed countries, even those with living standards as high as or higher than our own, are not experiencing the same inequality. In Europe and Japan the difference between high- and low-paying jobs is much narrower. Furthermore, a comparison of similar jobs in different countries reveals considerable variation. No economic law is imposing some uniform structure of wages in all countries. Consider, for instance, pay in the financial industry. In the United States, the average pay is only 84 percent of the average manufacturing wage. But in Japan it is 134 percent and in Germany it is 122 percent.[23] A variety of social, legal, and economic forces interact to determine the relative level of pay from one country to another. Countries that have been much more engaged in the international economy than the United States have been able to compete while also protecting lower-end wages. This situation can be traced to different social standards about what constitutes reasonable unskilled pay, to stronger unions, higher and more vigorously enforced minimum wages, and much more generous social welfare benefits, which allow workers to refuse low-wage jobs. In short, there is not some single path into the future that is dictated by abstract, uncontrollable economic or technological forces. Economic, political, and social choices will heavily influence the direction of the U.S. economy.

The Shift to Services and Local Economic Development

Some may concede that when national data is used to compare service jobs to manufacturing jobs, services don't look so bad. But they may point out that national averages obscure local reality. Looking at non-metropolitan America and considering the replacement of mining, logging, farming, and manufacturing jobs with trade and service jobs, they may insist, reveals the degeneration of the local economy. Local economic development has to be built around goods production if it is to have any hope of success.

This is a mix of truth and confusion. First of all, local declines in goods production are almost never caused by a local shift toward services. Local services are not "displacing" goods production. In general, goods production has entered a long-term decline that would be taking place regardless of what is happening with local services. In that sense, the shift to services is a fortunate counterbalance to what would otherwise be an even more disruptive adjustment. In addition, although there are exceptions in highly unionized industries (and many natural resource industries fall into that category), U.S. manufacturing activities located in nonmetropolitan areas tend to pay relatively low wages. U.S. nonmetropolitan areas became industrialized precisely because firms were seeking relatively low-wage, nonunion work forces. The lowest manufacturing wages are found in nonmetropolitan areas. As a result, there is not always a significant difference between local manufacturing and local service wages. One is an approximate substitute for the other.

Communities hard hit by manufacturing losses are not good candidates for the expansion of services—pessimists about the service sector are right in this regard. Depressed communities whose economies are contracting are unlikely to attract private investment of any kind. This makes turning the corner all the more difficult.

In general, however, diversification of the local economy into services represents a viable path to boosting total income in the community, reducing poverty and unemployment, and maintaining a reasonable distribution of income among the local population. Service and trade firms contribute directly to local economic development, trapping and holding dollars within the local economy that would otherwise leak out more rapidly. In addition, developing a more sophisticated set of locally available goods and services makes the community a more attractive location for residents and other businesses. Diversification reduces economic isolation and its associated costs.

From a development point of view, it is also cheaper for a community to enhance the range of locally available goods and services than to recruit manufacturing by participating in the national sweepstakes for footloose firms. Given the limited resources nonmetropolitan communities have for economic development, this is a significant advantage of a services-based strategy.

Although it is difficult to separate the impact of expanding services from that of contracting goods-production, empirical analysis of current transformations in nonmetropolitan America appears to confirm the viability of building local economic development around the expansion of service-producing industries. One recent analysis studied the role of services in community development in the Mid-Atlantic states.[24] It found that even the growth of low-wage services raised the level of a community's aggregate income, with the effect being the strongest among rural communities. High-wage services also appeared able to substitute, at least partially, for manufacturing maintaining aggregate income level. Among rural communities, service-sector growth was associated with expansion of middle-income groups and contraction of lower-income groups. Growth in both low-wage and high-wage services increased the number of families in the lower-middle and upper-middle groups, while it was associated with decline in the number of lowest-income families.[25]

Such changes do not appear to damage the local economy. What they do is simply expand the range of local opportunity. One might wish that traditional manufacturing and extractive activities were not in relative decline, and that one could enjoy the benefits both of that historical economic base and of diversification into services and trade. But as we shall see, this could be a dangerous wish. Manufacturing and extraction are not always conducive to local economic health. Of course, local communities cannot stop national and international economic trends, and wishful thinking is not productive when local economic development strategies are being considered.

Mismeasuring Local Economic Well-Being

The economic activity that is replacing the mill and the mine and the factory is more decentralized, and smaller businesses, being less visible than the large factory of earlier days, leave the impression that nothing is replacing lost jobs. For simple survival, it seems, we have to search desperately for and support any commercial activity that is willing to locate in our area. As if to confirm declining economic fortunes in local areas, average incomes in most nonmetropolitan areas—all but the most densely settled areas on the East and West coasts—are significantly below the national average. This would seem to prove the case that beggars can't be choosers, and that to protect the local environment will be more costly than the area can afford. Average incomes, however, are a seriously misleading measure of local economic health.

Average Income As an Index of Local Economic Well-Being

Average-income statistics are accurate indices of local economic welfare only if the following conditions are met:

- The cost of living is the same in all areas. The dollar's purchasing power does not vary by geographic area.
- All important goods and services are either provided through commercial markets or are equally available in all locations.
- There are no significant tradeoffs between productive noncommercial activity (such as child rearing, leisure, home-based work) and income-earning activity, or if there are, patterns of choice between these do not vary across geographic areas.

In fact, none of these conditions hold in the real world.[26]

It has long been recognized that there are significant differences in the cost of living from region to region and between metropolitan and nonmetropolitan areas. Until 1981, the U.S. Bureau of Labor Statistics' data documented cost-of-living differences between several dozen metropolitan areas. A variety of academic and nonacademic efforts have been made to estimate these differences. One recent study showed a 53 percent difference between high- and low-cost states and a 45 percent difference within one state, Illinois, between the most expensive and cheapest counties.[27] The American Chamber of Commerce Research Associates' data indicates similar large differences—up to 60 percent—in cost of living among American cities.[28]

Economists regularly warn users of income data to correct for differences in local cost of living. In 1981, for instance, a National Academy of Sciences panel on rural development policy recommended that a rural cost-of-living index be developed so that rural/urban income differences could be accurately gauged.[29] Analysts studying the long-debated wage differential between Northeastern and Southeastern states have pointed out that if cost-of-living differences are accounted for, the differential disappears or reverses itself.[30] Relative average-income statistics do not, by themselves, indicate which area is better off than another.

Local cost of living is just one geographically specific factor to which local wages and income are likely to adjust in a compensating way. Business firms in cities with a high cost of living have to pay higher wages to attract and hold workers than their counterparts in areas with a relatively low cost of living. That is, wages and income tend to adjust so that the real purchasing power of wages is about the same in all areas. If this did not happen and all other factors were equal, there would be continuous migration from one area to another until it did.

But there are other local features that individuals find important in determining their overall economic well-being, among them, climate, recreational opportunities, low crime, little congestion, clean air and water, good schools, and cultural amenities.[31] The major shifts in the U.S. population over the past fifty years can be largely explained by the pursuit of such amenities. People care where they live and commit significant resources to obtain access to nonmarketed services that are important to them. Put slightly differently, people get two "paychecks" as a result of their choice of residential location, the usual monetary payment associated with productive activity as well as valuable payment from the flow of services from the local social and natural environments. Together, the two paychecks determine aggregate economic well-being. Labor markets do not ignore that second paycheck.[32] As a result, local wages and income adjust to compensate for a local area's deficiencies or attributes. Areas characterized by amenities draw people. People clamoring for employment so they can reside in an attractive area put downward pressure on wages. As a result, the area (other things such as cost of living being equal) will have lower wages and income. A less desirable area will tend to have higher wages and income. But these income variations do not reflect variations in well-being. On the contrary, they offset other local factors to leave migrants no better or worse off than if they had migrated somewhere else.

The issue at hand is whether some or all of the higher income paid in large metropolitan areas is simply compensation for the disadvantages of living there: high cost of living, pollution, congestion, crime, and so on. Put the other way around: How much of the lower income that characterizes nonmetropolitan areas is explained by their amenities? If nonmarketed goods and services account for some of the lower income, it cannot be taken as a measure of lower well-being.

Not all productive human activity takes place in the context of commercial business. Some of the most important and satisfying activity involves child rearing, home making, and leisure pursuits. The choice to engage in such activity usually entails financial sacrifice (less money income per family member). If, despite that, people pursue such nonmarket choices, we have to assume that is because they want to improve their own or their family's well-being. In these circumstances, reduced average income is not a sign of lower well-being.

The pattern of household choices varies geographically. Households in Utah have 40 percent more dependents than households in Washington, D.C. This is partially the reason that Utah appears so poor and Washington, D.C., appears so prosperous. Fifty percent more women participate in the labor force in Michigan, Minnesota, and New Hampshire than in West Virginia, and 25 percent more than in New York, New Mexico, and Kentucky.[33] These differences have a significant impact on measured per capita income, an impact that does not entirely reflect differences in well-being.

The average number of work hours per week is approximately forty in manufacturing, transportation, and public utilities. In retail trade and services, it is as low as thirty. Different states have different mixes of employment and, as a result, different average hours worked: 12 percent of South Dakota's employment is in manufacturing, 50 percent in trade and services, while in South Carolina, 24 percent of employment is in manufacturing, 10 percent in trade and services.[34] If any value at all is placed on time out of the labor force, then the difference in per capita income that results from a difference in the number of hours worked does not accurately reflect the difference in welfare.

Some choices to pursue "home production" can be seen as having been forced on households by lack of economic opportunity. But even in those circumstances, the additional leisure time and household production is worth something. Furthermore, the choice not to join the work force or to limit one's participation to less than 40 hours a week is increasingly recognized as a choice, not something dictated by the larger economy.[35] In either case, the implications for gauging local economic well-being are daunting. The adjustments that have to be made in average income data before it accurately reflects differences in local cost of living, site-specific amenities, and choice of work are complex and numerous.

Partial Solutions: "Deflating" Local Income Data

Cost of living and the value of local amenities interact in a way that makes them difficult to separate for the purposes of analysis. Consider the high cost of living in Hawaii. That state has many natural amenities for which people are willing to sacrifice. The large numbers seeking to live on Hawaii's limited land mass have caused rental values to rise and, with them, the cost of housing, the cost of other locally produced goods, and the cost of living. Isolation from the mainland has added to the cost of living. Because potential residents are willing to make sacrifices to live in Hawaii, wages do not have to rise to entirely cover the higher cost of living. It would be difficult to adjust incomes in Hawaii only for cost of living and compare them to incomes in, say, Vermont, in order to determine relative economic well-being. Valuing local amenities apart from cost of living is difficult, but such a separation may not be necessary.

If the array of amenities in one area is relatively more attractive than in another, migration will take place until wages, cost of living, and, possibly, amenities themselves adjust, making neither area more attractive for the marginal migrant. At that equilibrium point, wage differentials will indicate the dollar value residents place on the particular "bundles" of cost of living and amenities in the two areas. If we can accurately measure equilibrium wage differentials, it will give us a dollar measure of the value a population attaches to local nonwage features. The measure is what economist Ed Whitlaw calls the "second paycheck" that supplements the money income of residents.[36]

One must assume, of course, that equilibrium has been reached in national labor markets, which may not be the case. A certain amount of migration continues to take place. Nonetheless, over the past half century, during which period tens of millions of people relocated, major differences in per capita income among states and local areas have remained. It seems safe to assume that, to a considerable extent, differences in wages and incomes represent equilibrium differences.[37]

How much of a difference would it make in our characterization of the economic health of various regions if we attempted to "deflate" local incomes to account for differences in cost of living and local amenities? Assume that the major sources of variation in amenity and cost of living are population size and density, which are associated with such phenomena as congestion, pollution, crime, and social conflict. Urban economic theory supports, at least in part, the connection between population size and cost of living.[38] If we are trying to evaluate economic well-being in nonmetropolitan areas relative to the metropolitan areas in which almost three-quarters of the U.S. population lives, this approach may make some sense.

If average incomes are statistically analyzed on the assumption that differences primarily reflect variations in cost of living and amenities associated with urban *size*, we can derive a set of "deflators" to adjust local incomes to more accurately reflect local economic well-being. Deflators are derived by studying how income varies from one area to the next across the nation and (with linear regression techniques) identifying those variations associated with changes in population size alone—which are assumed to be tied to urban disamenities and cost of living (table 3-5). These factors, divided into local income, yield a result that can appropriately be compared to average national per capita income. Put slightly differently, if per capita money income in a county were 20 percent below the national average and the deflator was 0.8, this index would indicate that in welfare terms, average local economic well-being was actually equal to the national average. The deflator for New York City (the only city in the 9+ million category) would be 1.217. Income in the New York metropolitan area should be divided (deflated) by this factor before any welfare comparisons are made with other areas. A per capita income there about 22 percent above the national average would represent the same well-being as the national average. If this factor is combined with that of a small southern county, an income level 57 percent higher in New York would represent the same level of economic welfare as in the southern county. Put the other way, an income level in the nonmetropolitan southern county that was only

TABLE 3-5.

Compensating Wage-Differential Deflators Based on Urban Size and Region

	Normalized Deflator (1.0 = U.S. average)
Population (thousands)	
< 1	0.957
1 ≤ 2.5	0.930
2.5 ≤ 5	0.913
5 ≤ 10	0.896
10 ≤ 25	0.892
25 ≤ 50	0.913
50 ≤ 100	0.948
100 ≤ 250	0.957
250 ≤ 500	0.974
500 ≤ 1,000	1.000
1,000 ≤ 9,000	1.070
> 9,000	1.217
Regions	
Northeast	1.000
North Central	1.061
South	0.909
West	1.071
Alaska	1.414
Hawaii	1.061
Nonmetropolitan Areas	
Contiguous	0.975
Noncontiguous	0.950

Note: As an example of the application of these deflators, a county with a population of 25,000 to 50,000, located in the South and not contiguous to a metropolitan area, would have a deflator of $(0.913) \times (0.909) \times (0.95) = 0.788$.

Source: Irving Hoch et al., ca. 1983, pp. 5, 23, and 27.

64 percent of an income level in New York City would represent the same level of economic welfare.

Thus what appear to be dramatic differences in economic well-being among communities may not actually exist. If deflators are applied to average metropolitan and nonmetropolitan per capita income, the gap narrows considerably (table 3-6). A gap of about 10 percent

TABLE 3-6.

Metropolitan and Nonmetropolitan Per Capita Income Deflated

	Unadjusted Per Capita Income As Percent of United States				
	1973	1978	1981	1985	1992
United States	100.0	100.0	100.0	100.0	100.0
Metropolitan	106.4	107.01	107.5	106.3	105.7
Nonmetropolitan	83.0	81.6	80.5	76.7	77.3
Ratio of Nonmetropolitan to Metropolitan	0.78	0.76	0.75	0.72	0.74

	Per Capita Income Adjusted for Cost of Living and Quality of Life As Percent of United States				
	1973	1978	1981	1985	1992
United States	100.0	100.0	100.0	100.0	100.0
Metropolitan	102.0	102.8	103.3	101.9	101.4
Nonmetropolitan	94.5	92.7	91.7	87.0	88.1
Ratio of Nonmetropolitan to Metropolitan	0.93	0.90	0.89	0.86	0.87

Sources: Hoch et al., ca. 1983, p. 26; BEA REIS, 1993 data for 1985 and 1992.

still exists when nonmetropolitan areas are compared with metropolitan. But compared with the 25 percent gap that unadjusted data indicates, this is modest and should moderate the urgency of calls for a public policy fix.

When deflators are applied to the incidence of poverty in metropolitan and nonmetropolitan areas, the results are not as dramatic but they are informative. Adjusting local income with deflators reveals a lesser incidence of poverty in nonmetropolitan areas and a higher incidence in metropolitan areas.[39] That is, higher wages in large metropolitan areas (to compensate for a higher cost of living) mask the full extent of poverty.

Adjusting per capita income for cost of living and the disamenities of urban density has a dramatic impact on the apparent distribution of low income across the United States. A glance at the nonmetropolitan counties that in 1984 had per capita personal income 25 percent below the national average would suggest that almost the entire southern tier of states except for southern Florida and California are poor, in addition to a thin tier across the northern boundary of the nation (figure 3-5a). A substantial part of the nation would seem to be deprived of the

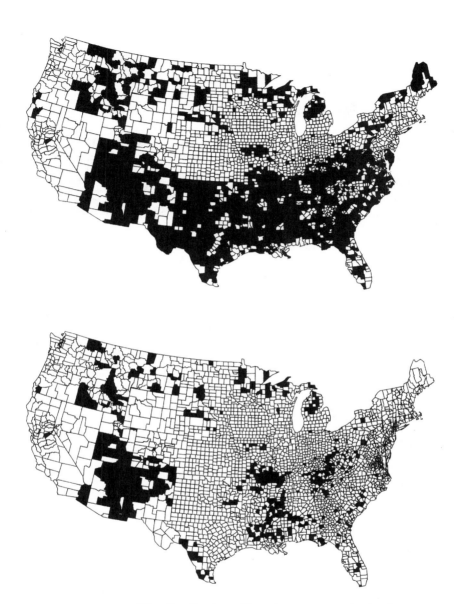

FIGURES 3-5A AND B. The distribution of low-income counties in the United States. Figure 3-5a shows counties with per capita incomes more than 25 percent below national averages in 1981. Figure 3-5b shows the same when cost of living and value of amenities are taken into account. For adjustments, see table 3-6. (*Data sources:* BEA REIS.)

full benefits of the national economy. The strange thing about this picture is that the southern belt of states has been the fastest-growing U.S. region for several decades. People, voting with their feet, have apparently been migrating into poverty. But when the crude equilibrium wage adjustment for cost of living and amenities is made, the picture changes dramatically (figure 3-5b). We are left with scattered low-income pockets that match our empirical awareness of areas that are in fact poor: the Appalachian–Cumberland Plateau area of Kentucky and Tennessee, the Ozark region of Missouri, the Mississippi Delta region, and the Four Corners area in the Southwest.

In conclusion, if one uses average money income statistics to evaluate the health of local economies, most nonmetropolitan areas will appear to be in moderate or serious trouble. That statistical result may be used to justify almost any steps to boost local commercial activity. When, however, adjustments are made to account for differences in cost of living and quality of life, most of nonmetropolitan America appears relatively healthy. Communities should be extremely cautious in their handling of unadjusted per capita income data. They are not an accurate indicator of local economic health.

Moving the Mountain to Seize the Ounce: Mineral Extraction and Local Well-Being

In the casual economic geography most of us learned in school, mining and related processing and manufacturing activities are the economic foundation of vast, sweeping arcs of rural America: most of the western states, Appalachia, the Midwest, and the belt stretching from Louisiana through Texas and Oklahoma into the Old West. Wages in mining and mineral extraction are the highest of any large industrial group: 250 percent more than the pay in retail trade, 66 percent more than the pay in services, and 50 percent more than the pay in manufacturing.[1] Mining looks like a real economic plum, one of the few remaining high-wage industries in the United States and one of the only industries in many rural areas. Not surprisingly, mining is seen as the mainstay of rural communities where it has been the traditional employer and as a godsend to rural economies that mining companies are considering for new operations.

Mining Towns Where Mining Didn't Matter

Because mining and mineral-related economic activity bring a large flow of income into rural or small-town economies, mining is assumed to be a powerful stimulus to local economies. As income gets spent and respent within the local economy, it is assumed to generate additional income and jobs. Ultimately, the thinking goes, mining is responsible for many spinoff jobs.

Because mining activity is relatively unstable owing to new discoveries, fluctuating commodity prices, exhaustion of deposits, the impact

of world competition, and labor-management disputes, it is a laboratory of sorts in which to study the impact of changes in one sector's employment and income on the rest of the economy. Because mining is
part of the economy, a rise or fall in mining employment or income will,
simply as a result of arithmetic, have at least a short-term impact on aggregate employment and income. But many believe that mining has a
more pervasive influence on the economy, that nonmining (nonexport
or nonbasic) sectors will closely and inevitably follow the fortunes of
the mining sector. That is, the mining sector is the economic engine
driving the rest of the economy. To test this assertion empirically, we
need to look at how the rest of the economy behaves as mining employment or income fluctuates.

Beginning in the early 1980s, the silver-mining and smelting operations in Idaho's Silver Valley began to shut down. This was not unique
to Idaho. Silver and copper operations across the West were shutting
down. Between 1981 and 1987, the Silver Valley lost over 80 percent of
the income it had once earned in mining and metal smelting. In 1981,
metal-industry income represented half of all personal income received
in the area. But as this assumed economic base collapsed, the rest of the
economy not only did not follow suit, it expanded slightly and then held
remarkably steady (figure 4-1).

Salmon is a relatively isolated town in the mountains of central
Idaho, along the Montana border. As its name indicates, it sits along
headwaters of the Salmon River. Its export-oriented economic activities have traditionally been ranching in the Lemhi Valley to the south,
timber processing from surrounding federal lands, and mining. During
the 1970s a local mining operation was developed, operated, and then
shut down. About 500 new jobs were added to the "economic base"
only to be lost. For a town of 3,000 this was a major change. But
tracking what happened in the rest of the economy (nonexport sectors)
reveals that the operation neither stimulated the other sectors nor (after
its collapse) inhibited their expansion. The rest of the economy, in fact,
expanded more rapidly when the "economic base" was in decline
(figure 4-2).[2]

During the late 1980s in south central Montana, the nation's only
platinum mine was opened in the mountain valley of the Stillwater River.
The mine boosted total income flow within the local economy by almost
40 percent and almost quadrupled the "export base." Yet this major expansion in basic industry had no impact on income received in the rest
of the economy. Equally startling is the fact that during an earlier period,

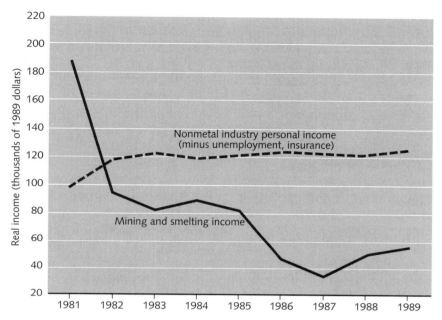

FIGURE 4-1. Metal industry versus other income, Silver Valley, Shoshone County, Idaho. The collapse of the mining and smelting industry in Idaho's Silver Valley did not have a multiplier impact on the rest of the economy. (*Data sources:* BEA REIS deflated by CPI.)

when the economic base was cut in half, the rest of the economy expanded modestly but steadily (figure 4-3). Again, mining activity did not play the dominant economic role that is usually assumed.

For nearly a hundred years the economy in Butte, Montana, centered on copper mining and smelting. As late as 1975 almost three-fourths of Butte's economic base was estimated to be associated with the Anaconda Copper Company. By 1983 the mines and smelter had shut down. One would assume that Butte would shrivel into a ghost town. But nothing could be further from the truth. After the initial shock, during which the area's population and employment fell by 20 percent and real income declined by 15 percent, the economy proved remarkably resilient. Five years later the economy had achieved a level of diversity that caused the chief executive officer of the Butte–Silver Bow government to comment, "Now that I look back at it, one of the best things that ever happened to this community was Anaconda's leaving."[3]

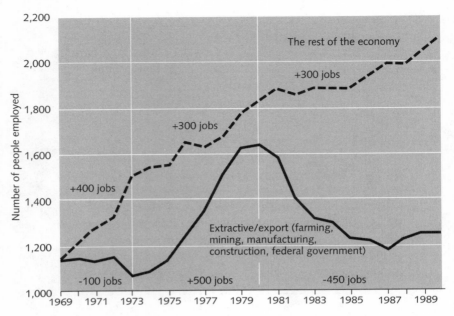

FIGURE 4-2. Jobs in the extractive industry versus in the rest of the economy, Salmon, Lemhi County, Idaho. Employment outside the extractive sectors in Salmon did not track fluctuation in employment in the extractive sectors. (*Data sources:* BEA REIS.)

Shifting from the micro view of mining's impact to the role mining has played in the economies of states assumed to be heavily dependent on it, the same pattern or, more accurately, lack of pattern is visible. Analysis of the relationship between employment in mining and employment in all other sectors for each of the twelve western states during the 1980s reveals that there was either no significant impact from mining or a negative relationship, with higher mining employment associated with lower employment elsewhere in the economy (table 4-1).[4] Between 1980 and 1990 over a third of all mining jobs (93,000) were lost in the West. But during that same decade, 6.5 million new jobs were created.[5] That is, despite a catastrophic collapse of mining employment, the region's economies were able to expand significantly (figure 4-4). By no means is mining dictating economic conditions in the West.

Why isn't this sector leading the rest of the economy at either the local, state, or regional level?

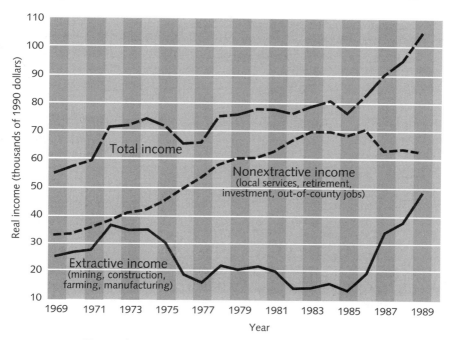

FIGURE 4-3. Extractive and nonextractive income, Stillwater County, Montana. (*Data sources:* BEA REIS CD-ROM deflated by CPI.)

Yesterday's Gold Rushes, Today's Ghost Towns?

For more than a century, metal mining, especially gold, silver, and copper, has been an integral part of the vision people have of the American West. The cultural image we have of the Old West is tied to the images that Hollywood and the popular press have refined for over a century. Miners searching for precious metal and the retail trade that followed them compete only with the gun-toting cowboys as the dominant myth of how the West was settled. To this day, residents of western states tend to regard mining as a central element of the industrial base on which their lives depend.

There is, of course, some truth to this story. Gold rushes did bring thousands of new residents to California and Alaska. The urban centers of Montana were originally mining towns. The industrial base in

TABLE 4-1.

Impact of Changes in Mining and Manufacturing Employment on Total Employment, 1980–90

	Impact of Change in Mining (*t* statistic)	Impact of Change in Manufacturing (*t* statistic)	*R* Square
Alaska	Not different from 0	Not different from 0	0.36
Arizona	Not different from 0	6.0 (*t*=6.0)	0.81
California	-26.0 (*t*=-4.7)	4.0 (*t*=7.7)	0.91
Colorado	Not different from 0	Not different from 0	0.52
Idaho	-8.5 (*t*=-2.11)	4.2 (*t*=4.2)	0.75
Montana	Not different from 0	3.4 (*t*=2.54)	0.49
Nevada	Not different from 0	Not different from 0	0.61
New Mexico	Not different from 0	Not different from 0	0.24
Oregon	Not different from 0	3.8 (*t*=5.6)	0.82
Utah	-4.4 (*t*=-1.99)	3.0 (*t*=5.2)	0.51
Washington	-2.7 (*t*=-1.95)	3.6 (*t*=5.2)	0.79
Wyoming	2.6 (*t*=2.26)	Not different from 0	0.46

Notes: 1.0 was added to the regression coefficient to create a total employment multiplier. The *t* statistic is an indicator of the reliability of the statistical relationship. A *t* value less than 2.0 would indicate a statistically unreliable result. The *R* square is a measure of the fraction of the variation in total employment that has been explained by mining and manufacturing employment.

Source: Data from BEA REIS.

the inland West (Arizona, New Mexico, Utah, Idaho, and Montana) was tied to mining and associated metal manufacturing. There is no doubt that metal mining played an important role in the early development of the western economy. But the important question is whether that historical experience is an accurate guide to current and future economic reality in the West.

When the current economy is seen through the rearview mirror, the image is disturbing. Over the long term, mining has been shrinking in both relative and absolute terms, and whether measured by employment or income. In the short term, both employment in and income from mining have been unstable. With the sector's decline having produced some of the West's best-known ghost towns, it is easy for communities to conclude that their very existence is tied directly to the strength of the mining industry.

But in most cases such fear is unfounded. A direct look at the cur-

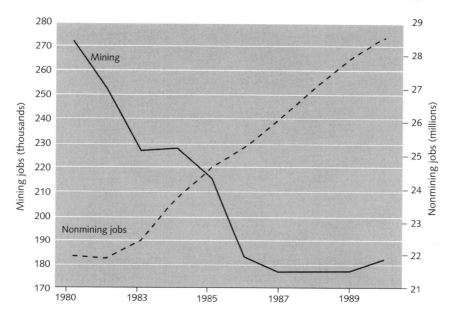

FIGURE 4-4. Mining and nonmining employment in the western states, 1980–90. The collapse of mining employment in the 1980s was accompanied by a major expansion in nonmining employment in the West. (*Data sources:* BEA REIS CD-ROM.)

rent and evolving economies of the western states reveals that the importance our historical and cultural images have attached to mining is greatly exaggerated.

Mining and Local Economic Reality in the West

In contrast to our cultural image, metal mining makes up only a sliver of the overall economy of the West. For the twelve states there, slightly more than one-tenth of 1 percent of total employment is directly associated with metal mining (figure 4-5). That is, only one job in a thousand in the West is in metal mining.[6] No matter what "multiplier" one might use to amplify this number, the result will not indicate a significant part of the overall western labor market.

The relative importance of metal mining as a source of employment in the aggregate western economy is minimal and shrinking. Between 1980 and 1990, it fell by half (figure 4-6). During that period 25,000

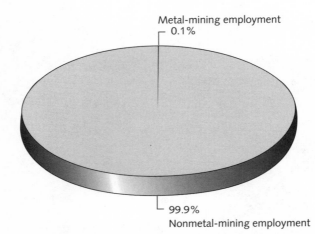

Metal-mining employment
0.1%

99.9%
Nonmetal-mining employment

FIGURE 4-5. Metal mining as a source of jobs in the western mining states, 1990. Metal mining accounts for just a sliver of total employment in the West. (*Data sources:* BEA REIS, Wage and Salary Employment.)

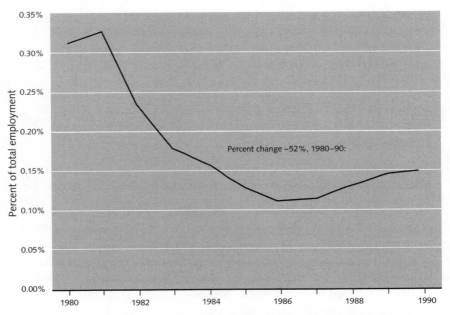

Percent change −52%, 1980–90:

FIGURE 4-6. Metal mining as a percentage of total employment in the western mining states. Metal mining as a source of employment in the West declined by more than half during the 1980s. (*Data sources:* BEA REIS, Wage and Salary Employment.)

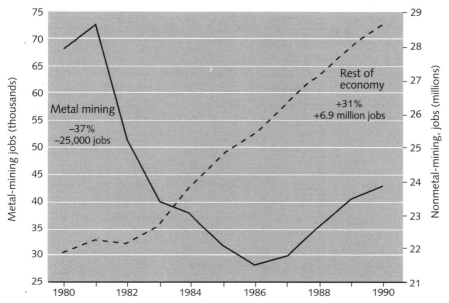

FIGURE 4-7. Metal-mining and nonmetal-mining jobs in the western mining states. While metal-mining employment declined by almost 40 percent in these states, employment in the rest of the economy expanded by almost a third. (*Data sources:* BEA REIS, Wage and Salary Employment.)

jobs were lost in metal mining, while the overall western economy significantly expanded, adding almost 7 million jobs (figure 4-7).

For individual states in the West, the relative importance of metal mining varies. In Nevada almost two out of every hundred jobs (2 percent) are in metal mining, while in California and Oregon only one in ten thousand jobs (one-hundredth of 1 percent) are directly supported by this industry (table 4-2). All states but Nevada, Montana, and Alaska saw metal mining decline in relative terms as a source of employment; usually the decline was significant. In absolute terms, the number of jobs in metal mining declined in three-quarters of the western states.

If the importance of western metal mining is analyzed in terms of the income paid to workers, the results are similar to the employment analysis. Because mining jobs pay relatively high wages, the industry's relative importance in terms of income is slightly higher, 0.19 percent compared to 0.15 percent for employment (figure 4-8 and table 4-3).

TABLE 4-2.

The Relative Importance of Metal Mining Employment, 1990

	Total Employment	Average Job Growth, 1985–90	Metal-Mining Employment	Metal Mining As a Percentage of Total Employment
Alaska	329,602	3,047	1,053	0.32
Arizona	1,871,875	50,988	10,531	0.56
California	16,547,911	464,279	2,375	0.01
Colorado	2,009,216	25,744	3,889	0.19
Idaho	537,991	13,217	2,776	0.52
Montana	426,145	4,697	2,605	0.61
Nevada	738,240	36,924	12,833	1.74
New Mexico	741,081	15,277	2,094	0.28
Oregon	1,605,446	49,298	105	0.01
Utah	2,775,357	22,164	3,055	0.11
Washington	890,281	100,842	963	0.11
Wyoming	261,978	(701)	751	0.29
Western United States	28,735,123	684,934	43,030	0.15

Sources: BEA REIS, CA25 and CA27 Employment Files and County Business Patterns.

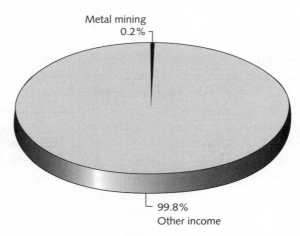

Metal mining
0.2%

99.8%
Other income

FIGURE 4-8. Metal mining as a percentage of total income in the western mining states, 1990. (California, Oregon, and Washington income is estimated.) Metal Mining provides only a sliver of total income in the West. (*Data sources:* BEA REIS CD-ROM deflated by CPI.)

TABLE 4-3.

The Relative Importance of Metal Mining
in the West As a Source of Income, 1990

	Metal Mining Earnings (thousands of dollars)	Total Personal Income (thousands of dollars)	Metal- Mining Income As a Percentage of Total Income
Alaska	68,415	11,933,122	0.57%
Arizona	486,606	58,923,252	0.83%
California	97,455	619,761,886	0.02%
Colorado	207,234	62,279,699	0.33%
Idaho	108,120	15,422,975	0.70%
Montana	106,318	12,232,536	0.87%
Nevada	571,021	23,313,824	2.45%
New Mexico	82,900	21,659,648	0.38%
Oregon	5,494	49,158,605	0.01%
Utah	139,564	24,185,159	0.58%
Washington	28,717	92,181,288	0.03%
Wyoming	34,048	7,363,418	0.46%
United States	2,794,000	4,664,057,000	0.06%
Western States	1,935,892	998,415,412	0.19%

Note: Disclosure problems resolved using the ratio of metal-mining employment to total mining employment. This was applied to total mining income.

Source: BEA REIS, CA05 Personal Income Files.

That is, about $1.90 of every $1,000 dollars earned in the West is directly associated with metal mining. From 1980 to 1990, metal mining was a shrinking source of income for all but three states, Nevada, Alaska, and Montana. For most states, the relative decline was dramatic (figure 4-9). Despite the industry's overall decline in earnings, total regional income moved significantly in the opposite direction, rising 37 percent in real terms as population and economic activity expanded (figure 4-10). Clearly, earnings in metal mining are not driving the western economy.

Metal Mining on Federal Land

Much of the West's land is owned by the federal government. The state percentage of publicly owned acreage varies from a low of 25 percent in Montana to a high of over 80 percent in Nevada. Excluding Alaska, slightly less than half of the land base in the region is federal land. It is

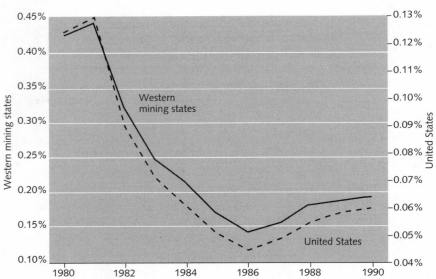

FIGURE 4-9. Metal-mining real income as a percentage of total income. Metal mining has declined by more than half as a source of real income, in both the western states, where federal mineral ownership is extensive, and in the United States as a whole, where federal ownership is much less important. (*Data sources:* BEA REIS CD-ROM deflated by CPI.)

highly likely that significant mineral deposits are located on federal land and that mining companies will seek to extract them. This scenario has led to controversy for two reasons: fear of environmental damage, and a law governing metal mining on federal land that was passed in the nineteenth century.

The 1872 Mining Law gives mining companies a right to develop any resources they discover. For almost no payment to the federal government, minerals and the land in which they are deposited can become private property. No matter what the environmental damage, it is nearly impossible to block a mine development. Efforts have been launched to reform the law and make it consistent with late-twentieth-century environmental and mineral leasing laws. That, in turn, has provoked outcries from the mining industry that any significant reform of the nineteenth-century free-access legislation would undermine the West's economic base.

But all metal mining in the West does not take place on federal land.

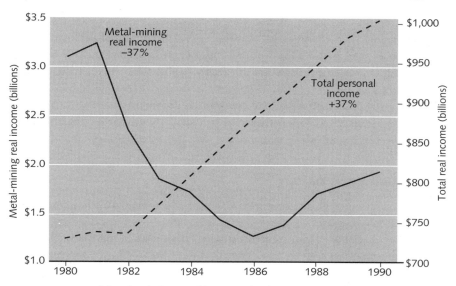

FIGURE 4-10. Metal-mining real income in the western mining states. (*Data sources:* BEA REIS deflated by CPI.)

If that part of metal mining that takes place on federal land and that might be subject to a change in the law is considered alone, the sliver of economic activity associated with the industry is even thinner.

Because so much of the West is in federal ownership, it is often assumed that most mining must take place on federal lands. This is misleading. Some of the dominant mining districts in the West are almost exclusively on private land, for example, the copper operations in Utah and Arizona, Homestake's gold operations in the Black Hills, and some of the largest gold mines in Nevada. In addition, the 1872 Mining Law allowed those who discovered commercially viable mineral deposits on public land to convert the land to private ownership. As a result, many western mines have been converted to private ownership. Thus, estimating the percentage of metal mining being done on federal lands requires careful measurement, mine by mine.

Federal land and mineral-management agencies do not regularly collect information relevant to this question. However, in 1992 the General Accounting Office surveyed all of the hard-rock mining companies the Bureau of Mines had identified as operating in the twelve western states; the intention was to identify what portion of production took place on federal land, and it turns out to be about 15 percent.[7]

That would suggest that in the West only about one in six metal-mining jobs is tied to the extraction of minerals from federal land affected by reform of the Mining Law. Total employment associated with metal mining on western federal land is about 7,000—four-hundredths of 1 percent of total employment, or 1 out of every 2,500 jobs (table 4-4). Obviously, the economies of western states are not dependent on metal mining on federal lands. Legal reform that reduced mining on federal land would certainly not cause serious economic disruption.

Instability and Decline

Because mining produces standardized products that are traded on international markets—oil, gas, coal, gold, copper, silver, and so on—the profitability of any mineral development operation is determined by the commodity prices set by those markets. As commodity prices change, the commercial viability of mineral development operations changes,

TABLE 4-4.

Two Estimates of Metal-Mining Employment on Federal Land, 1990

	Metal-Mining Jobs	Percentage of Total Mining Jobs on Federal Land		Metal Mining Jobs on Federal Land		Percentage of Total Metal-Mining Jobs on Federal Land	
		Estimate 1[a]	Estimate 2[b]	Estimate 1	Estimate 2	Estimate 1	Estimate 2
Alaska	1,053	65.0	36.3	684	382	0.21	0.12
Arizona	10,531	11.0	6.1	1,158	646	0.06	0.03
California	2,375	48.3	27.0	1,147	640	0.01	0.00
Colorado	3,889	29.8	16.6	1,159	647	0.06	0.03
Idaho	2,776	60.6	33.8	1,682	939	0.31	0.17
Montana	2,605	28.2	15.7	735	410	0.17	0.10
Nevada	12,833	30.0	16.7	3,850	2,148	0.52	0.29
New Mexico	2,094	25.0	13.9	524	292	0.07	0.04
Oregon	105	52.3	29.2	55	31	0.00	0.00
Utah	3,055	8.7	4.9	266	148	0.01	0.01
Washington	963	29.6	16.5	285	159	0.03	0.02
Wyoming	751	46.5	25.9	349	195	0.13	0.07
Western States	43,030	27.3	15.2	11,751	6,556	0.04	0.02

Notes: a. Estimate adjusted using GAO survey, 1990.

b. GAO estimate distributed to states.

Sources: U.S. General Accounting Office 1992, p. 6; Rogers and Carlson 1992, p. 21; and BEA REIS, Wage and Salary Files.

opening up new opportunities when commodity prices rise, hurting operations when commodity prices fall. And commodity prices fluctuate widely. Recall the swift rise in oil and natural gas prices in the late 1970s and early 1980s: both more than doubled in real terms, setting off extensive exploration and development aimed at bringing to the market resources that previously had not been worth even looking for.[8] The oil and gas industry swept across the West, seeking to explore nearly everywhere, including Glacier National Park and the adjacent Bob Marshall Wilderness and managed to obtain oil and gas leases on much of the region's public land. Small towns buzzed with exploration activity. Then the boom collapsed as oil and natural gas prices dropped to their previous levels (figure 4-11). The bust had a devastating effect across the Great Plains. From Texas through Oklahoma up through Wyoming and eastern Montana, tens of thousands of oil and gas workers were thrown out of work. Mineral tax revenues plummeted, pitching state and local governments into fiscal crises. States like Wyoming and Montana saw significant outmigration of families forced to move on. Drilling rigs were abandoned and sold for scrap-metal prices.

It is not only the energy side of the mineral extraction industry that has had to cope with the boom and bust phenomenon associated with international commodity prices. During the first half of the 1980s the price of copper, in real terms, fell by half.[9] That led to the shutdown of most copper mining and smelting operations in a belt from Arizona and New Mexico up through Utah into Montana. Tens of thousands of mining and ore-processing workers were thrown out of work. Most were never rehired. Unlike oil and gas exploration workers, they were not a mobile professional work force. Layoffs hit mining towns like Butte and Anaconda, Montana, that had been tied to copper production for most of this century. Starting in 1986, copper prices began rising again. The 70 percent increase in price between 1986 and 1989 led to the reopening, with much smaller work forces, of many of the West's copper mines. In 1989 copper prices began to tumble again, falling by almost 40 percent and threatening the modest recovery. Then in the mid-1990s prices doubled. The recent copper industry roller coaster is a dramatic example of the unstable conditions affecting mining operations and the communities where they set up (figure 4-12).

Sky-rocketing prices during the second half of the 1970s led to a boom in gold mining. After 1971, when the federal government ceased pegging the price of gold at $35 per ounce (about $120 in 1994 dollars) and allowed the market to determine prices, they steadily rose to

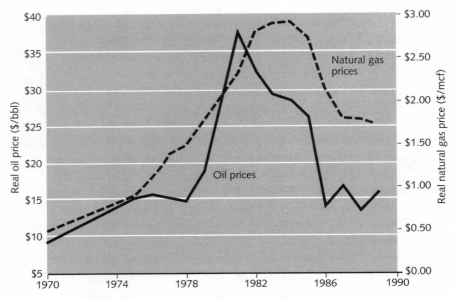

FIGURE 4-11. Real oil and natural gas prices. These prices (adjusted to remove inflation) have fluctuated widely. (*Data sources: Statistical Abstract, 1994*, table 1171.)

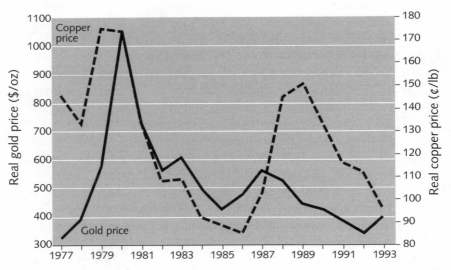

FIGURE 4-12. Real gold and copper prices. These prices go through boom and bust cycles. (*Data sources: Statistical Abstract, 1994*, table 1171.)

a peak in 1981 of over $1,000 per ounce (1994 dollars). Prices at that level made the development of very-low-grade gold ores feasible. Technologies developed that made it economically feasible to process huge volumes of ore, even when it contained only a tiny fraction of 1 percent of the precious metal. A new industry was born. But as mines came on line, the price of gold began to fall. After falling to half its previous peak level it recovered for a while in the mid-1980s, then resumed its decline to roughly a third of the peak level. Though in real terms this put the price at a level over three times higher than the price at which the federal government had once fixed it, the drop threatened many of the new gold-mining operations. At the very least, the depressed prices of the mid-1990s made further investments in gold exploration and development less attractive. Without higher prices to support new mines, the gold mining boom leveled off and, ultimately, declined (see figure 4-12).

Even with the recovery of copper mining in the second half of the 1980s and the gold mining boom throughout the 1980s, the decline in energy mineral development and metal mining in the first half of the 1980s led to a dramatic overall decline in aggregate mining employment in the western states. A third of all mining jobs were lost (see figure 4-4). The disruption was worse than this aggregate figure suggests, since the oil and gas workers laid off in the Great Plains were unlikely to have seen gold-mining jobs opening up in Nevada as employment opportunities available to them.

The instability of the mineral market appears to have increased over time. During the 1960s and 1970s, many mineral industries in developing countries became state-owned and -operated enterprises. Production from the operations has been driven by the objectives of national employment and foreign exchange earnings for debt payment rather than by market profit. As a result, when markets weaken, prices fall even further than they did in the past because a significant part of supply is not curtailed. To this source of instability that plagues the mineral market has to be added the increased volume of international speculative capital that now follows commodity trading, as well as shifting investments among alternative stores of value, for example, gold, foreign currencies, international equities, and real estate, which cause currency values to fluctuate.[10]

Unstable and depressed mineral commodity prices are not the only trend reducing employment in mining. There is also the increasing mechanization and automation of mining and processing. New processes and new equipment have steadily reduced the direct labor content of an ounce of gold and a pound of copper and a ton of coal. Labor productivity and commodity prices are at least partially linked. The new production techniques, adopted worldwide, have increased supply potential, driving commodity prices down worldwide and adding to the pressure on all mining operations to further reduce costs, including labor costs.

The reduction in labor per unit of mine output has been impressive. While economists and policymakers wring their hands over the slow growth in productivity in the overall American economy, productivity in mining has been growing rapidly. During the 1970s and 1980s three-quarters of American industries saw productivity grow by less than 2 percent per year; in mining it grew 5 to 10 percent per year, putting the sector in the top 10 percent of American industries for this measure.[11]

If demand for a mineral is limited by national and international markets, rising labor productivity is likely to translate into declining employment, and if demand is going up, improved labor productivity can satisfy demand without increased employment. The impact on employment potential can be substantial. Metal-mining productivity growth of 10.8 percent per year over a decade would reduce the direct labor content of metal ores by two-thirds. Coal mining productivity rising at 7.3 percent per year over a decade would reduce the direct labor content of coal by half.

The decline in mining employment during the 1980s largely confirms the impact of limited markets and rising productivity. In metal mining, coal mining, and oil and gas extraction, employment has fallen by about 40 percent (figure 4-13). Although rising commodity prices may open up commercial opportunities in the future, there is no reason to believe that improvements in labor productivity have come to an end. One can expect limited markets and rising labor productivity to continue to exert downward pressure on the employment potential of the industry. In the future, mining is not likely to be a source of economic vitality for America's communities.

Local Employment and the Promise of Mineral Development

Because mining jobs are among the highest paying available, a mineral development proposal can plausibly be presented to a commu-

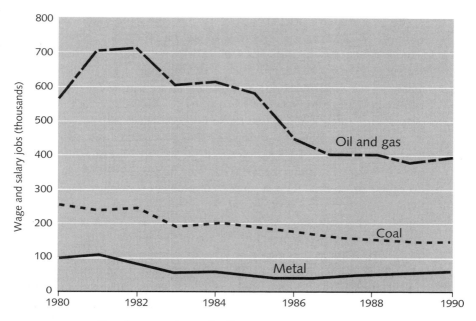

FIGURE 4-13. Employment in coal, oil and gas, and metal mining. Employment in the various sectors of the mineral industry declined during the 1980s. (*Data source:* BEA REIS, Wage and Salary Employment.)

nity as a solution to the low income, poverty, and limited employment opportunity that are said to characterize rural areas. The casual assumption that mineral development will directly improve the well-being of residents masks a broad array of uncertainties that need to be analyzed.[12]

Typically, mineral projects first come to public attention when companies seek permits to explore for minerals. Often this involves construction of roads, extensive exploratory drilling and/or seismic exploration, and excavation. At the time permits are sought, employment associated with ultimate mineral development will be offered as the central justification for the environmental damage that might be associated with the exploration. However, employment is not a certainty, even if permits are granted. Actual employment will depend on the size and quality of the mineral resource, if any is discovered, and the future level of commodity prices and mining costs.

Just as a chance to win $100 does not have the same value as the receipt of a $100 prize, the possibility of 500 high-paying jobs is not the same as 500 actual high-paying jobs. There are standard methods for evaluating events with known probabilities of occurring.[13] If a person is neither risk averse nor enjoys risk for risk's sake, one usually converts uncertain values into an expected value by weighting the value of each outcome by the probability that that outcome will actually occur. Thus a 1 percent probability of winning $100 has an expected value of 1 percent of $100 dollars, or $1. If you repeatedly buy lottery tickets with such a chance of winning the $100 and paid $1 for each ticket, you will, over time, break even. In that sense, the value of the opportunity to win $100 can be said to be worth $1.00. The same is true of uncertain jobs. Exploratory gas drilling that promises 1 chance in 75 of a small commercial find that would employ 100 people is not the same as actual jobs for 100 people. The expected value of the employment is 1.33 percent (1 chance in 75 times 100), or slightly more than one job. Of course, there may well be several or many other possible outcomes. In drilling for oil or gas, one may find a small commercial field, or a large field, or a major find requiring nearby processing or refining operations. Each of these has some likelihood of occurring; the expected value of the employment would be the sum of the products of the incremental employment associated with each possibility, multiplied by the likelihood of that occurrence. A proposal might have an employment potential of 650 high-paying jobs if the most optimistic results actually occurred. But when weighted by the probabilities of various occurrences, expected employment might be only a single job (table 4-5). An employment value of 650 jobs might justify a public policy decision that would not be justified by an employment value of a single job. Mineral developers will emphasize the 650 potential jobs. It is important to temper that number with considerations of probability. What are the chances that the jobs will actually be created?

Is the mineral development proposal appealing because it promises jobs to local residents who are currently unemployed or employed in low-paid jobs? Most exploration and development jobs, because they involve specialized skills and are of short duration in any particular area, are unlikely to go to existing local residents. Mobile professionals will be brought in for this type of work. Only a tiny fraction of the jobs will go to existing residents. The same is likely to be true of the construction work force that may be required. Even production jobs will attract many nonresidents to the area. To get the workers it needs, the

TABLE 4-5.

Expected Employment from an Uncertain Mineral Development

Type of Find	(a) Potential Employment	(b) Probability of Find	(c) Decimal Weight (same as b)	(d) Incremental Employment (increase in a)	(e) Expected Employment (c × d)
Major (including refining)	650	1 in 3,750	0.000267	550	0.15
Medium	100	1 in 225	0.004000	50	0.20
Small Commercial	50	1 in 75	0.013300	50	0.67
No Commercial	0	99 in 100	0.986700	0	0.00
Total					1.02

mining company may even have to advertise and recruit in locations far removed from the mineral development operation. Underground miners, for instance, are often recruited from outside. In addition, word of large mining projects tends to spread rapidly, drawing to the area unemployed workers from a fairly large geographic area. Mobile, experienced, relatively aggressive outside job seekers will compete with local residents for jobs. And if more outsiders arrive than there are new jobs available, the overflow may stay and compete with local residents for existing lower-paid jobs. This could actually reduce employment opportunity for existing local residents.

It is almost certain that a significant percent of new mining jobs will go to nonresident inmigrants. For long-term production jobs, this could be as high as 50 percent. For shorter-term exploration and development jobs, it could be as high as 80 to 90 percent.[14] These are important considerations, given that the public policy intent of supporting mineral development is usually to solve local unemployment problems, not unemployment problems in far-removed areas. A decision that might be justified by the creation of 500 high-paying jobs for residents might look quite different if, say, only 100 of those jobs actually went to locals.

The opening of a mine or the development of an oil or gas field or the construction of a processing plant usually requires many times more workers than will actually be employed once the facility is operational. Some exploration, development, and construction jobs last only a few months, some a year or more. It is not clear that temporary employment will solve the economic problems facing rural areas. Large, temporary work forces are more likely to disrupt the local economy than improve it. What local residents want is stable, permanent employment. What local merchants want is reliable (and, no doubt, high) income flows into the community to support their businesses. Five hundred jobs of nine months' duration will not be the economic salvation of a small community.

A business concern that regularly lays off a substantial part of its work force for extended periods is not the same as business that offers fairly stable employment. Extended layoffs and strikes affect an entire community, disrupting the income flow upon which much of its economy relies and slowing economic development. It is important to consider the instability of mineral markets and prices when evaluating the contribution mining can make to local economic well-being. An economic activity that randomly and frequently throws large numbers of people out of work is not a boon to the local economy. This is especially true of local economies that are already specialized in and dependent on mining. More of the same is not necessarily economic development. Putting more eggs in one basket may simply compound the effect of the boom-and-bust cycle the community endures.

The employment impact of a proposed mineral development is often exaggerated by promoters, who will add "indirect" and "induced" employment to direct-employment figures. Indirect employment is associated with the mine purchasing inputs for its operations (fuel, tools, equipment, professional services). Induced employment is caused by employees spending their earnings in local businesses and the employees of local businesses respending that income.

The prediction of such "extra" employment impacts is so unreliable that for two decades the U.S. government has not allowed them to be counted as a benefit when doing benefit-cost analysis on federal projects.[15] One of the difficulties with extra impacts in relation to mineral developments is that they often take place in relatively isolated locations with little commercial infrastructure. Because of that few local businesses can take advantage of the new spending potential and income leaks out of the local area quickly, flowing to communities some distance away. This problem is compounded when a significant portion of the work force consists of commuters, temporary residents, and recent inmigrants. These workers are likely to direct their spending away from the immediate area.

Another problem is the assumption that if spending associated with the mine did not take place, indirectly employed workers would be permanently unemployed. This is not reasonable. People don't sit around waiting for a project paying high wages to open up nearby so that local spending can rise and put them to work. Most people put to work in induced and indirect jobs have been working at some other economic activity, not just sitting idle. While it is probable that alternative employment would not be as attractive in terms of pay and working conditions, for most of those filling secondary jobs there would be alternative employment. Most of what are calculated as "indirect" jobs do not represent net new employment.

Direct employment can be easily measured empirically. Indirect and induced employment are concepts associated with a particular model of the local economy that may or may not be relevant or empirically accurate. As discussed earlier, empirical analysis yields little support for such assumed employment multipliers in the mining industry. Changes in mining employment and income have not had the expected multiplier effect on the rest of the economy. What multipliers primarily do is amplify the assumed economic importance of the mining industry. This may be politically useful to some groups, but it is a questionable guide to public economic policy.

Elusive Prosperity:
High Wages, Depressed Communities

In the folk economics that dominates public discussion of economic policy, it is taken for granted that more high-wage jobs are a cure for whatever economic ills may plague a community. If an economic activity like mining pays wages that are as much as twice the average local wage, the community will prosper. This rosy assumption is contradicted by the brute reality of economic conditions in towns dominated by mining. Butte, Montana, Lead, South Dakota, and Kellogg, Idaho, looked run-down and depressed even during periods of peak production in the recent past. The same could be said of almost any of the mining areas of the nation: the coal belt stretching from Pennsylvania to West Virginia and Kentucky, the copper towns of Arizona and New Mexico, the iron and copper mining areas of northern Minnesota. The instability endemic to mining discussed above is primarily responsible for their sluggish economies. But "monoculture" mining does more than cripple local economies. It leaves in its wake massive environmental degradation.

Because mining income is unstable, fluctuating as it does with world commodity prices, competition with developing countries, changes in technology, and labor-management disputes, those who rely on it have to take steps to protect themselves. One defensive strategy is to minimize the fixed investment that is tied to a mining operation and its location. Business owners in mining towns are cautious about investments in commercial infrastructure that might be stranded by another mine shutdown, and miners are wary of setting down roots in a mining-dependent town. Employees will live in temporary residences, retain residences elsewhere, and commute long distances to work. Others will leave their families behind and move temporarily to the mine site. The result is a transient work force with personal and economic commitments elsewhere, which keeps down local investment.

The environmental degradation associated with most mineral operations compounds the problem. Mining gnaws away at the earth, producing toxic effluents that kill streams and poison ground water. Smelting and refining causes air pollution that at best is unpleasant and at worst is toxic to both vegetation and human health. Many mining towns are environmental wastelands with air and water of questionable safety. This has a real impact on decisions about where to locate homes and businesses. Miners won't live in degraded environments if they have a choice, and those not connected with the mine avoid it altogether. Thus much of the income that is earned in mineral production never flows through the local community. The low level of commercial and residential investment and the unstable mineral operation itself mean a depressed tax base and poor public services. The result is an area of industrial sacrifice, a center to which workers travel daily but which derives little economic benefit from all of the wealth it generates.

High wages are not the only relevant economic variable when evaluating whether a particular type of economic activity will contribute to the well-being of a local community. Stability and tenure of employment, the number of jobs going to residents, and the impact on noncommercial but crucial economic resources such as environmental quality and public services are also of central importance. "More jobs and income" is a slogan, not an economic development policy.

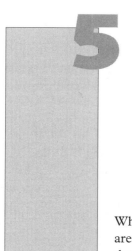

5 All That Glitters: Mineral Development and Mineral Policy

When mineral extraction is proposed in a natural area primarily devoted to recreation and wildlife, the common assumption is that the mineral values will dominate no matter how carefully and completely one estimates the economic values associated with recreation and wildlife. Mineral values such as gold and natural gas are believed to represent concentrated forms of economic wealth that require the sacrifice of only a relatively small amount of land for large economic returns. Disturbance of a few square miles can produce resources earning tens or hundreds of millions of dollars. Meanwhile, it is assumed, recreation and wildlife, because they are dispersed, lose little of their land base. Only a few hikers, hunters, or anglers are inconvenienced, only a few big game animals or fish are disturbed. Clearly, the conclusion is, mineral values will almost always exceed environmental values.

This type of informal analysis is seriously flawed and oversimplified. It ignores the dynamic context in which both mineral values and environmental resources should be evaluated.

It should be noted that in the following analysis we shift our focus from the vitality of the local economy to the economic values derived from mineral commodities and from undisturbed natural landscapes. This is the primary way economists evaluate economic activity. The purpose of economic activity (at least to economists) is not primarily to put people to work but rather to produce the goods and services that satisfy their needs and desires. That is not to suggest that protecting the environment has no positive impact on local economic vitality. As discussed earlier, because people value high-quality living environments, what is good for the environment, in general, is also good for the local economy.

The Value of Mineral Deposits

If a particular mineral deposit that is proposed for development is not developed, it does not mean that the nation or the world will be forced to go without the value that could have been created at that site. At any given moment, all known mineral deposits are not under production. Only the most profitable deposits are producing. The rest are left undeveloped because the costs associated with extracting them are too high. Consider America's coal resources. Almost all fifty states have some significant coal resources. But not all states are significant coal producers. Even states like Montana that are major coal producers do not have most of their coal resources under production. A good part of the eastern half of Montana contains coal resources. But coal is being mined at only a handful of locations.

The same can be said about metal ore and oil and gas resources. Only resources whose extraction is cheap relative to commodity prices are brought into production at any given time. There are abundant supplies of mineral resources that could be brought into production if the price and cost were right. There are also alternative sources of supply for any particular mineral deposit. What is lost if a particular site is not brought into production is the advantage that site has over other sites that would be brought into production. If the alternative site is a more expensive one, the economic loss associated with not developing the cheaper site is the cost differential, not the value of the commodity. When there are many alternative sites, as there are for coal, oil, gas, and most metal ores, the cost differential between sites may be low. Because of that, the economic cost associated with not developing any particular site is also likely to be low.[1]

This consideration of alternatives when evaluating the economic value of a particular location extends beyond alternative sites. If, for instance, drilling for natural gas in a particular area was not allowed, and this was the only new source of natural gas available, it would not mean that people's homes would be colder or that industrial operations would have to be curtailed. There are substitutes for natural gas—alternative fuel as well as the potential to improve the efficiency of natural gas consumption. What would be lost if a particular natural gas site is not developed is the cost advantage it has over all of the alternative ways we might satisfy the need that natural gas serves. Given the huge potential for cost-effective conservation of resources in this country, it may be that there is no cost advantage associated with supplementing supply as opposed to improving the efficiency with which we use current supply.[2] In that case, not only would there be no economic loss associated with the failure to develop a mineral site, but there may be an economic gain as more cost-effective means are used to satisfy our needs. The value of the mineral deposit in place is only the cost advantage that particular source has over alternative ways of satisfying the same need. One cannot evaluate the potential economic loss associated with deciding not to develop a mineral resource unless one considers the alternatives.

In general it would be incorrect to estimate the economic value of a mineral deposit by multiplying the physical quantity of the mineral that might be extracted by the commodity price of the refined product. A gold deposit with the potential of producing 20 million ounces of gold is not worth $8 billion simply because the price of gold is $400 per ounce. At the very least, one has to subtract from this value the costs of developing the mine, extracting the mineral, processing the ore, refining the metal, and transporting it to market. It is only after all of these costs have been incurred and the metal is delivered to the market that it has the $400 value. Given that at any particular time, a significant number of mineral operations are financially marginal, barely able to provide a competitive return on investment, the value of those deposits after costs are deducted is often near zero.[3]

Then there is the risk that the mineral deposit will not be as rich or as cheap to produce as expected. Perhaps commodity prices will fall, making the operation financially unviable. Perhaps environmental problems will halt the operation, or cumulative environmental problems will impose a liability on the mining company. The actual net economic value of the output of a mineral development operation is uncertain, especially before development gets under way. The projected mineral value must incorporate uncertain outcomes and their probability of occurrence. If, for instance, there is only a 50 percent probability that a mineral operation will realize a yield at a cost and be sold at a price that will make the development viable, the economic value may be only half the potential amount associated with a successful mine.[4]

In moving from the commodity value of the finished mineral product to the economic value associated with a particular mineral site, the adjustments discussed above are cumulative and multiplicative. If a mineral-development proposal is very risky and the site at issue does not have a great cost advantage over other sites, the economic value of that site's mineral potential could be extremely low compared to the "value" one might calculate by multiplying the quantity of mineral times the commodity value of the finished product—as little as a fraction of 1 percent of the commodity value of the finished mineral product. If there is a probability of successful production and the site has significant cost advantages over alternative sites, the economic value of the site's mineral potential is higher but still likely to be only a small fraction (perhaps a fifth or a sixth) of the nominal value of the potential finished product (table 5-1).[5]

The primary point here is that one cannot evaluate a gold deposit or a natural gas development by taking the market price of the commodity and multiplying by the physical quantity that might be recoverable. That would produce a value as much as a hundred times larger than the actual economic value of the site for its mineral potential. Because mineral production is usually risky and barely profitable, and because there are almost always readily available alternative sources of supply, the economic loss associated with not developing a site is often very low. Mineral potential does not necessarily represent concentrated wealth.

A mineral that is not extracted now because of environmental concerns is not lost. In the future, if the value of the mineral were to rise, or the value of the environmental resources threatened by its development were to fall, or technological developments were to reduce the environmental impact of extraction, the mineral could be developed and its economic value realized. The choice not to develop a mineral resource today is not an irreversible decision.

This is important for two reasons. First, technologies may develop that significantly reduce the environmental costs associated with extraction. For instance, where extensive roads in a natural area might be needed now for oil and gas development, in the future slant-rig or directional drilling might allow the resource to be developed without the environmental disruption of road construction and site development. Or consider metal mining. Currently, low-grade ores are processed by moving huge quantities of ore to chemical treatment facilities. The results are massive scarring of the landscape and water pollution. Alternative processing methods in the future could considerably alleviate such problems.

Second, those who are concerned about the future scarcity of raw materials should be even less concerned about delaying mineral production at a site. If, as some believe, supplies of fossil fuel and other minerals are running out, then the value of mineral resources should rise in the future. Undeveloped mineral resources would be like money in the bank, increasing in value over time. And if real commodity prices

TABLE 5-1.

The Economic Value of Mineral Deposits in Place

	Development, Production, and Processing Costs As a % of Price	Cost Advantage of This Site over Others (%)	Probability of Successful Development and Operation As Planned (%)	Economic Value As a % of Price
Scenario 1	75.0	30.0	70.0	15.8
Scenario 2	60.0	25.0	60.0	9.0
Scenario 3	50.0	15.0	10.0	0.8

increase faster than the real return that can be earned elsewhere in the economy, no economic value is lost by leaving mineral resources in place for the time being.[6] Of course, during the delay in development, the value of a deposit could evaporate either because the market has declined or because cheaper sources have been discovered. If value were lost as the result of a delay, mining interests could argue that the economic value of the deposit had been wasted. Alternatively, it could be argued that the delay prevented a valuable natural area from being permanently damaged in the production of something that was about to become cheap and unnecessary anyway.

The Value of Preservation

Mineral development usually causes significant environmental degradation, an economic cost as real as that associated with the depletion of any other scarce and valuable resource. People's sacrifices in the pursuit of high quality living environments have demonstrated how valuable clean air and water, beautiful landscapes, wildlife, and recreation are. There is little dispute these days that environmental damage lessens human well-being.[7]

The cost associated with environmental damage has to be evaluated, however, in a dynamic context. When permanent or semipermanent changes are made in the landscape, the economic value lost is not just that associated with current nonconsumptive use and value. Losses will continue, and there is reason to believe that the size of annual economic losses will grow. The reasons for this expectation are tied to conventional supply-and-demand analysis: the supply of undisturbed natural landscape is shrinking; the demand for such landscape as a source of environmental services (recreation, scenic beauty, water quality) is rising. Thus the value of natural landscape can be expected to rise relative to commodity values over time. Increasing commodity values will be constrained by the availability of substitutes, technological change, recycling, and so on, mitigating forces that are not available to increase the supply of natural landscape. The rise in the economic value of environmental resources relative to commodities is important in evaluating any mineral development proposals in natural areas.[8]

Natural landscapes and ecosystems take centuries or millennia to develop, landscapes and ecosystems modified by short-lived mining may take decades or centuries to recover. Human economic activity is constantly nibbling away at the remnant natural areas in the country and the world. If human-built landscapes such as Disney World or urban park systems that have been developed over the last century are good substitutes for natural ecosystems, then human activity can supplement the shrinking supply of landscape and offset its impact. But to most individuals, human-built landscapes are not a close substitute for intact natural areas. While Disney World or a contemporary "open" zoo may be impressive human constructs with their own particular values, they are no match for intact natural ecosystems. What people seek in nature is its nonreproducible gifts. This is especially true of relatively unique natural areas.[9] In addition, the satisfaction people get from natural areas comes from experiencing them directly; they are not just intermediate inputs in production processes that, like coal, can be replaced by something else when technological change or some other factor makes substitution possible. With nature it is the resource itself that people wish to experience.

While the supply of wild lands cannot be enhanced and will probably shrink, demand will probably grow. The demand for environmental goods and services, like almost all goods and services, increases with income and population. In addition, increasing importance seems to be attached to environmental quality. There is no sign that this will change in the near future. At the very least, when calculating the value of environmental losses associated with mineral development, one has to build into the analysis expected growth in the economic value of preserved landscape.[10]

Environmental losses associated with mineral development, processing, and refining are not limited to small geographic areas. These activities physically modify landscapes and often allow toxic chemicals that had been geographically and chemically stabilized to become mobile in the environment.[11] Through erosion, leaching, and seepage, toxins enter surface and ground water. Refining activities compound air pollution. Environmental disruption can extend for miles beyond the mining site and is anything but trivial in effect. The Clark Fork River in Montana is a good example. Mineral waste from copper operations in Butte and Anaconda have left toxic deposits for a hundred miles downstream, creating the largest Superfund waste site in the nation. Air pollution from the Anaconda smelter damaged the Anaconda-Pintlar Wilderness as well as the health of residents living adjacent to the smelter.[12] To produce timber for the underground mining operation, the Anaconda Company stripped the surrounding hills of forests and logged the Blackfoot River basin a hundred miles away. Mining is rarely a local event.

Mineral deposits do not necessarily represent a concentrated form of economic wealth that outweighs the nonconsumptive values associated with natural landscapes. The high cost and risk of mineral development can strip a project of its economic value. In addition, mineral operations produce uniform commodities that can be obtained from hundreds of different sites. This is another way of saying that minerals from any given site are dispensable. Yet what is threatened by mineral operations may be unique, irreplaceable gifts of nature. There would be something seriously wrong with any economic analysis that regularly concluded that a resource that is unique and irreplaceable should be sacrificed to a resource that is abundant and easily replaced.

Natural landscapes house different resources with different values. Some, like mineral resources, are developed through commercial means. Others, such as wildlife and scenic beauty are noncommercial. Often the pursuit of commercial and noncommercial resources conflict. In that situation we face a familiar economic problem: We have a scarce resource that if put to one purpose cannot be used for another. A choice has to be made: Which use of the landscape will yield the greatest value? There is nothing in economic theory or empirical economic experience to suggest that commercial economic value is always greater than noncommercial economic value. In fact, that often will not be the case. Any analysis that assumes that commercial uses reign supreme is not economic analysis, for it fails to perform the basic economic task of evaluating all conflicting choices. When economic analysis is approached objectively, there is no way of presupposing any particular result. Certainly it would not be odd to discover that nonconsumptive, noncommercial environmental values exceeded commercial values in some cases. Backpacking and wildlife may very well hold more economic value than a gold mine.

Reforming Mineral Policy

Mineral development offers a glittering prize: high-paying jobs for rural areas whose traditional economic bases have deteriorated and stimulus to regional metropolitan centers that provide financial and service support for development. In areas where mineral development has traditionally been important, proposals for new developments promise to reverse past losses and bring back the "good old days." Such offers are difficult to refuse. But experience with mineral development should temper our response to the promise of mineral-based well-being. Mineral development, rarely the basis for sustained local prosperity, is more often associated with ghost towns and areas mired in sustained depression. Hard-rock mining (metals and other nonfuel minerals) alone has left behind as many as a half million abandoned sites, many with serious ongoing environmental problems.[13] To this legacy has to be added the environmental impacts of past coal, oil, and gas development. The damage from coal mining, both underground and strip, is extensive and long-lasting, in many cases nearly permanent.

These are not minor, largely aesthetic concerns. The Blackfoot River in Montana and the Alamose River in Colorado are just two examples of rivers that have been severely damaged by mine waste. The Upper Clark Fork Valley in Montana and the Silver Valley in Idaho's panhandle are sprawling Superfund toxic waste sites, the result of mineral development. The coal fields of eastern Pennsylvania, West Virginia, and Kentucky are testimony to the ravaging impact of strip mining. The heap leach gold operations in the Black Hills of South Dakota, the Rocky Mountains of Montana, and the desert ranchland of Nevada are more recent examples of the near-permanent scarring of the landscape in the pursuit of mineral wealth.

Given that people care where they live and that economic activity does shift to where there is an adequate work force, communities have to be concerned about the long-run impact of turning their landscapes into open pits or toxic waste sites that systematically release poisons. Empirical research confirms that the presence of significant sources of air or water pollution, smelters, petroleum processing, and Superfund sites increases the rate of outmigration and decreases the rate of inmigration.[14] In permanently degrading the landscape and releasing toxins into the air and water, mining can threaten a community's long-run economic future.

If mineral development is going to boost and sustain well-being, the environmental disruption it causes has to be contained. For a broad range of mining activities that is not currently possible because of the nineteenth-century mining law designed to promote mineral development on public lands. This limits the ability of land managers to reject mining proposals when projections of environmental damage appear too high. Since the law also allows ownership of the site to shift to the mining company for almost no cost, future control over the land is also lost. Furthermore, mining companies are legally protected against cleaning up sites that are too costly to reclaim; they can simply abandon their ruin, leaving cleanup and restoration costs to the public to bear. The result is thousands of abandoned sites that will cost tens of billions of dollars to clean up.[15] Faced with a fiscal crisis, the federal government lacks the funds for cleanup. As a result, mining regions and their populations have had no way of repairing the damage done by mining to their environments and economies.

Federal mining law reform would attempt to solve these problems in several ways. First, federal land managers would be given the authority to reject mining on public lands when the environmental costs are judged to be too high. Second, more realistic mine-reclamation bonds would be required so that as wealth is removed, an adequate fund to repair the landscape is simultaneously created. Third, the government would charge annual rental fees to those who hold federal mineral claims and collect a royalty on all mineral wealth removed. The revenue raised from these sources would help fund reclamation. Finally, the practice of "patenting" mining claims, which allows public lands to be transferred to private ownership, would be abandoned. Taken as a package, mining law reform would reduce the damage done by new and existing mines and fund the repair of the cumulative damage associated with past mining. This would be doubly beneficial to local economies, both protecting or enhancing their amenities (thereby holding and drawing people and business) and pumping money into local economies as people go to work reclaiming old sites.

Opponents to mining law reform have argued that the proposed hard-rock royalties and rents would have a dramatic impact on the economy of the West and of the nation, shaking "the very foundation of

America's industrial base."[16] By forcing mines to shut down, royalties and rents would create ghost towns in the West.[17] The reforms would result in the "wasting of a significant portion of U.S. gold ore reserves," possibly as much as 60 percent.[18] A proposed 8 percent royalty would result in the loss of 47,000 jobs, more than all of the workers now employed in metal mining in the West, and render "most of the domestic mining industry non-viable."[19] Such claims cannot help but catch the attention of concerned citizens and policymakers. Fortunately, not one can be supported by facts.

The Assumed Impact of Mining Law Reform: The Doomsayers

Predictions of economic catastrophe resulting from mining law reform stem from analyses based on insupportable assumptions.

Assumption 1: The West's hard-rock mining industry cannot handle the equivalent of an 8 percent decline in the commodity value of metal ore that a federal royalty would impose. In fact, the hard-rock mining industry has always had to cope with wide swings in the value of its output. In just the first six months of 1993, for instance, gold prices rose from $330 to $405 per ounce, almost six times more than the effective rise the proposed 8 percent federal royalty would have prompted at the beginning of 1993. If the industry were able to survive without a federal royalty payment at the beginning of 1993, it most certainly would be able to survive with a federal royalty in mid-1993. Between 1987 and 1992 real gold prices declined by $200 per ounce, a change more than fourteen times greater than the effective impact of the proposed royalty. The U.S. gold industry not only survived this drastic price decline but almost doubled its output. In an industry as used to shifting economic conditions as hard-rock mining is, modest royalty payments could not possibly cause the catastrophic collapse now projected by the mining industry.

Assumption 2: Mining companies operating on federal lands cannot afford to pay a royalty similar to what is regularly paid by mines operating on private, state, tribal, and other federal mineral lands. But mineral royalties are not rare and unusual. In the United States the owners of all mineral deposits except for hard-rock deposits on federal land demand and get royalty payments. Moreover, the typical royalty is a "gross" royalty—like the royalty proposed for federal hard-rock minerals—based on the value of the mineral product as it leaves the mine. Royalty rates paid to other mineral owners are similar in size to those proposed for federal hard-rock minerals. Given that the collection of such royalties has not blocked mineral development on private, state, tribal, and other federal mineral lands, there is no reason to believe the case will be different on federal hard-rock lands.[20]

Assumption 3: Mining is an important part of the nation's and the West's economic base. As discussed in the previous chapter, this simply is not the case. Mining is responsible for only a sliver of total employment and income, a tiny fraction of 1 percent. In addition, if mining activity lessened slightly in the United States, it would not harm American manufacturing because mining products are readily available from alternative sources of supply at about the same price as in the United States. Excess international supply is what has regularly depressed commodity prices. Contrary to the national myth, mining is not a crucial part of the nation's or the West's "industrial base."

Assumption 4: All future metal mining in the United States will have to take place on federal land, where it will be subject to the proposed royalty. Only a small fraction of hard-rock mining takes place on federal land—in the West, about one-seventh of production. Even in a state like Nevada where 82 percent of the land is in federal hands, the most notable "gold strike" in a hundred years was made on private land (Newmont's Carlin and Gold Quarry mines on the T Lazy S Ranch.[21] Alaska excluded, most land in the West is not federally owned. And, of course, the West is not the only geographic region with hard-rock potential.[22] Nonfederal land will continue to compete with federal land as a source of minerals and as a major supplier.[23] Mining law reform will simply eliminate the current economic incentive to prefer federal sources because of the lack of royalties.

Assumption 5: The quantitative impact of a federal gross royalty is indicated by the nominal percentage royalty multiplied by the commodity price of the finished product. But an 8 percent royalty on the gross value of the mineral product as it leaves the mine does not have the same financial impact as an increase in costs equal to 8 percent of the commodity value of the finished product. For instance, an 8 percent gross royalty on copper when the commodity price of copper is a dollar a pound is not the equivalent of an eight-cent increase in the cost of mining copper. The financial impact is closer to half of this, because royalties are deductible in calculating federal and state income taxes, state net proceeds mineral taxes, and net royalties. In addition, the royalty applies to the value of the mined mineral, not to the value of the smelted and refined product delivered to commodity markets.

Assumption 6: Claim-holding fees will be paid on all current hard-rock mining claims, draining an enormous amount of capital from the mining industry and imposing huge financial costs. This assumes that mining companies will behave in an irrational and nonbusinesslike manner. The thinking is that mining companies holding relatively unpromising claims will sacrifice such activities as promising exploration and development, valuable research, and productive management just to hang on to each and every claim they hold, no matter what the cost of maintaining that claim and no matter how unpromising it is. No business person would behave in that manner. Holders of hard-rock mining claims will have to make an economic calculation comparing the expected payoff associated with marginal claims and other uses to which the cost of claim maintenance could be put. Only claims with the most likely payoff will be maintained through payment of claim-holding fees. Others will be abandoned, though of course the minerals will not be lost. They will be available for development if mining economics change.

Assumption 7: The price of gold will remain depressed, in the $350-per-ounce range. But gold prices are notoriously volatile. Basing ten-year projections for the industry on recent low prices is not a very reliable approach. As mentioned, gold prices rose over $80 per ounce during the first half of 1993. This has a dramatic impact on any analysis of the profitability of gold mining. During most of the 1994–1996 period gold prices hovered just below $400 per ounce, a price rise that more than offset the 8 percent royalty that was first proposed in 1991 and was reintroduced to Congress in 1993.

Assumption 8: Cost-price relationships in hard-rock mining from 1990 or 1992 will remain frozen for the next decade. But costs have been fluctuating wildly over the last decade or so. Produc-

tivity has risen steadily, and new mining, extraction, and benefaction·
processes have developed, changes that will continue. In addition, the
per-unit costs of mining can be controlled by mine operators who vary
the quality of the ore they process. This is dependent on the price of the
commodity. When the price is high, it pays to process lower-grade ore
and accept higher per-unit costs. When the price falls, per-unit costs
can be cut by going after higher-quality, less costly ore. Between 1991
and 1992, for instance, the average cash cost of gold production declined almost 4 percent, or $10 per ounce.[24] That decline would have
offset almost three-quarters of the effective impact of an 8 percent royalty. There is nothing "fixed" about the costs associated with hard-rock
mining ten years or more into the future.

***Assumption 9: Federal expenditures of hard-rock-mining royal-
ties and fees supporting state and local government programs
and administering hard-rock-mining programs, including
mine reclamation, will bring no local economic benefit.*** But such
federal expenditures are like any other expenditures within the local
economy: they put people to work, they purchase supplies, materials,
and services, and to the extent that they reduce taxes, they increase disposable income. It is not reasonable to predict job losses when mining
companies spend less money and not predict similar job gains when
state, local, and federal governments spend more money.

These are just some of the tortured assumptions that have been
made in mining-industry analyses of the economic impact of federal
mining law. Many other, more specialized, but equally unacceptable arguments have been put forth. The point is, industry studies have had to
stray far from fact and economic reality to develop their self-serving
catastrophic scenarios.

The Economic Impact of Mining Reform

When some of the faulty assumptions are abandoned, one can use information on the average total cost of production at various mines to
estimate the impact of the proposed federal royalty. As an example,
here we analyze the impact on employment in gold mining if the royalty
and rent proposals embodied in the 1993 mining law reform were
adopted. Gold mining is the type of hard-rock mining most likely to be
affected, since a larger percentage of it (about a third, much more than
the industry average) takes place on federal lands. Almost all mining of

copper, the next most important hard rock, is done on private land.[25] Thus, if the percentage reduction in gold-mining employment caused by federal mining law reform is applied to all hard-rock mining, the impact of reform is significantly exaggerated.

If all active gold mines were on federal land, and if the commodity price of gold were $400 an ounce, the proposed royalties and rents would reduce long-term gold production by about 2 percent over the next decade. The drop would be about 3 percent if gold were $375 an ounce (figure 5-1). The federal royalty is allowed to increase the total cost associated with each mine. The break-even point is where the total cost (including a competitive return on investment) is equal to the value of the output. Looking at the point where the price line intersects the total cost curve, one can see the impact on the viability of different mines as the federal royalty raises the costs of production.

But all gold mines do not operate on federal land. If only 30 percent of marginal production were on federal land—only 30 percent of total production comes from federal land—the employment reduction would be about 1 percent or less. To the extent that the royalty caused mineral production to shift from federal to nonfederal land, the long-term impact would be even smaller because there would be an offsetting increase in employment on nonfederal land.

If, to be conservative, the employment impact of the proposed royalty on gold is increased by 50 percent to 1.5 percent and applied to other metal mining, including copper (although in fact almost all copper mining takes place on nonfederal land and would not be subject to the federal royalty), it would result in the loss of about 640 metal-mining jobs across the West. This job loss represents about 1 job out of every 10,000 projected to be created over the next two decades in the West. Even if one assumes a 15 percent decline in production in federal hard-rock mines and assumes that almost a third of all production will be on federal land (an impact thirty to sixty times greater than what the cost analysis indicates), job loss comes to only two-hundredths of 1 percent of the job creation expected in the region.

In analyzing the employment impact of mining law reform, it is important to realize that proposed royalties, rents, and fees would not simply represent income draining out of western states. Most of the revenue collected by the federal government from mining would be returned to western states to support reclamation and other state and local government programs. In fact, more jobs would be created as a result of this local reinvestment of royalty proceeds than can be expected

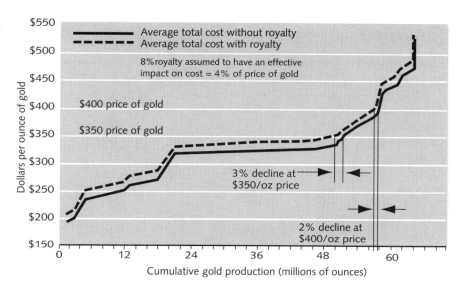

FIGURE 5-1. Long-run impact of an 8% gross royalty on gold production. The impact would be quite modest for gold prices in excess of $325 per ounce. (*Data sources:* J. L. Dobra and P. R. Thomas, 1992, "The U.S. Gold Industry, 1992," Nevada Bureau of Mines and Geology Special Publication 14, University of Nevada, Reno, Mackay School of Mines.)

to be lost in mining owing to the federal royalty. This is true because much of the new federal revenues would come from claim-holding fees that would not have an impact on mine production. In addition, as pointed out above, the royalties would have little negative impact on mining operations but would be available to fund extensive reclamation activities. As a result, federal reclamation spending could be expected to create an additional 1,400 jobs. Even in the worst case, a net of about 300 jobs would be created (table 5-2).

It is important to keep in mind that mining law reform would provide more control over the environmental impact of mining and would work systematically to repair the damage done in the past. The result would be to protect and enhance western landscapes, water resources, recreational opportunities, wildlife, and communities. These are the characteristics that have drawn people to the West during the 1990s, revitalizing the region's economies. Environmental protection

TABLE 5-2.

The Employment Impact of Federal Mining Law Reform (8% royalty on federal hard-rock minerals)

	Expected Job Loss Due to Royalty	Maximum Job Loss Due to Royalty	Expected Job Gain Due to Expenditure of Fees and Royalty	Expected Net Job Impact	Net Job Impact (using maximum job loss)
Arizona	126	139	584	458	445
California	92	442	86	-5	-356
Colorado	45	134	156	111	22
Idaho	36	218	130	94	-89
Montana	42	119	136	94	18
Nevada	195	585	596	401	11
New Mexico	26	64	89	63	25
Oregon	9	47	6	-3	-41
Utah	41	35	154	114	119
Washington	24	71	48	24	-23
Wyoming	9	42	22	13	-20
Western States	644	1,757	2,043	1,400	286

Source: Power 1993, tables 3 and 4.

strengthens an important part of the region's economic base and contributes to its ongoing development. When this positive economic force is taken into account, one can expect that mining law reform would contribute to job creation on a scale that far exceeds the calculations provided here.

The Toxic Legacy of Summitville Consolidated

While still contemplating how to cope with the toxic legacy of a century of mining, we are already creating a whole new set of mine-related environmental catastrophes. The Summitville mine on the Alamosa River in the San Juan Mountains of Colorado is the best-known recent example. The Summitville Consolidated Mining Company tore off the tops of the mountains and filled in a valley to serve as its cyanide heap leach base. Toxic flows poisoned local creeks and groundwater, and acid-laced runoff attacked aquatic life for 17 miles along the Alamosa. The company, faced with the cost of cleaning up the disaster, declared bankruptcy. When the State of Colorado tried to hold its parent company, Galactic Resources of Canada, responsible, it too declared bankruptcy. The state, unable to carry the costs of control and reclamation, turned the site over to the U.S. Environmental Protection Agency. Now U.S. taxpayers will foot the bill to contain an environmental sore that will probably never be healed.[26]

Meanwhile, those living in the vicinity of the abandoned mine and downriver have to cope with the consequences. The mine only operated for six years. In exchange for the limited economic benefits of that brief operation, residents now have to live permanently with a degraded landscape. Clearly Summitville, like many other mineral development operations, was no boon to the well-being of local residents.

Not all mineral development activity has to have such a negative impact on local economies. But it will if it is not closely regulated. In areas that cannot support development with current mining technology, land managers have to be able to say no. In other areas, strict environmental controls and substantial reclamation bonds should be required. In addition, all ongoing mining operations should have to contribute to the funding of state and federal reclamation of mining sites abandoned in the past. There is a toxic legacy here for which the entire industry should be partially responsible. Only if progress can be made to eliminate the environmental destruction wrought by mineral development activity should new development activities be allowed. The lure of exaggerated contribution to local wages and employment should not override the environmental controls needed to protect an area's future. Mining contributes too little to local economic development to justify its permanently scarring local environments while disrupting local communities

Not Seeing the Forest for the Trees: Local Economies and the Timber Industry

In heavily forested areas, the economic dominance of the timber industry is usually taken for granted. Forested land prevents agriculture and urban development. With these activities excluded, it seems logical to conclude that the economic well-being of residents will be tied directly or indirectly to the timber-producing potential of the forest. The timber industry is lord, the community his inevitable domain. This conclusion is similar to that reached about the importance of agriculture in landscapes dominated by crop or grazing lands.

Trees of a Thousand Kind: American Timber Policy through the Centuries

The heated debate over timber harvesting and the management of America's public timberland is hardly new. It goes back more than a century. The practice of clear-cutting trees from huge tracts of land goes back even further, having been the practice since Europeans first arrived in the New World. The disruption of the lives of workers, their families, and their communities that accompanies the exhaustion of regional timber supplies is also a national tradition. Over the last two centuries the center of timber production has constantly shifted as supplies were exhausted and sought elsewhere.

Europeans first became interested in North America because of the continent's timber. Vikings came to the New World five centuries before Columbus for the express purpose of cutting trees to support their

settlements in Greenland.[1] One of the impressive features of the New
World reported by Columbus was its extensive forests with trees "of a
thousand kind and tall."[2] Along the Atlantic seaboard as much as 90
percent of the landscape was covered with forests,[3] stretching more
than halfway across the continent to the Great Plains. From the Pacific
Coast, especially the Pacific Northwest, huge towering forests of red-
wood and Douglas fir stretched inland.

As European settlement proceeded, the forests were seen as a mixed
blessing. While providing valuable building materials, fuel, chemicals,
and naval stores, they inhibited settlement and agriculture, the dominant economic activity. Trees, plentiful beyond comprehension, were a
"noxious weed" covering potentially valuable farmland. They had limited value, and that could only be realized by their removal.

Colonial attitudes toward forestland could be downright hostile. The
natural forest was a wild, threatening place that God intended hu-
manity to tame, "a waste and howling wilderness where none inhabited
but hellish fiends and brutish men."[4] This European attitude is well de-
picted in the Grimm brothers' fairy tales taught to us as children. Recall the forest into which Hansel and Gretel were led.

The hostility of European immigrants to America's natural forests is
understandable if we consider that in Europe most of the remaining
forest lay on the periphery of human settlement, acting as a refuge for
the marginal elements of society, outlaws, pagans following the old pre-
Christian ways, Robin Hoods retreating into Sherwood Forest to escape the forces of organized civil society. European hostility, in somewhat muted form, continued to dominate the philosophy of American
foresters well into the late twentieth century: natural forests were
chaotic and wasteful places crying out for the taming hand of hu-
mankind. Moreover, only through the intervention of forest management could the forest's "health" be maintained.

From an economic perspective the European attitude was also understandable. To Europeans trying to establish settlements and steadily
expanding and unlimited trade, forest resources exceeded local needs
and the demands of international trade. They represented a cheap and
inexhaustible resource to be mined as quickly as was economically feasible, or wasted through girdling and burning if markets did not support
commercial harvest of trees that stood on potential agricultural land.

Fueled by such attitudes, timber harvesting moved systematically
across the growing nation. States like Maine and Pennsylvania that had

dominated timber production in the nation's early years yielded leadership to Michigan, then Wisconsin and Minnesota. From there the industry swept through the Gulf South, then the Pacific Northwest, and finally the northern Rocky Mountains. With timberland available in the West or South for as little as $1.25 an acre, northeastern and mid-Atlantic states could continue to compete only by innovating, cutting costs, and expanding the scale of their operations. The economic dynamic in play left little room for considerations of conservation or environmental impact. In the Great Lakes region and throughout much of the South, a pattern was established of deforestation, abandonment, erosion, and poverty.[5]

Beginning in the late nineteenth century, as the timber industry reached the end of the frontier, leaving in its wake a devastated landscape, demands for reform mounted. One result was a significant shift away from the privatization of public land. In fact, during the first half of the twentieth century, deforested private land abandoned after logging, reverted to public ownership as both state and federal governments adopted reforestation and forest-reserve programs to fight local poverty, erosion, and flooding. Many of the state forests across the nation had their origins in these conservation efforts, as did the national forest system itself.[6]

America's experience with destructive timber harvesting is the foundation of the current conflict over the management of public forestland as well as the debate over the imposition of state forestry standards on private timberland. At the same time, there has been a profound shift in the public attitude toward the nation's forestland during this century, even in states dominated by the timber industry. What was once seen as an inexhaustible supply of trees to be raided and an expanse of wilderness that confounded civilization is now seen as an extremely limited resource. Only small remnants of once-expansive forest ecosystems remain. What was once in excess supply is now in short supply relative to demand. What was once seen as a threat to civilization is now seen as a precious gift of nature threatened by the demands of civilization. The value of forests is no longer seen as primarily that of the trees themselves or the agricultural potential lying beneath them. Forested landscape is increasingly viewed as the natural backdrop that sustains civilization both physically and spiritually. It is the conflict between this new set of values and the old that is currently being played out both on the land and in the political life of our communities.

Community Stability and Social Forestry

The impact of timber harvest policies on local communities has long been recognized. Deforestation changes the possible mix of economic activities and has the potential to change watersheds and local climate. Clearly, communities can be and often are dependent on forests.

This social reality has colored discussions of American forest policy from at least the middle of the nineteenth century, when citizens of Maine and Pennsylvania began worrying about the future of their timber industries. Since then, forest policy has been entwined with concerns about social policy. Public dialogue on forestry practices has typically been couched in terms of "social forestry." The general idea that communities can depend on forest resources for their well-being, and that well-being is affected by forest management decisions, was converted into a vague concept of community stability that has been touted by almost every interest group concerned with public forest policy. Community stability has meant many different things to many different people. We need to understand its shades of meaning if we are to understand the social ramifications of timber politics.

One of the early concerns about the timber industry was its unstable work force that moved from lumber camp to lumber camp as the harvest frontier shifted. Social commentators decried the "depravity of rootless existence" connected with the industry.[7] They saw the rough, marginal labor force as a threat to decent society, one that needed to be tamed and incorporated into stable communities where normal family life was possible. Their descriptions of logging camps—which does not sound all that different from portrayals of the mining camps of the West or the early ranching settlements that western novels and movies have mythologized—still have a ring of truth. Forested regions have continued to support a rural population living in relative isolation and poverty and exhibiting a marked hostility to urban dwellers and the "government." The backwoods still exist as a social and economic reality in many regions of the United States. Community stability in this context entails developing industrial economic opportunities that will support the work force and constructing a social infrastructure of educational and health services, especially for children, in an attempt to break the cycle of poverty.

For at least a century and a half, there has been concern about stabilizing the flow of logs from forests so that regions do not have to endure logging booms and busts. The poverty that can result from deforestation, erosion, and flooding has been recognized since early in the twentieth century. Community stability in this context means guaranteeing a continuous long-term supply of raw material from the forest to the local mill.

From the mid-nineteenth century through the mid-twentieth, there has been concern that competition from the development of new timberland would force the value of timber products down and threaten the economic viability of long-established milling operations. As we have seen, timber supplies in the Great Lakes and Gulf regions threatened the industry in Maine and Pennsylvania, while the timber supply in the Pacific Northwest threatened the viability of the industry in the Great Lake and Gulf states. The harvest from federal lands threatened the value of private industrial timber holdings and the viability of lumber mills based on them. "Excess" competition among producers would lead to a "race to the bottom of the well" that in turn would result in a deforested landscape and future timber shortages. In the meantime, long-established mill towns would go bankrupt. Community stability in this context largely means maintaining existing stability through publicly assisted monopoly control of the level of timber harvests, which would prop up wood product prices.

As the Great Depression faded and was replaced by a building boom in the 1950s and 1960s, the idea of restricting output to protect the existing industry gave way to the idea of boosting production on federal lands to help Americans realize a part of the American dream, home ownership. Community stability came to mean anything that increased employment and income in the local area. Higher yields of timber were always better than lower. Community stability became a code word and justification for boosting the cut on public lands, even if the expanded harvest was financially feasible only because of public subsidies. Below-cost timber sales were justified as a type of rural "make work" policy. The timber industry was encouraged to build mills in areas that had never had a commercial timber industry, while communities were encouraged to become dependent on the timber industry. Since average income is usually lower in rural than in urban areas, and since the range of economic opportunity is usually more restricted in rural areas, the U.S. Forest Service had no difficulty explaining its plans for expanded harvests in social terms: more cut timber meant less rural poverty and more jobs.

To professional foresters the issues were more technical and less social: What should be the appropriate harvest pattern over time, given the existing inventory of old growth and the productive potential of the land for wood-fiber production? The forestry concept of sustained yield is not as close to the contemporary concept of sustainable economic development as it sounds. Discussions of sustained yield, even flow, nondeclining even flow, and planned "departures" from these tend to be obtuse and technical and are seldom directly related to the economic health of communities. Despite the debate over alternative harvest schedules, the degree to which community health is influenced by different schedules for logging has rarely been investigated.

Community stability obviously means a lot of different things to a lot of different people. It carries a lot of emotional and rhetorical weight, especially undefined, and dominates public discourse on forest policy while doing little to inform that discourse. For most of the last several decades, the U.S. Forest Service has interpreted community stability to mean boosting the flow of raw materials from public lands to private lumber mills.

The Shifting Timber Frontier

Concern about the impact of the industry on the economic well-being of timber-dependent communities dates at least as far back as the middle of the nineteenth century. While the nation looked to the rich timber frontier of the Gulf South, the Great Lakes states, and the Pacific Northwest, political leaders in earlier logging states, Pennsylvania and Maine, were calling for reforestation of their harvested lands and more conservative harvesting practices. Their concern was to ensure a continuing supply of logs for a market that had grown and on which both states' economies depended. Deforestation seemed to threaten the long-run viability of the industry and the prosperity of both states.[8] The concern was legitimate. In the mid-nineteenth century the American timber industry began leapfrogging from one temporary center of logging activity to another, into Michigan, Wisconsin, and Minnesota in the second half of the century, on to the south next, and by the mid-twentieth century, to the Pacific Northwest. Now, as the century draws to a close, the industry is shifting back to the South, leaving distressed lumber towns throughout the Pacific Northwest.[9]

With each shift, a timber center has gone into decline, disrupting communities and entire regions (figure 6-1). What the Great Lakes states experienced a century ago, the Pacific Northwest is experiencing

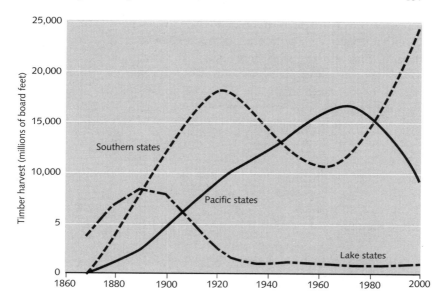

FIGURE 6-1.

Geographic instability of the logging industry. Since the mid-1800s regional timber harvests have expanded and contracted because harvest levels have not been sustainable. (*Data sources:* "Lumber Production in the United States, 1799–1946," USDA Miscellaneous Publication No. 669, October, 1948, table 4; 1950–1990 from Bureau of Census Lumber Production, Current Industry Report MA-27T; post-1990 lake and south from "The South's Fourth Forest," USDA Forest Resource Report No. 24, 1989.)

now: timber harvests in excess of what is sustainable cause downsizing of the regional industry and expansion elsewhere.[10] Seeing as this cycle has been repeated for almost a century and a half, it would seem prudent for any community to avoid becoming a timber town. Timber booms appear to have a life span somewhere between thirty and forty years.

This is not inevitable, just probable in light of history. A region might harvest its trees on a sustainable basis, but regions usually do not have the regulatory tools to arrange that. When, as is almost always the case, private ownership of timberland dominates, it is the private owners who decide the rate at which the trees are harvested. Sometimes the harvest is conservatively spread over long periods. Other times the "excess" inventory of trees on the stump is "liquidated" in little more than a decade. This is partly what happened in the Pacific Northwest in the 1980s. As a result of the financial pressure created by junk bond–financed hostile takeovers, some industrial timberland owners accelerated their harvest. This boosted their cash flow either to help fend off takeover threats or to make payments on the high-interest junk bonds that financed a takeover. In any case, harvests moved to nonsustainable levels and there was nothing the public could do about it.

In theory, public lands could be managed to offset this pattern, but political pressure operates in an altogether different way. Higher levels of harvest mean more jobs now, and politicians rarely plan further ahead than the next election. The pressure on public land managers is to keep the level of harvest up and increase it if possible. That type of commodity-oriented public-land management is seen as improving community well-being, even when it will almost assuredly result in community disruption and decline. Because of short-lived economic and political pressure, timber harvests that could be sustainable rarely are. Instead, the industry continues to leapfrog from one stooped, dependent community to another, promising prosperity with each leap but rarely delivering it.

Timber Dependence and Community Well-Being

Timber harvesting and processing are usually touted as one of the few high-paying and reliable sources of local employment and income. The argument is straightforward: the timber industry will significantly increase income-earning potential and employment opportunity in otherwise backwoods areas. The tax base from the mill and logging equipment will fund public infrastructure and services. Education, roads, parks, and law enforcement will improve, and with them the quality of life. Is this picture accurate, or just a deceptive lure?

Income Stability

Solid-wood products (lumber and plywood mills) is one of the most volatile manufacturing industries in the American economy.[11] Because a significant part of its output flows directly into the housing industry,

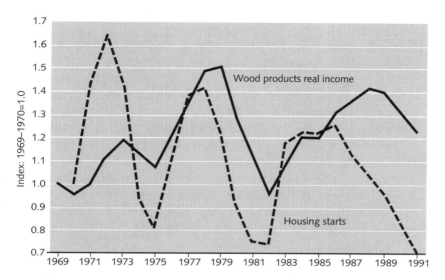

FIGURE 6-2. Timber income and housing starts. Earnings in wood products fluctuate widely as housing starts fluctuate. (*Data sources:* Housing starts from *Statistical Abstract,* various years; wood products real income from BEA REIS deflated by CPI.)

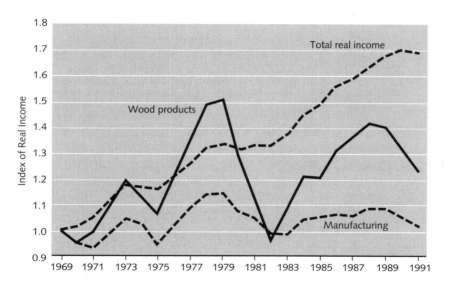

FIGURE 6-3. Income stability in wood products, manufacturing, and the total economy. Real earnings in the wood products industry go through deep cyclical swings. (*Data sources:* BEA REIS deflated by CPI.)

the demand for wood products fluctuates with the volume of home building (figure 6-2). Housing starts in the United States fluctuate widely, doubling in a matter of a year or so, then falling to half of their former level, depending on demographic changes, interest rates, and confidence in the national economy. The swings in income earned in wood products are two to four times as large as those in manufacturing as a whole (figure 6-3). Real total income rarely declines by more than a few percentage points even in the worst recession, but real income from wood products can decline by as much as a third. During the 1970s, income from wood products boomed, expanding by 50 percent after adjusting for inflation, and then crashed, returning to the levels of ten years earlier. In the mid-1980s the industry recovered only to lose much of its gain in the late 1980s and early 1990s. When fluctuations in the national economy are compared to the ups and downs of the wood products roller coaster, the national economy looks like a smooth ride up.

Analysis of counties in timber states where wood products provide a large percentage of total income illustrates the destabilizing impact of this industry. For instance, in western Montana where the timber industry is considered dominant, the larger the industry is as a source of county income, the larger the declines in total county income over the last two decades. The relative importance of the wood products industry in any given county explains about 90 percent of the variation in income decline. A similar pattern of income decline tied to the predominance of the wood products industry can be found in the timber counties of Oregon. The more important the industry is to the local economy, the larger the periodic downward pressure on that economy is likely to be.[12]

Job Stability

One important aspect of economic well-being is the reliability of employment. Variability of income does not always reflect what has happened to employment in a particular industry. But this is not the case with wood products. Incomes fluctuate widely along with employment. For example, while overall employment has grown steadily over the last two decades in the Pacific Northwest, employment in wood products has fluctuated considerably (figure 6-4). From 1979 to 1982, 55,000 jobs—a third of all wood products employment—were lost. After some rebound and fluctuation during the 1980s, employment in the early

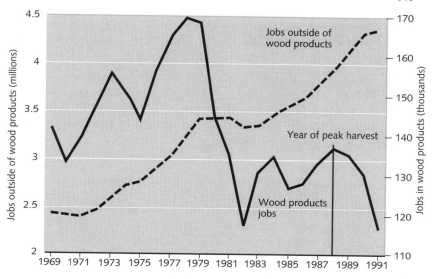

FIGURE 6-4. Pacific Northwest wage and salary employment in wood products and all other sectors. Employment in wood products declined by 35,000, even though timber harvests reached peak levels in 1988 in the Pacific Northwest. Employment outside of wood products expanded by 500,000 during the same period. (*Data sources:* BEA REIS, Wage and Salary Employment.)

1990s was as low as it had been during the timber "depression" of the early 1980s. It should be kept in mind that although timber supply constraints had begun to limit production in the early 1990s, the catastrophic drop in the early 1980s was purely demand related. The market for wood products deteriorated, as it does cyclically, throwing tens of thousands of people out of work. Compounding the lost employment was a reorganization of the industry that focused on producing a smaller number of standardized products with much more highly automated mills. Logging also became more capital intensive as huge machines replaced workers.

National statistics on workers who have lost their jobs because of temporary or permanent, partial or total shutdown of plants show that during the 1980s over 100,000 wood-products-industry workers were displaced. Workers in wood products were over three times more likely to be displaced than workers elsewhere in the economy.[13]

An alternative way of measuring the job security in the wood products industry is to study the way unemployment rates in timber states vary county by county relative to the importance of the wood products industry. For example, in the Pacific Northwest, counties where the timber industry was responsible for a larger percentage of total jobs had statistically significant higher unemployment rates.[14] A simple correlation of this sort, of course, does not necessarily imply cause, but the results of a large number of alternative measures of economic instability do indeed suggest that the presence of a dominant wood products industry causes employment instability.

Higher Income

In most areas the wages paid to wood products workers are relatively high, especially compared with those received outside of the manufacturing sector in nonmetropolitan areas. High wages are one of the primary benefits touted in justifying health, safety, and environmental problems associated with the industry. The wages are said to have a spillover effect, boosting average wages in the rest of the local economy.

When one looks for signs of the spillover effect, something quite different appears. For instance, in Montana and Oregon, the more important the wood products industry is as a source of income in a county, the lower the average income is—in other words, the poorer the local economy is, if one accepts average income as a measure of economic well-being. In Idaho, although there is not a significant negative correlation between the industry and income, there is also no evidence of any positive relationship. Again, significant negative correlations between the relative importance of the wood products industry and average income do not necessarily establish a causal relationship. But they do cast doubt on the assumption that the timber industry is associated with relatively high income.

These results are not attributable to wood product firms being primarily located in rural areas, where average income tends to be lower. In Montana the industry is concentrated in the larger urban areas, yet lower average income is still associated with areas where the industry is more dominant. And in the Pacific Northwest the industry is not primarily located in counties with smaller populations. Some other explanation has to be offered for lower average income in timber-dependent communities.

These empirical results are consistent with most other studies of the relationship between economic reliance on the timber industry and local well-being. The vast majority of available studies show that despite the "high wage" character of wood products employment, community specialization in wood products either has no positive impact or a negative impact on a broad variety of indicators of local well-being.[15]

Paul Bunyan's Dying Breed: Wood Products, Economic Stability, and the Future

Employment in wood products, besides being vulnerable to short-run housing cycles and national economic fluctuations, is in long-run decline. Wood products manufacturing is a mature industry serving a specific market for building products, and the housing market, at best, is likely to grow only as fast as the overall economy grows. As competition from nonwood building materials rises, the market may grow more slowly than the rest of the economy. In addition, technological change will probably continue to boost productivity as capital and energy are substituted for labor. This has already been taking place on an impressive scale. Automated stud mills producing a few uniform products have replaced sawmills that produced a variety of products. Total output has risen while employment and labor income have declined. Logging is shifting from workers with saws and axes in hand to large machines that hold, cut, delimb, and load in one step. A single machine can replace a half dozen workers.

What is the impact of automation on employment? Consider wood products output in the Pacific Northwest. It was higher in 1988 than in 1978, yet the jobs associated with that output had fallen by 35,000, or 20 percent (see figure 6-4). During the 1980s lumber mill production nationwide rose by almost 2 percent per year, while lumber-mill employment declined by 2 percent per year.[16] Even increased harvest and production do not necessarily mean reliable employment. The wood products industry is likely to slow down local economies in the future, not provide them with a boost.

Analysis of the historical impact of the lumber industry on rural towns confirms this expectation. One study of forest-dependent communities in the Northeast found that forestry communities had unstable populations and economies as well as high rates of divorce, poverty, and ill health.[17] Communities tied to wood products fared worse than agricultural, mining, or tourist communities in terms of both economic and social health.

The Timber Industry As a Way of Life

Economic dialogue can be arcane, incomprehensible, or tedious. Partisans have to breathe political life into discussions of public economic policy if they want to get attention to their issues. Faced with a sluggish local economy, a chamber of commerce, rather than saying that it would like to boost the value of its own businesses, may point instead to young people being forced to move away in search of employment. That tugs strongly at the heart. The fact that young people tend to move away from their parents regardless of the rate of local economic growth is irrelevant.[18] The emotional punch, not the truth, is the point.

Similar emotive rhetoric has been heard regarding job losses associated with protecting the last ancient forests in the Pacific Northwest against a final and irreparable act of overcutting. During the 1980s the economies of this region expanded briskly, adding about 150,000 jobs *per year.* This figure should be compared with *total* wage and salary jobs in regional wood products—about 120,000. Thus economic development has been systematically replacing jobs lost in primary production with other jobs. This is the pattern accompanying economic development across the nation over the last two centuries as extractive jobs have given way to jobs in manufacturing and services.

One way to emotionally charge this normal and positive transformation of the economy is to raise the issue of disrupted ways of life. Several generations of families work in the timber industry, harvesting and processing trees. A community is established, complete with its own values and culture. Now with logging jobs threatened—even if they can be replaced by other jobs—a way of life, a part of American culture and history, will die. Who could be in favor of that? Loggers and mill workers have an aura that teachers, accountants, and computer consultants lack. There are no Paul Bunyan legends about service workers.

But is logging and lumber mill work a way of life, like farming and ranching, handed down from one generation to another? Or is it just another job that people move into and out of with considerable frequency? Data suggests the latter. In 1991 the median tenure of employment in lumber and wood products firms was 4.2 years, in sawmills 4.6 years, and in miscellaneous wood products 2.7 years.[19] That is, over half of the employees in any given wood products firm worked there for only 3 to 5 years. And the median tenure as a worker in the industry was only 5.3 years. This is hardly what one would expect in an industry around which so much romanticized folklore has gathered. In fact, these job tenure statistics are lower than for the economy as a whole, where median job tenure is 4.5 years and median tenure in the industry is 6.5 years.[20] People working in wood products hold those jobs for a shorter time than workers elsewhere in the economy. Notably, service workers, though they have about the same tenure with their current employers as wood products workers, about 4 years, have a much longer tenure in the industry, almost 7 years.[21] The much-maligned service jobs that are increasing while wood products jobs disappear provide longer job tenure. If we are interested in promoting ways of life built around stable job tenure, maybe we should abandon the myth of the wood products industry.

What is actually being threatened by the downsizing of the wood products industry is not a time-honored profession passed down from generation to generation but rather high-paying jobs for relatively uneducated white males. High-school dropouts used to instantaneously enter the middle class by taking a wood products job. That particular route to a middle-class lifestyle is what is being closed. Following the alternative routes takes considerably more training and time. At any rate, white males are a politically powerful group and a potent symbol of middle America. It is not surprising that their way of life has attracted so much attention.

Another concern about job loss in wood products that has considerable emotional punch is forced outmigration. When longtime residents are forced to move away in search of work, the social fabric of a community is indeed damaged. But as mentioned above, the relationship between local economic conditions and outmigration is much more complicated than emotive rhetoric might suggest. Consider in- and outmigration over the last two decades in Oregon, the nation's most timber-dependent state. Outmigration actually rose during the boom years in the later 1970s (when inmigration was also rising). Then when the Oregon economy slipped into a depression in the early 1980s, the rate of outmigration actually declined. The same pattern appears on a smaller scale in Oregon's timber-dependent southwest counties. When the economy collapsed, outmigration was cut almost in half.[22] This pattern is not unique to Oregon or to timber regions, as analysis of Great Plains counties from 1970 to 1990 shows.[23] Hard economic times, then, are not what primarily drive outmigration. Good economic times can cause far more disruption in a community by boosting both inmigration and outmigration. This is not as surprising as it may seem. Outmigration is closely linked to the demographic and migration characteristics of the local population. For example, young, well-educated workers who have had personal experience with migration tend to move away regardless of local economic conditions. And when inmigration is high, outmigration is also likely to be high because of the presence of more and more relatively mobile workers.[24] In any case, "revving up" a local economy does not stabilize the community by reducing outmigration and population turnover.

If wood products' jump-starting of local economies is of dubious value, there are other aspects of the industry that give more reason to pause. Forestry is one of the most dangerous occupations around.[25] No other has a higher injury and mortality rate. The rate of disabling injuries in the lumber and wood products industry is 40 percent higher than in the construction industry and three times higher than in mining and manufacturing. In logging itself, in 1991, the average number of work days lost per worker due to injury was twice that in mining and construction and three times that in manufacturing.[26]

The timber industry's record of investment in its workers is equally distressing. For instance, in 1990, 99 percent of the timber workers laid off in Oregon had no more than a high-school education, and 25 percent had not even completed high school.[27] Local lumber mills have induced many young people to drop out of school, a decision that in an unstable industry can have serious negative consequences for them and for the community in the long run.

The timber industry does not represent a way of life that needs public subsidization. Rather, it is a mature primary industry that is in relative decline along with mining and agriculture as the U.S. economy continues to develop, shifting resources, including labor, from products that are less in demand to those that are more in demand. There is nothing special or central about the timber industry that should cause the government to give it privileged access to public resources.

Community Stability Revisited

Although the timber industry favorably compares its wages to the income earned in most other nonmetropolitan economic activities, timber towns tend not to be prosperous. Both households and businesses are hesitant to invest in communities that are heavily dependent on lumber. But it is investment in new housing and business that renews a community physically. Those investments are the tax base that finances public infrastructure—schools, parks, streets, libraries, public health services, and other facilities and institutions. A negative cycle can easily develop in which economic uncertainty associated with the timber industry leads to reduced private investment and flagging local economic health, which in turn leads to a deteriorating infrastructure that keeps people and business from migrating in. The local community slides slowly downward over the years despite high-paying jobs in the local mill.

In the case of the timber industry, economic development and vitality are not to be achieved with more of the same—more harvest of more trees. Diversification is the only antidote to the instability and tendency toward decline associated with the industry. In theory, the Forest Service has recognized this since at least 1982, when it officially adopted its Guidelines for Economic and Social Analysis.[28] Community stability, the guidelines say, is "the capacity of a community to absorb and cope with change without major hardship to institutions or groups within the community." The emphasis is on adaptation rather than preserving a timber-dependent status quo. But Forest Service officials have shown almost complete disregard for this concept of community stability. Instead, they have concentrated on expanding timber harvests as the way to enhance community stability.

A graphic example is what happened in western Colorado in the 1980s. There the Forest Service sought to set timber harvests at levels far in excess of what local mills could handle.[29] This was seen as a way of supporting and stabilizing relatively poor rural communities. Many local people and state government officials opposed the effort to expand an environmentally destructive industry on the grounds that it would destabilize the economy and threaten a rapidly growing economic base built around natural amenities and recreation. But the Forest Service was adamant about what was good for the local communities, rejecting all appeals and defending the harvest goals against court challenges. Finally the secretary of agriculture, who oversees the Forest Service, overruled the agency, agreeing with critics that the expanded harvests would be destabilizing.

By the early 1990s, the Forest Service was de-emphasizing community stability as a justification for intense resource extraction. Declining employment and income potential in timber-dependent communities as well as the diversification of local economies made the notion of stabilizing communities by "getting out the cut" suspect. In addition, the Forest Service, with some help from the courts and citizen appeals, began to recognize that forests were seriously threatened by heavy timber harvesting. Given the evident shift in what the public expected from the Forest Service, the agency began to re-evaluate its management priorities.

It is still too early to say what the result of this re-evaluation will produce. There are signs, however, of sophisticated political jujitsu. The Forest Service appears to be in the process of transforming its environmental opponents' concept of ecosystem protection into "ecosystem management," a new justification for intensive management of almost all public forestland. The general idea is that the mission should be to keep forest ecosystems healthy by widespread salvage logging to remove decaying and diseased timber.

This would represent a move back to the nineteenth-century forester's vision, which viewed natural forests as unproductive, chaotic, and dangerous. Ecosystem management appears to revive this attitude in late-twentieth-century jargon. Our forests have become disease-ridden, overmature, choked by understory vegetation, veritable tinderboxes that at any moment can explode into fires beyond our control. The Forest Service knows how to save us from danger; we need only give it the budget and authorization to proceed with widespread timber harvests that will mimic natural processes, which, coincidentally, will also increase the flow of logs to commercial lumber mills. The more things change, the more they appear to stay the same.

Healing the Scars: Forest Management and Local Well-Being

Folk economics suggests that the dominant economic connection between a forested landscape and a local economy is the commercial timber harvest. The forest is seen for its trees and their commercial value as harvested. Expanded harvests will enhance the economy, restricted harvests will shackle it. Since public policy has little power to influence the rate of logging on private land, concern about the appropriate rate focuses on public land, particularly federal. The widely shared extractive view is that timber harvests from federal land, for better or worse, drive the economies of timber-dependent adjacent communities, and that restricting harvests to protect the environment depress them. This is far too limited a view of the role that forestland plays in influencing local economies. In evaluating that role, it is important to look at the total economy, not just the extractive sector (figure 7-1).

Federal Forestland and Local Economies: The Timber Connection

Most of the public controversy over forestland management centers on federal land controlled by the U.S. Forest Service and Bureau of Land Management, two agencies that control tens of millions of acres of forestland. Federal land managers face pressure on one side from those who want to see as much commercial development of forest resources as possible, and on the other from those who want to protect forests for

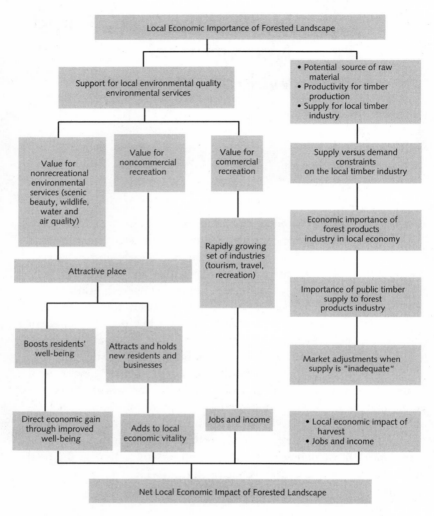

FIGURE 7-1. Factors that determine the local economic value of a forested landscape. The economic links between the forested landscape and the local economy are many. A change in public land use cannot be analyzed simply in terms of commercial harvesting.

their noncommercial value. To protect large areas of federal land from commercial extractive activities, proposals are regularly made for federal wilderness classification; creation of national parks, monuments, and recreation areas; protection of wildlife habitat, especially for endangered species; wild and scenic river designation; and ecosystem protection. During the mid-1990s congressional proposals were made to ban all logging in federal roadless areas and all logging in national forests.[1] Such proposals are attacked by timber industry supporters as threatening the economic health of adjacent communities by "locking up" the raw materials needed to keep the local economy afloat.

The Mirage of Timber Productivity

If federal forestland were to be managed for something besides logging, the "opportunity cost" of pursuing the other objective would be equivalent to the land's commercial timber value. However, not all forestland has equal commercial timber value. In fact, many forested areas have no such value because the costs of gaining access to and harvesting the timber are too high. Obviously, if these costs exceed the value of the timber, there is no economic loss incurred by choosing not to harvest. Thus in evaluating the opportunity cost of putting certain lands off-limits to harvest, one has to analyze their timber potential. The total number of acres does not tell us anything about the opportunity cost of managing land for nontimber values.

This consideration is especially important for federal land because the more productive timberland passed into private ownership years ago. The national forest reserve system created at the end of the nineteenth century included only land that no one had yet claimed for private use, primarily the mountainous lands of the West. Early in this century, the federal government bought up much of the land that had been logged and abandoned in the East, and today this land makes up most of the eastern national forests' 24 million acres.[2] Generally, timber productivity on federal forestland is significantly lower than on nonfederal forestland.

The Forest Service's own classification of forestland as part of a commercial timber base is not tied directly to an economic measure of commercial viability. To be included in the Forest Service's commercial timber base, the commercial value of the trees does not have to exceed the cost of managing the land for its timber value. If potential timber productivity exceeds certain minimal levels, the land is assumed suitable for timber management regardless of those costs. Land that no private owner would judge as having commercial value is added to the Forest Service's timber base, and as a result its commercial value is overestimated.

Still, a substantial amount of national forestland whose management is currently being debated has not been classified as having commercial timber potential. This is true, for instance, for over 80 percent of the remaining roadless National Forest land in the Northern Rockies (table 7-1).[3] The decision to manage this land for its nontimber value costs the nation nothing. In fact, it saves the nation the losses the Forest Service would incur in trying to manage the land for timber. In the past, land set aside as wilderness or national parks tended to be steep, dramatic, and inaccessible and with little commercial timber value. In that setting, the current debate about "locking up" the timber resource involves gross exaggeration.

The timber-producing capability of land can be determined in purely biological terms. A site can be studied for such factors as temperature, moisture, sunlight, nutrients, and competition from various plants. Then calculations can be made about what species to plant, how frequently they should be thinned, what pesticides and herbicides should be applied to control biological pests, and so on. This will produce an estimate of the wood fiber the site is capable of producing—but it won't be a measure of the site's timber productivity in economic terms. Potential biological productivity is not economic productivity.

To realize economic productivity, expensive access roads have to be built and maintained for 50 to 150 years. The area has to be planted, thinned, and nurtured for decades before the harvest. The value of that distant harvest is what has to justify all the high up-front costs. As might be expected, those future timber harvest values may not always justify the costs of realizing it.

The Forest Service tends to base its estimates of a site's timber value on biological potential, not economic productivity, requesting congressional budget support for intensive timber management regardless of the economic losses. Sites with almost no commercial timber, even relatively bare sites, are considered highly productive forestlands. In the Forest Service's evaluation of resource tradeoffs associated with wilderness protection in roadless areas, such exaggerated site productivity has been used to boost the apparent timber opportunity cost of wilderness preservation, thereby protecting the agency's ability to harvest the trees.[4]

It is not only the dollar cost of intensive management that constrains the timber productivity of federal land. National forests are not private tree farms that can be operated without regard for the environmental impacts. Legislation guiding the management of national forestland makes clear that timber is just one of many forest values that are to be

TABLE 7-1.

The Percentage of Northern Rockies Ecosystem Protection
Act–Protected Land That Is Suitable for Timber Harvesting

National Forest

Montana

Lolo	30	
Bitterroot	22	
Gallatin	16	
Helena	15	
Beaverhead	12	Cumulative 18%
Custer	23	
Deerlodge	21	
Kootenai	22	
Lewis and Clark	13	
Flathead	20	

Idaho

Clearwater	45	
Idaho Panhandle	50	
Nez Perce	36	
Boise	17	
Caribou	3	Cumulative 21%
Challis	3	
Payette	10	
Salmon	10	
Sawtooth	1	
Targhee	51	

Eastern Washington and Eastern Oregon

Colville	47	
Malheur	36	Cumulative 26%
Umatilla	32	
Wallowa-Whitman	21	

Northwestern Wyoming

Big Horn	28	
Bridger-Teton	10	Cumulative 11%
Shoshone	8	

Overall percentage is 20%.

Source: Power 1993.

protected and developed, and timber is not identified as the dominant value.[5] In addition, the Forest Service must see that its management decisions are consistent with state and federal clean-water laws, the Endangered Species Act, and other environmental regulations. The point is that economic, legal, and environmental constraints limit theoretically calculated timber productivity. The relevant measure in evaluating nontimber management of landscape is realizable economic productivity.

For any particular parcel of the federal forestland, there are likely to be overlapping constraints that set the maximum realizable timber harvest well below the theoretical biological maximum. Adding another constraint or removing one or more may have little impact on the realizable harvest. Where that is the case, one constraint may have little or no timber opportunity cost because other constraints have already limited timber harvests. If, for instance, watershed or endangered species considerations block timber harvest in a particular drainage, classifying that land as wilderness does not cause any further reduction in harvest. Extra protection, in other words, won't further limit logging. Moreover, maximum biological potential is probably irrelevant when discussing tradeoffs between timber and other realizable forest values.

Distinguishing Supply from Demand

The possible physical output of both U.S. timberland and U.S. mills exceeds the quantity that customers are willing to purchase. At any given time, not all sources of timber are under production and not all the productive capacity of mills is being utilized. It is demand and the costs associated with available alternative sources that determine the actual level of local extractive activity. This is another way of saying that demand matters as much as supply, and that supply is affected by costs, not merely quantity available.

Except when a region has been overharvested, the quantity of available trees rarely limits logging and milling operations. Even when the quantity of available trees forces a reduction in timber operations in one area, the industry overall is unlikely to be affected because operations will be expanding elsewhere. The periodic and painful disruptions in operations that affect almost all timber regions are not tied to constrained access to the forest's raw material but rather to lack of demand for the products that forests and mills are physically capable of producing.

As mentioned earlier, demand for lumber products is determined by such factors as demand for new housing, the level of national economic activity, the value of the American dollar, and interest rates. When Americans are not buying new homes, when the relative value of the American dollar encourages the importation of Canadian wood products and discourages the export of American products, when high interest rates discourage construction of all sorts, or when the national economy is in a recession, the demand for timber products falls. In the first half of the twentieth century, this was a recognized fact. During that period efforts to protect the economic health of timber-dependent communities focused on the problem of excess supply and inadequate demand. Clearly, shortage of wood fiber was not what was destabilizing American forest communities.

Similarly, periodic declines in lumber production from the late 1960s through the early 1990s had nothing to do with limits on supply (see figure 6-3). The cause of idle mills was lack of demand for their products. Confusing supply constraints with limited demand is to stand economic reality on its head. But this is what has often been done in discussions of the relationship between forested landscapes and local economic health. Expanding the supply of trees available for harvest when it is depressed demand and low lumber prices that limit production solves nothing. In fact, it could lead to overharvesting, additional environmental disruption, and additional downward pressure on lumber prices.

The Relative Importance of Federal Timber Supplies

Some discussions of federal forest management give the impression that federal timber supplies are the dominant source of wood fiber for U.S. mills. The implication is that it is federal forest managers who determine whether there is enough wood fiber available to assure adequate housing for Americans and jobs for forest industry workers. This is an exaggeration. The Forest Service is rarely the sole or even most important local source of wood fiber. The Forest Service controls about 18 percent of the nation's commercial timberland but only 14 percent of annual fiber growth. That is, only one seventh of America's timberland productivity is controlled by the Forest Service. In the eastern half of the nation, the federal government controls an even smaller part of the total wood fiber supply, about 8 percent. Even in the West, where the national forest system is concentrated, federal land represents a minority, about 40 percent, of total timberland, and as mentioned, it tends to be less productive than private timberland.[6]

It would stand to reason, then, that manipulation of federal supplies cannot control the timber industry or the future of America's timber-dependent communities. In some areas the Forest Service will have more influence than in others, but it is misleading to assume that federal land management decisions are the dominant determinants of economic activity in timber communities. The Forest Service is just one player, and a minority player at that. This fact is obscured in public debate over federal forest use. Private timberland use is not subject to similar public comment, though it can have a much greater effect on the local community. Private land-use decisions are accepted, fatalistically by many, as an aspect of a private enterprise society. That is not true of less consequential federal land-use decisions. They get vigorously and emotionally debated, which lends them an air of exaggerated importance.

In evaluating the impact of a federal forest management decision, the relative importance of the federal timber supply has to be taken into account. Public policy should never be built on the assumption that 15 percent of supply determines the industry's overall fortunes.

Federal and Private Timber Supplies:
A Case of Dynamic Interaction

Because timber sales from federal land flow into a national and international market, their impact on the overall timber industry cannot be determined in isolation. A competitive market generates interaction between federal and private timber supplies. When one source of supply is reduced, prices tend to rise, stimulating production from other sources of supply while reducing exports and increasing imports. As timber prices rise, so does the profitability of harvesting trees. Logs that were previously exported unprocessed to more lucrative foreign markets may now find the domestic market more profitable. Canadian sources of supply will find the American market more attractive. As a result, the net impact of reduced supply is significantly smaller than the initial reduction in federal harvest.

The point is that a reduction in supply is not simply met passively by the industry. A drop in supply triggers a complex set of adjustments that tend to reduce its potentially disruptive impact. The relative importance of such interaction between sources of supply (as well as of demand) can be seen in the net impact of the reduction in federal timber supply associated with protecting spotted owl habitat in the Pacific Northwest. In 1991, the Bureau of Land Management sought an exemption from the Endangered Species Act to log spotted owl habitat in southern Oregon. About 220 million board feet were at stake. Forest Service modeling of the impact of not pursuing that source indicated that the regional timber supply would be reduced by only a quarter of this, 55 million board feet. The expected offset came from reduced log exports from the region and increased harvesting on private land. As federal supplies shrank, the price being bid for logs would rise significantly, diverting logs from export and attracting private landowners into considering timber harvests on their land.[7] An earlier analysis of the potential impact of legally prohibiting clear-cutting on national forestland projected a reduction in national forest harvests of as much as 50 percent. Since national forests were expected to contribute 20 percent of the nation's harvest, that contribution would have fallen to 10 percent. But half of that impact was expected to be offset by increased imports, decreased exports, and increased private harvests.[8] As a result, the impact of cutting Forest Service harvests in half was to reduce national supplies by 5 percent, not catastrophic.

In evaluating the economic impact of reducing the federal timber supply, full market adjustments involving other sources of supply (and demand) have to be taken into account.[9]

Local Supply and Local Mills

Another factor in the matrix of market relationships in which local Forest Service supplies and local mills are embedded is the growing geographic market. Federal timber supplies are sold in a competitive bidding process in which any firm anywhere can participate. For that reason, timber sold from national forests adjacent to timber-dependent communities need not go to local mills. It may be purchased by a mill hundreds of miles away or, through displacement, exported unprocessed. Highway and rail transportation are cheap enough to allow the hauling of logs a considerable distance. Local mills may be purchasing logs from national forests far from the local community, even from a different state. Meanwhile, the local federal supply may be "cross-hauled" to communities outside of the national forest's area of economic influence.

This market reality makes it difficult to relate timber sales from a particular national forest to the economic well-being of a particular community. The demand for logs in the Pacific Rim nations led to substantial log exports from Pacific Northwest ports during the second half of the 1980s. Federal legislation forbade the direct sale of unprocessed timber from federal lands in the export market. But the exporting of logs from private land led to intensified bidding for federal timber supplies to replace the exported logs. Because of a shortage of logs west of the Cascades, mills bid for logs east of the Cascades. That forced mills east of the Cascades that were losing their traditional supplies to mills west of the Cascades to look further inland for logs. Log displacement had the effect of indirectly drawing logs from western Montana's national forests 600 miles away to serve the Pacific export demand.

The Timber Industry and the Local Economy

The impact of federal timber supplies on the local economy is ultimately determined by the relative importance of that industry in the local economy. A raw material supply that may be crucial to the survival of a particular industry may be of only minor importance to the local economy if that industry is a meager source of local jobs and income. As mentioned earlier, the relative importance of the timber industry in an area dominated by a forested landscape is often significantly exaggerated. The mere presence of trees does not make the industry processing them the linchpin of local economic vitality. And history is not necessarily a good guide to current economic reality. Despite its nostalgic lure, the view through the rearview mirror should be replaced by a close look at exactly where a community's jobs and income originate.

It is highly unusual for the timber industry to be responsible for more than 10 percent of total personal income in a county. In western Montana, an area usually assumed to be economically dominated by the timber industry, only two counties rely on wood products for significantly more than 10 percent of their income. In Oregon, one of the nation's two most timber-dependent states, only four of the state's thirty-six counties rely on wood products for significantly more than 10 percent of total income.

The dependence of most communities on the timber industry is much more modest than folk economics would suggest, 5 percent or less of total income even in timber regions. Thus even fairly significant changes in federal timber management policy will have little effect on the local economy. Suppose a local national forest is considering a 25 percent reduction of its timber program. Assume that the Forest Service has traditionally provided 40 percent of the local raw material. Also assume that 25 percent of the federal reduction will be made up by expansions in private, state, and tribal harvest. In that situation, a 25 percent reduction in federal harvest would directly reduce local income by less than a half of 1 percent (25% × 75% × 40% × 5% = 0.375%). Even if one believed in rigid income multipliers of 2 to 3, the impact would be a loss of 1 percent or less of local income. That would hardly be devastating to the local community.

Pushing the Economy with a Wet Noodle

The relationship between the number of acres of local Forest Service land that is managed primarily for commercial timber production and the jobs and income earned in the local wood products industry is tenuous to say the least. Federal forestland does not necessarily represent a significant source of commercially viable timber. Federal land is not the only or even the dominant source of wood fiber in most areas. Besides, timber supply is not what usually determines the level of employment and income in the wood products industry. In addition, local logs cannot be directed to local mills. Finally, the timber industry is rarely the only or most important economic show in town, even in so-called timber-dependent communities. Given the tenuous relationship between federal land-use decisions and income earned in the wood products industry, attempts to influence local economic well-being by manipulating the acreage allocated to timber management are like trying to push something with a wet noodle. The tools in the hands of federal land managers are too weak compared with the market forces that buffet the wood products industry. The limited capacity of federal forest management policy to move local economies in particular, planned directions needs to be recognized. The illusion of power and influence is rarely a sound basis for good public policy.

Seeing beyond the Trees: The Economic Value of Natural Forests

By statute, national forestlands are not simply warehouses of commercial timber waiting to be harvested. The multiple uses or values associated with forestland have long been officially recognized. The watershed, wildlife, scenic, recreation, biological, historical, cultural, and spiritual values associated with America's forests have been acknowledged for most of this century. But there is a big difference between these and timber values: timber produces considerable cash flow and has organized industry backing, while the others do not. That has led many to accept timber as the number-one priority in the management of federal forestland. However, it is a serious economic error to assume that only those economic values are significant that are given commercial expression.

America's forest landscapes are the environment in which growing numbers of people are choosing to live. They have economic value simply for the environmental goods and services that flow from them.

Residential and Business Location

Attractive natural landscapes influence the location of economic activity. Denuded, biologically sterile landscapes are economic disaster areas. They lose residents and businesses. Forested landscapes can create economic vitality simply by attracting and holding residents. From Vermont to the Carolinas across the South to the desert Southwest and from the Rocky Mountains to the Pacific Northwest there are hundreds of communities whose natural and social amenities have drawn people and businesses.

Western Montana—where it is often incorrectly asserted that over half of all jobs and income derive directly or indirectly from the timber industry—offers two examples of economic vitality despite dramatic declines in timber harvesting of National Forest land (figures 7-2 and 7-3). Montana's harvest from National Forest land peaked in the late 1960s, after which increasing environmental constraints forced harvests dramatically down. Nonetheless, western Montana has seen ongoing growth in jobs, income, and population. In the Bitterroot Valley south of Missoula, Montana, federal timber harvests have fallen to a small fraction of what they once were, and over the last two decades mill after mill has closed. Despite the collapse of what is often asserted to be its economic base, the Bitterroot Valley has seen sustained economic expansion largely tied to inmigration. A similar phenomenon can be observed in the Flathead Valley in northwest Montana. Here too federal harvests have declined dramatically, but the area has led the entire state in economic growth. Some of the decline in federal harvesting has been offset by expanded harvests on private land. The point is that timber from federal land is not what has been driving the local

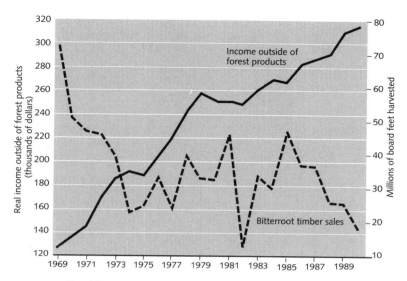

FIGURE 7-2. Real income and timber harvesting in Bitterroot Valley, Ravalli County, Montana. Drastic declines in harvests from federal land in the Bitterroot Valley coincided with rapid expansion in the nontimber economy. (*Data sources:* Income from BEA REIS deflated by CPI; timber harvest from Region 1, U.S. Forest Service, Missoula, Montana.)

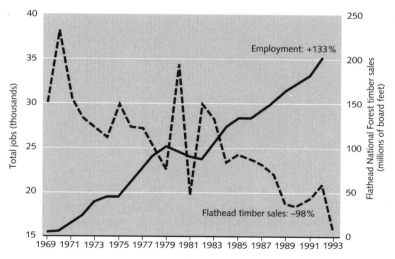

FIGURE 7-3. National forest timber sales versus jobs: Flathead National Forest and Flathead County, Montana. Major declines in harvests from federal land in the Flathead Valley coincided with rapid growth in total employment. (*Data sources:* Employment from REIS; timber harvest from Region 1, U.S. Forest Service, Missoula, Montana.)

economy. Almost no one disputes the role of spectacular natural amenities—among them, Flathead Lake, Glacier National Park, the Bob Marshall Wilderness, and the Flathead River—in the economic health of the area.

Recreation

One important noncommercial amenity of a natural landscape is outdoor recreation such as fishing, birding, hiking, rafting, and hunting. Over the last several decades economists have made an effort to quantify the economic importance of recreation, as has the Forest Service. It is important to realize that the primary economic connection between many federal forests and adjacent communities is through recreation, not logging. In eight of Montana's ten national forests, for instance, wildlife and recreation provide three times as much employment as timber harvesting.[10] In Wyoming's northwestern national forestland, recreation provides nine jobs for every one associated with the timber harvest.[11] Timber often isn't king and recreation is usually anything but trivial.

Commercial Recreation and Tourism

In addition to their value to residents, recreational amenities attract tourists. Although tourism is not the dominant force in most local economies—and many people wouldn't want it to be because of the potentially disruptive impact—it is one of the fastest growing industries worldwide. During the last decade it was the only natural resource–based industry that did not suffer a serious decline. Dispersed recreation—not Disneyland extravaganzas but activities of the sort provided largely to urban residents by backcountry outfitters, fishing guides, whitewater guides, and ranches—can also redistribute income from urban to rural areas, boosting their economies.[12]

Choosers Aren't Beggars: Preservation and the Local Economy

During the 1980s many forest-dependent communities lost their lumber mills and were forced to make adjustments to the new economic reality. As painful as the losses were, these towns did not fade into the ghost towns that were predicted before the mills shut down. Their economic vitality and that of many other forest-dependent communities facing a similar change hold important lessons for local communities.

Dubois, Wyoming

Until 1987 Dubois, Wyoming, a town of about 1,000, hosted one of the largest stud mills in the nation. That mill provided a third of both the jobs and the tax base in Dubois. It consumed an enormous number of trees. Supplying them from the Shoshone and Bridger-Teton National Forests grew more and more controversial as roads were built through wildlife habitat and recreation land. Controversy over the appropriateness of sacrificing the forest to keep the mill alive caused tension between Dubois and the neighboring communities of Pinedale and Jackson, whose economies were more clearly recreation oriented, and it split the population of the county, Fremont. Some argued that the survival of Dubois and of the regional economy was at stake. Others insisted that the mill's voracious appetite could never be satisfied, and that seeking to satisfy it in the short run would destroy the recreational economy that was developing in the area.[13]

The Forest Service, after years of feeding the mill and leaving the woods with huge, spreading scars, decided that it could not continue to provide the flow of logs the mill required. The mill shut down amid protests that Dubois would "up and blow away." By 1993 the mayor was bragging, "Now our economy is steadier and stronger than ever."[14] Real-estate agents "were delighted to get rid of that mill."[15] As retired economics professor and long-time Dubois resident John Murdock pointed out during the timber harvest debates in the late 1980s, even before the mill shut down the area had begun to attract residents and businesses because of its outdoor amenities.[16]

The Dubois area, less than 100 miles southeast of Grand Teton and Yellowstone National parks along a major highway, is home to the largest bighorn sheep herd in the country. To the south rise the Wind River Range and to the north the Absaroka, the highest mountain ranges in Wyoming. The town sits on the Wind River. One would think that the economic potential of such a spectacular setting would have been obvious. But to the majority it did not become obvious until the lumber mill shut down. The director for economic development in Fremont County claims that this area "may be one of the few places in the country basing our economic revitalization on wildlife and wild-land rehabilitation."[17] Local officials are formally implementing this commitment, opposing extractive developments such as oil and gas development that may threaten wildlands and the economic vitality that relies on them. In 1993 a National Bighorn Sheep Interpretive Center opened in Dubois and is expected to draw 120,000 visitors annually. This is just one of the many signs of the town's "somersault from logging camp to nature camp," and it has taken place in a short five years.[18] In the years following the mill closure, real income in Dubois grew by 8.5 percent per year while the Wyoming economy showed almost no real growth and the national economy grew at less than a third of this rate—hardly the doom that proponents of feeding the landscape to the mill had forecast.[19]

The Pacific Northwest

As a result of overcutting and cumulative environmental damage, timber harvests in the Pacific Northwest and the northern Rocky Mountain states were significantly reduced in the early 1990s. In the Pacific Northwest federal court orders were issued to protect the remaining patches of ancient rain forest that provided habitat for endangered species such as the northern spotted owl and several stocks of oceangoing salmon. Even without court-ordered limits, timber harvests would have been cut because the old growth had been aggressively removed on both private and public timberland during the 1970s and 1980s, and the second growth was decades away from harvesting.[20] The Forest Service and private timberland owners clearcut huge tracts of the mountainous landscape in western Montana, northern Idaho, and eastern Washington, causing erosion and sedimentation that damaged trout fisheries. The roads and clear-cuts fragmented wildlife habitat, compounding the threat to the grizzly bear and the woodland caribou, both endangered species. Because many of the Rocky Mountain forests have relatively low timber productivity and are steep, environmentally sensitive terrain, they can be managed for timber only at a loss to the U.S. government.[21] Both the White House and Congress have been increasingly critical of such below-cost programs, while the scars left by clear-cuts and roads have generated mounting public opposition to logging. This was the political climate that led to the plummeting harvest in the northern Rockies in the early 1990s.

Oregon has been called the timber basket of the nation. Small cities and rural areas stretching south along the Cascade range are thought of as lumber towns. In western Montana and northern Idaho, more than half of all jobs and income are imagined to be directly or indirectly tied to timber, the region's only major commodity export. It is not surprising, given such preconceptions, that the dramatic reduction in federal timber sales was accompanied by warnings of massive economic disruption. In the Pacific Northwest some industry spokespersons claimed that 100,000 jobs would be lost.[22] In western Montana, with its much smaller population, over 10,000 jobs were said to be threatened.[23] Economic calamity, the timber industry insisted, was certain unless the federal government boosted the harvest.

As of the mid-1990s, no such thing has occurred. In Oregon, western Montana, northern Idaho, and northeastern Washington unemployment rates are at their lowest levels in twenty-five years and tens of thousands of new jobs are being created annually. Displaced wood-products workers have been quickly absorbed into the expanding economy at wages within 10 to 15 percent of what they previously earned. Real earnings rose. Once depressed timber towns had growing populations and mini–building booms. As one observer commented, "Economic calamity never looked so good."[24]

The primary explanation for such vigor in the wake of timber industry downsizing is that these economies had already started the transition from underdeveloped extractive economies to diversified service-based economies. Forestland was an amenity that drew people and businesses, and inmigration set off a dynamic that was self-sustaining, expanding the range of economic activities that made the Pacific Northwest even more attractive to households and businesses. In a different manner the forests continued to support economic activity, providing stability during a time of change. This case and others contradict the Forest Service's belief that boosted harvests create community stability. Reduced logging protects the environmental base that is becoming the foundation of local economic vitality. As the mayor of Springfield, Oregon, one of that state's so-called timber-dependent towns, put it, "Owls versus jobs was just plain false. What we've got here is quality of life. And as long as we don't screw that up, we'll always be able to attract people and business."[25]

Kremmling, Colorado

Kremmling, population 1,200, is located on the Colorado River about 125 miles northwest of Denver. In 1992 Louisiana-Pacific closed its waferboard mill there, eliminating about 220 jobs, about a third of the town's jobs. The change came as a shock. But Kremmling reacted quickly and resiliently. The theme that emerged over and over again in town planning meetings was that above all, the citizens wanted to preserve their quality of life. Large-scale tourism, following the example of Steamboat Springs, Vail, and Aspen, was voted down. Not that Kremmling is ignoring the recreational economy: new motels are being constructed; discussions are under way to bring Amtrak service in; the town is seeking to designate the road west of Kremmling as a scenic byway; recreational facilities are being upgraded; and the Wilderness Society and Forest Service are working with the community to develop dispersed recreational opportunities nearby.[26] Meanwhile, an "assisted-living center" is being built for senior citizens so that they do not have to move to Denver or Steamboat Springs for nursing home services. Retaining a senior citizen in a community (or attracting one) can have a cash flow value similar to that provided by a lumber mill job.

It is interesting how quickly attitudes toward the local economy changed when the extractive industry was eliminated—not by government fiat or local opposition, but by impersonal market forces. Once the traditional industry died, there was almost no support for replacing it with another environmentally threatening firm. In fact, the residents were emphatic about the importance of protecting the social and natural environments. What is also interesting is the confidence the community developed: it didn't have to be a beggar instead of a chooser. The community saw itself as something special, endowed with human and natural resources that could build a future. Optimism carried the community beyond passive dependency and gave it a handle on its own future.

Twenty Million Acres of Additional Wilderness: Locking Up Resources, or Creating Jobs?

One of the most contentious issues of public land management is wilderness classification. Because federal land classified as wilderness under the 1964 Wilderness Act is off-limits to commercial extraction and motorized vehicles, many people argue that the classification "locks up" resources that would otherwise support the local economy. The above cases suggest otherwise.

Beginning in the late 1980s, a coalition of environmental groups in the northern Rocky Mountains of the United States and Canada began advocating legal protection for almost all of the remnant roadless areas on public land that did not already have wilderness or national park classification. In the United States, this took the form of proposed federal legislation, the Northern Rockies Ecosystem Protection Act (NREPA), that would prohibit almost all commercial extractive activity on Forest Service roadless areas in Montana, Idaho, eastern Washington and Oregon, and northern Wyoming.

The NREPA represents a growing awareness among environmentalists that natural landscapes cannot be protected in piecemeal fashion. "Island" areas cut off from biological exchange with larger ecosystems cease to be natural or healthy. The NREPA seeks to save roadless areas that serve as wildlife "corridors" between existing national parks and wilderness areas and that provide habitat critical to the survival of the region's wildlife—grizzly bears, timber wolves, salmon, bull trout, woodland caribou, and other species that represent almost the complete set of natural fauna present when European settlers first arrived. Many of these species are on the verge of extinction because of human encroachment on their habitat. Under the NREPA, nearly 20 million acres of roadless natural landscape would be given official protection from further encroachment.

Extractive interests were upset by the proposal. From their point of view, the NREPA would lock up tens of millions of additional acres in nondevelopment status. The act would take logs from mills, block metal mining, prevent oil and gas development, and limit grazing on public land, impoverishing local communities by cutting them off from the natural resource base on which they depended.

However, a detailed economic analysis of the impact this preservation proposal would have on the industry most affected, timber, indicated that the negative impact on extraction would be minor and that the overall impact on the economy was likely to be positive.[27] All twenty-eight national forests involved were analyzed, going roadless area by roadless area using Forest Service data. The timber industry, it was estimated, would directly lose about 1,400 of the five-state region's 1.2 million jobs, or about one-tenth of 1 percent of total employment. On average, over the last decade this number of jobs has been created every three weeks by growth in the overall regional economy. That is, the employment cost of protecting 20 million acres of natural landscape would be a three-week pause in normal job creation.[28] Even this relatively modest setback for timber employment was expected to be more than offset by jobs gained from granting permanent protection to the environment and from recreational activities that were already the driving force in the region's economic growth.

The NREPA analysis explained the relatively minor disadvantages to local economies of putting 20 million acres off-limits to timber extraction in terms that should be familiar by now:[29]

- The Forest Service has found 80 percent of the roadless acres in the northern Rockies to be unsuited for timber management. That 80 percent could be put off-limits to timber harvest with no impact on the wood products industry (see table 7-1).

- In many cases in the region, and notably in Montana and Wyoming, the primary connection between national forestland and the local economy is not logging but recreation.

- The timber industry was already a declining source of employment in the northern Rockies. During the 1980s employment per million board feet of timber harvested declined by over 30 percent. And automation and shifts to less labor-intensive products are reducing the employment potential associated with each thousand board feet of timber harvested.

- During the 1980s when employment in extractive industries was unstable and declining, the nonextractive sectors expanded. As a result, the relative and absolute importance of extractive industries as a source of employment declined. That nonextractive sectors were able to expand despite the collapse of extractive sectors dramatizes an economic vitality unrelated to extraction and offsetting the depressing effects of its decline. The natural environment has much to do with the region's vitality.

- The Forest Service exaggerated the level of timber harvesting that is possible in the region's roadless areas. Plans drawn up on the basis of inaccurate timber inventories and site productivity data ignored legal constraints on harvesting adjacent to previous clearcuts. The Forest Service, having assumed that it would be able to meet water quality and fish habitat standards, has found that it cannot. Nor did the plans adequately account for old growth and endangered species protection. As a result of such error, the allowable sale quantities the Forest Service originally projected as coming from roadless areas cannot be realized. Almost all national forests in the region are now reducing planned sales to well below those originally projected in Forest Service plans.

- Roadless areas are the most costly and least productive lands from a timber management point of view, and most can be harvested only at substantial losses to the U.S. taxpayer. Congress and the White House are putting increasing pressure on the Forest Service to end such below-cost timber management. As a result, many roadless areas will have to be removed from the suitable timber base. They will not provide trees to local mills even if the NREPA is not adopted.

Juggling Extraction and Amenities

The timber industry is unstable and in long-term decline as a source of jobs and income. Logging, especially the massive clear-cutting of recent years, seriously threatens other forest amenities that support local economies. Landscapes stripped bare, silted streams with dead fish, fragmented ecosystems devoid of wildlife—this isn't what draws people and business. Lessons abound from America's past: aggressive logging in northern New England, the Great Lakes region, and the South left desolate landscapes and poverty behind.

The economic health of a community in a forested landscape does not depend on as high a rate of extraction of wood fiber as possible. In fact, the long-run economic health of the community depends on something quite different: weaning from dependency through systematic diversification. The primary economic alternatives facing forestland communities are associated with their natural and social amenities. By no means does logging have to come to a halt, but it does have to be practiced in harmony with preservation. In situations where it unavoidably threatens other forest values, an economically rational choice requires that the positive economic values associated with preservation be weighed against the limited support expanded timber harvest offers the local economy.

The Forest Service's official definition of community stability, with its emphasis on helping places adapt to change, recognizes the amenity-driven diversification that is currently taking place in many forestland communities. Logging locations, methods, and volumes must be adjusted in ways that do not stop diversification. Modifying forest management policies to protect environmental services does not threaten the economies of forest-dependent communities, it protects and enhances them.

Agriculture: The Primordial Economy

Few Americans look at agriculture as just another type of economic activity. Agriculture was the first specific industry to get its own cabinet position in the executive branch of the federal government. There was a Department of Agriculture forty years before there was a Department of Commerce or Labor. Since the 1930s, huge federal support programs have targeted agriculture with billions of dollars of assistance each year. The federal government runs community stabilization programs that extend into almost every rural county and community in the nation, and most state governments have programs providing technical assistance to the agricultural sector through a network of extension offices. With a mix of cynicism and respect, representatives of other interest groups talk of the "agricultural exemption" to almost all burdensome regulations or taxes. We tend to be much more careful about the restrictions we place on farming and ranching than on other businesses, because, we believe, agriculture is in some sense more "fundamental" than the modern commercial enterprise.

Agriculture and Early Economic Thought: The Physiocratic Vision

The first efforts at economic modeling considered agriculture as the ultimate source of all economic value. In the mid-eighteenth century, a group of French intellectuals applied the newly discovered circulatory system of the human body to the national economy. According to these "physiocrats," the value created in agriculture flowed through and enabled all other activity in the economic system, moving from the grain grower to the miller to the baker to the mason and so on.[1] Their crude matrix depiction of the connections among economic activities provided the basis for modern mathematical input-output analysis. It also established the unique position of agriculture in the economy. Just as food provided the energy the human body needed to function, so agriculture provided the energy that drove the economy. All other economic activity simply processed the initial value created in agriculture; it did not add value.[2]

The policy implications of this view were clear. Mid-eighteenth-century France was a pre-industrial society in which agricultural innovation produced substantial surpluses that supported the landed aristocracy and the king, both of whom were engaged in what was soon to become a life or death struggle with the urban-based bourgeoisie. The intellectuals of the royal court provided a sophisticated rationale for giving the agricultural sector priority over growing urban-based production and trade. In fact, industrialization was seen as being fueled primarily by increased agricultural surpluses. The special place French physiocrats accorded to agricultural producers has endured to this day, if not in economic theory, then in the folk economics that dominates public policy.

Farming, Farming Everywhere

Agriculture is practiced in almost every place that urban residential and commercial activities have not claimed. Even in urban areas, people plant vegetable gardens and commercial nurseries set up business. Outside of urban areas almost every parcel of land is committed to one type of agricultural activity or another, if not crops, then livestock. At the very least, the grass crop will be cut and baled. Even on public lands, including designated wilderness areas, there is livestock grazing.

The ubiquity of agricultural activity reinforces the impression that it is important, or even central, to our economic well-being. Unlike agriculture, manufacturing and services do not fill in every "blank spot" in the landscape. But this is misleading. One cannot judge the economic importance of an activity or resource by its prevalence. A lot of agriculture represents marginal, default use of land. Where soil and rainfall permit rapid reforestation, woodlands may consistently challenge marginal agriculture, but where open land is capable of growing something, almost anything, entrepreneurs will seize that potential and harvest the grasses, stock the land with livestock, or otherwise put the land to agricultural use.[3] This demonstrates that the value of agricultural production at least covers the costs of making use of the land when its owners are paid little or nothing. In general, the costs of marginal agriculture nearly outweigh the benefits, generating almost no net economic value. Thus a substantial amount of marginal land could be withdrawn from agriculture with almost no economic loss.

Our Daily Bread

One reason for agriculture's special status is obvious: we all have to eat. In this sense agricultural production is a prerequisite of all productive economic activity. No other sector of the economy can make such a claim. We do not really have to have computers or automobiles or entertainment or finance in order to engage in economic activity at some level. But we must have food.

This fact of life was the foundation of the physiocratic vision. All economic activity, no matter how obscure or trivial or isolated, was linked to the agricultural sector through the physical flow of commodities and, in most cases, an opposite flow of payment for them. We should not be misled by this concept into according economic priority to agriculture. That something is required in an economic process does not establish its economic value. In most cases many different resources have to be combined to produce a product. Knowing that each resource is in some sense required does not tell us anything about the relative contribution each makes to the value of the final product. Healthy crops require the presence of certain trace minerals in the soil, without which profitable operations would be impossible. That does not mean that the dominant economic resources in crop agriculture are these trace elements.

It is not clear why advocates of special treatment for agriculture make their case by citing the human need for food. Humans also need air to breathe, water to drink, a tolerable climate, and certain vitamins and minerals. It is not possible from this biological knowledge to assign relative economic value to, say, Vitamin C or those who produce and distribute it to us.

What is missing from the "physical requirements" approach to economic relationships is any reference to the relationship between supply and demand. Air, though it is a prerequisite for all economic activity, is not generally an economic good because the supply is so large compared to the demand. Of course, heavy pollution can make clean air an economic good, in high demand and short supply. This has happened in the heavily polluted cities of Mexico City and Tokyo, where personal exposure to "shots" of clean air or oxygen can be purchased from vending machines. Economic value is established not by physical necessity but rather by the interaction of supply and demand. When an input is readily available at relatively low or no cost, its economic value is going to be low regardless of how crucial it is to an economic process. It seems unlikely that vitamin C will acquire much economic value in the future. That was not always the case. In the past, because so many sailors at sea developed scurvy owing to a deficiency of this vitamin, it was a valuable naval supply. But this commodity is unlikely ever again to be in such short supply relative to demand.

The relative economic importance of agriculture is established in the same way, by measuring supply relative to demand. If agricultural supply were to shrink relative to demand, it would have a profound impact on the rest of the economy. Just as interruptions in energy supplies in the 1970s and early 1980s disrupted the economy, falling agricultural production could have a cascading impact on the national economy. As supplies of an input shrink relative to demand, additional resources have to be diverted to the production of that input or the development of a substitute. The diversion means that things once produced will not get produced now, and we will be collectively poorer. If, to maintain food supplies, we had to reverse the centuries-old trend of reducing the percentage of our total resources committed to agriculture, the economic growth that has been facilitated by shifting resources out of agriculture into other productive activities would stop. Food prices would rise appreciably, and we would all be forced to spend more of our limited income on obtaining the same quantity and quality of food. In the process, the relative economic importance of agriculture would rise. A larger percentage of total resources would be committed to that sector and a larger percentage of total expenditures would be claimed by it. That, of course, would not improve our well-being, the cost of living having risen and economic development slowed.

What we have actually been experiencing, for many centuries now, is quite the opposite. Agricultural supply has risen faster than demand.

In general, food and fiber supplies have been more than adequate, although the distribution of food according to purchasing power causes a large portion of the world's population to suffer from malnutrition. In many areas, including North America and Western Europe, farms have been producing food and fiber in surplus amounts, driving agricultural prices down.[4] Agricultural innovation has allowed farms to survive and expand production despite falling commodity prices, but the work force has shrunk while the aggregate value of farm output has failed to keep up with the expanding economy. In other words, the relative economic importance of agriculture has steadily declined.[5]

One cannot establish the current economic value of agriculture by asking what the world would be like if there were not enough food or no food at all. Without question, if supplies were significantly different from what they have been, the relative economic importance of agriculture would be different. Certainly lots of things might happen to severely disrupt our economy and drastically change today's relative economic values. But hypothetical economic values are just that, hypothetical. Postulating severe supply constraints on various inputs into the economy may be useful in reminding us of how dependent we are on physical, social, and political interrelationships, sobering an otherwise facile confidence in the complex economic arrangements we have come to rely on. It is possible that we have become too specialized and too dependent on what will ultimately prove to be an unstable social system. But the very existence of interdependencies underlines the fact that agriculture does not play a particularly unique role in the economy. There is a big difference between hypotheses about having no agriculture at all (the foundation of folk economic support for special treatment) and analyses of the impact of having somewhat more or less agricultural production.

Puffing Up Agriculture

Numerous studies undertaken by the U.S. Department of Agriculture and by college departments of agriculture have set out to prove that agriculture is more important to the overall economy than the public and policymakers recognize. Is it better for the overall economy to have a larger rather than a smaller agriculture sector? Are there reasons why we would want to protect the relative size of agriculture in the national economy or even seek to expand it? To most people working in agriculturally related activities, these are silly questions. To them, the shrinking agricultural sector is ominous; the U.S. economy would be stronger if the industry were large and growing.

In analyzing the economic meaning of a declining agricultural sector, it is important to keep local economic adjustments to such change in perspective. It is certainly likely that as agriculture declines as a source of income and employment, communities that have been dependent on it will suffer some degree of economic dislocation. But dislocation is not necessarily a harbinger of long-run economic decline. Most communities in the United States were at one point dependent on agriculture; we used to be a nation of farmers. Who would argue that the displacement of irrigated agriculture along the Wasatch Front by the urban industrial complex of Salt Lake City impoverished the state of Utah? Who would argue that the development of California's Silicon Valley weakened Santa Clara County's economy because the computer industry that developed there displaced local agriculture and related activities?[6]

In economic development, certain economic activities necessarily displace others. The decline of one industry alone is not evidence that the overall economy is in decline. What is important from an economic point of view is not the sector in decline but what happens to resources that were previously used in that sector: labor, capital, and land. If these resources sit idle, clearly the economy is worse off, operating below capacity. But that is not generally what has happened to the resources freed up from agricultural activity. The displaced labor force has not remained permanently on the dole; it has been re-employed in economic activities that are in much higher demand. The productivity of the overall U.S. economy has risen significantly with the shift of labor from agriculture to other industries. Consider this: if agriculture employed 50 percent of the work force in 1990, as it did in 1880, there would be 56 million fewer workers in U.S. manufacturing and service production, making it impossible to satisfy the needs and desires that actually drive our present economy.

Land taken out of agricultural production is committed to commercial, industrial, residential, or other uses, and, judging from the successful bidding for such land, these tend to be more productive uses. Most agricultural land, however, stays in agricultural use. Ownership shifts from one person to another as smaller farms are consolidated into larger farms. In some circumstances, where the land is marginal for agriculture, it is given over to forest. As we have seen, this was the case with much of the East's former farmland in the late nineteenth and early twentieth centuries.[7] Forests, which have to grow, may not produce a cash "crop" for many decades. Forests ultimately maintained for such values as their nonmarket goods and services, wildlife habitat, watershed, recreation, and ex-urban residential sites may not ever produce a cash flow. The shift from agriculture, however, is evidence itself that agricultural value was lower than the nonmarket value of young forestland.

Given the capital-intensive nature of modern agriculture, it is unlikely that capital has actually been flowing out of agriculture. In any case, capital is highly mobile and certain to be re-employed elsewhere. The point is that resources either move into uses more productive than agriculture or stay productively employed in agriculture. They do not sit idle. It is almost certainly not the case that the overall economy suffers as a result of the relative decline of agriculture.

This can be put slightly differently. If we satisfy our needs for food and fiber using fewer of the total resources available in our economy, how can we be worse off? If we discover a way of heating our houses that uses less energy, how can we be worse off? It is the opposite of economizing to maximize resource use in the production of needed goods and services. Heightened agricultural productivity does not impoverish, it lays the foundation for ongoing economic development. There is no economic logic to keeping the same-size work force engaged in agriculture or, worse, the same percentage of the population employed in agriculture now as once was. Maintaining the same percentage of the work force in agriculture would lead either to greater surplus production and larger public subsidies or to higher-priced food and less production elsewhere in the economy. Neither consequence would improve the overall well-being of the population. Neither represents an economic improvement.[8]

The Value of Agriculture in a State Economy: A Case Study

All of us like to believe that what we do is important. Industries are no different. The more people believe that they rely on a particular industry, the easier it is to cast that industry's commercial interests in the role of serving the public interest. Industries that rely on public subsidies or government favors have an even greater need to demonstrate their importance. It is no surprise to find the truth stretched in industry-oriented analyses of the relative economic importance of such activities as mining, agriculture, and logging.

The usual measure of relative economic importance is a straightforward ratio:

$$\text{relative economic importance} \quad = \quad \frac{\text{contribution of agriculture}}{\text{size of the total economy}}$$

This ratio will exaggerate the relative economic importance of agriculture if either the numerator is overstated or the denominator is understated.

A study of the contribution of the agricultural sector to the economy of Utah done by the Agricultural Experiment Station at Utah State University is a good example of how such a measure can be distorted.[9] When measuring the relative importance of agriculture, it is common for agricultural advocates to combine all *food*-related activities and label them "agriculture- related." The Utah study counted employment and income in restaurants, supermarkets, other food stores, and wholesale food distributors as agriculture related, and implicitly claimed that Utah restaurants and food stores depend on Utah farms and ranches (figure 8-1). Of course, if food were not produced, restaurants could not sell meals and grocery shelves would be empty. But it is not plausible to argue that if agricultural products were not produced in Utah, Utah restaurants and food stores would not be able to obtain food and make sales. Many totally urban areas import food from out of state and operate restaurants and grocery stores. The people of Utah would not starve if food products were not produced in Utah. The implicit claim of Utah food's dependence on Utah agriculture conveniently increases the apparent economic importance of agriculture above the direct contribution it makes to income. Indeed, by including retail and wholesale food activity in the equation, agriculture's importance is inflated by almost 250 percent.

The Utah study claims as agriculture related a variety of economic factors of questionable relevance, for instance, salaries and employment in schools of agriculture. These schools are primarily supported by tax funds that flow directly from Utah citizens and businesses. That is, a burden is imposed on other economic activities to fund schools, so they cannot be treated merely as a contribution to the economy. The study also counts as agriculture urban nurseries that supply residences

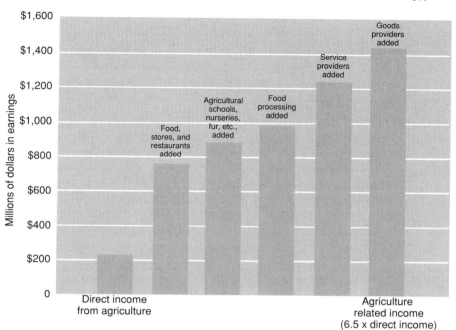

FIGURE 8-1. Inflating the farm-related sector in Utah, 1987. A number of steps can be taken to inflate direct income earned in agriculture to a larger "agriculture-related" value. (*Data sources:* D. L. Snyder and W. C. Lewis, 1989, "The Size and Role of Agriculture in Utah," Research Report 129, Utah Agricultural Experiment Station, Logan, Utah State University.)

and even fur farms. Counting such nonfarm activities inflates the impact of agriculture on income by 60 percent. Also included in the Utah study as agriculture related were service providers—accountants, lawyers, banks, real estate agents, and others—who have agricultural clients and businesses that supply goods to Utah's farms and ranches (fuel, electricity, equipment, buildings). Including suppliers triples the apparent size of the agricultural sector (see figure 8-1). There is some plausibility in counting suppliers' economic activities here. But the implicit assumption, that if agricultural activity did not take place, suppliers would not be employed within the local economy and would either have to move out or remain permanently unemployed, is questionable. Historically, this is not what has happened to the labor force displaced from agriculture and related economic activities. To repeat, it is the shift of population off the farm that has allowed economic development to take place across the nation. The work force's shift from less productive to more productive activities has allowed America's standard of living to improve.

In the ratio measuring agriculture's relative importance, the denominator can also be manipulated to make the total economy appear smaller than it actually is. The Utah study focused only on wage and salary income, ignoring income received by the self-employed and nonwage sources such as property and retirement income. Those nonwage incomes represent almost 40 percent of total state income. In addition, the study assumed that total wage and salary income was 13 percent smaller than federal statistics indicate. These adjustments alone cut the denominator by more than half, doubling the apparent importance of agriculture (figure 8-2).

The cumulative result of the Utah study's method is to portray agriculture as representing about 13 percent of the total Utah economy (figure 8-3). While it does not demonstrate overwhelming state dependence on agriculture, that figure does suggest that agriculture is one of the major sources of economic activity in Utah. But looking at the direct contribution Utah agriculture makes to income and employment, a quite different picture appears: agriculture directly generates only about 1 percent of total income. It certainly makes a difference to public policy whether agriculture is responsible for one out of every

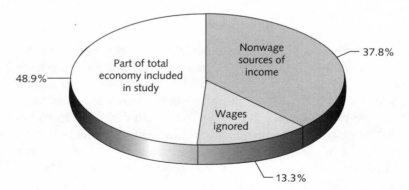

FIGURE 8-2. Shrinking the economy to enhance the relative size of agriculture. By ignoring nonwage sources of income and understating wage and salary income, the total economy is made to appear smaller and agriculture's role larger. (*Data sources:* BEA REIS.)

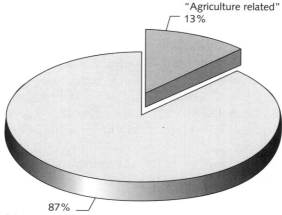

"Agriculture related"
13%

87%
Wages in the rest of the economy

FIGURE 8-3. Inflating the role of agriculture: Utah income, 1987–89. When the smaller wage economy is used as a reference point and agri-culture-related activities are included in it, agriculture appears to rep-resent a significant part of the total Utah economy. (*Data sources:* D. L. Snyder and W. C. Lewis, 1989, "The Size and Role of Agriculture in Utah," Research Report 129, Utah Agricultural Experiment Sta-tion, Loan, Utah State University.)

eight dollars earned in Utah or one out of every hundred. The latter is closer to the economic truth.

The Utah study is not alone in exaggerating agriculture's impor-tance. Furthermore, when the U.S. Department of Agriculture's methods of estimating the relative importance of agriculture are ap-plied to Utah, they increase the sector's apparent importance by a third over the state study's estimates.[10] The Utah study obviously did not push the envelope of exaggeration as far as it could be pushed.

Home on the Range: The Relative Economic Importance of Grazing on Federal Land

For the last decade and a half one of the more controversial public policy issues in the West has been the level of grazing on federal land and the appropriate fee to charge for grazing. Environmentalists see low grazing fees as encouraging and subsidizing overgrazing of public land, which results in the degradation of water quality, wildlife habitat, and recreation potential. On the other side, emotion is stirred up by the perception that most ranching operations depend on federal land, and that without access to it they would cease to be economically viable. Since, it is usually assumed, ranching is the backbone of the western economy, such a loss would have a devastating impact. Arguments of this sort successfully blocked most of the significant reforms of federal grazing policy attempted between 1975 and 1996.

Economic claims about the relative importance of federal grazing to the economies of western states can be analyzed by asking three question: What is the direct contribution agricultural operations make to the state economy? What portion of this total agricultural activity is associated with cattle and sheep operations? What portion of the feed for livestock operations is provided by grazing on federal land? To start with the last, for many western states, federal land provides only a small percentage of the total feed needed to support livestock herds. Montana, for instance, obtains only about 7 percent of its livestock feed from federal land. Washington, California, and Colorado get only 2 to 6 percent of their livestock feed from this source. Overall, the eleven western states obtain only an eighth of their livestock feed from federal land (table 8-1).[11] From a national perspective the reliance on western federal land is dramatically lower: only 2 percent of the feed consumed by beef cattle is provided by grazing federal land.[12]

This direct calculation of the degree of ranching dependence on federal land is to be contrasted with the method used by livestock interests in their efforts to make the case for protecting the status quo on western public land. A recent New Mexico study defined all ranches that obtained more than 5 percent of their forage from federal lands as federal grazing dependent. Using this arbitrary definition, even though ranches in the state of Washington only get 2 percent of their feed from federal land, they are classified as 45 percent dependent on federal land, a twentyfold exaggeration of their degree of dependence.[13] Other studies have gone further, treating all ranches that make any use of public land for grazing as dependent and then treating all livestock on those ranches as also dependent.

How can one estimate the contribution federal grazing makes to the economies of eleven western states? The percent of reliance on federal forage is multiplied by the percent of agricultural economic activity represented by cattle and sheep operations (table 8-2). This in turn is

TABLE 8-1.

Measuring Dependence on Federal Grazing

	Percentage of Ranches "Dependent" on Federal Grazing[a]	Percentage of Feed from Federal Grazing	Amount of Exaggeration of Dependency (percent)
Arizona	66	24	275
California	94	4	2,350
Colorado	53	6	883
Idaho	97	14	693
Montana	43	7	614
Nevada	100	43	233
New Mexico	51	20	255
Oregon	74	11	673
Utah	99	24	413
Washington	45	2	2,250
Wyoming	76	16	475
Aggregate Eleven States	69	12	575

[a]"Dependent" means more than 5% of forage from federal grazing.
Source: Godfrey and Pope 1990.

multiplied by the direct contribution agriculture makes to the economy in terms of both income and employment. For instance, in Montana, federal forage represents 7 percent of total livestock feed. Cattle and sheep operations are responsible for about 50 percent of the dollar value of all agricultural sales. Finally, agriculture is directly responsible for about 7 percent of total personal income in the state. Thus federal grazing is responsible for about one-quarter of 1 percent of all income in Montana.[14]

It should be kept in mind that livestock is not synonymous with cattle in the West. In many western states, among them Arizona and California, poultry raising is the dominant form of livestock production. In Washington, Oregon, and Utah only about half of the livestock are cattle and sheep. And in all eleven western states, only 60 percent of the livestock activity is associated with these two animals.[15]

Only about $1 out of every $2,500 in income received in the eleven western states is directly associated with grazing on federal land, and only 1 out of every 2,000 jobs is directly tied to federal land grazing. All grazing on federal land, of course, is not threatened by proposals to raise fees and protect habitat. Raising grazing fees to market levels

TABLE 8-2.

Employment and Income from Federal Grazing

Employment	Arizona	California	Colorado	Idaho	Montana	New Mexico	Nevada	Oregon	Utah	Washington	Wyoming	Aggregate Eleven States
Agricultural jobs as a % of total	1.07	1.63	1.90	6.18	7.01	2.54	0.65	3.83	1.89	2.74	4.55	2.06
Cattle and sheep jobs as a % of total	0.10	0.09	1.18	2.11	3.53	1.40	0.38	0.91	0.81	0.51	3.47	0.53
Federal grazing jobs as a % of total	0.11	0.00	0.07	0.30	0.25	0.28	0.16	0.10	0.19	0.01	0.56	0.06
Days of normal job growth to replace all federal grazing jobs	14	1	14	72	93	53	18	23	30	2	—	11
Federal grazing jobs	2,132	603	1,456	1,636	1,085	2,129	1,228	1,630	1,805	291	1,503	17,989

TABLE 8-2. CONTINUED

Employment and Income from Federal Grazing

Income	Arizona	California	Colorado	Idaho	Montana	New Mexico	Nevada	Oregon	Utah	Washington	Wyoming	Aggregate Eleven States
Agricultural income as a % of total	1.01	1.02	1.04	4.86	3.87	1.60	0.37	1.71	0.78	1.48	2.08	1.19
Cattle and sheep income as a % of total	0.10	0.06	0.65	1.66	1.95	0.88	0.21	0.41	0.34	0.28	1.59	0.31
Federal grazing income as a % of total	0.11	0.00	0.04	0.23	0.14	0.18	0.09	0.04	0.08	0.01	0.25	0.04
Days of normal income growth to replace all federal grazing jobs	18	0	6	57	30	25	8	10	9	1	—	6

Source: Power, 1994.

would simply remove the incentive to prefer federal to private forage. And excluding cattle from streamsides and adjusting stocking rates downward to protect vegetation and habitat would not result in zero grazing. The impact of any of the proposed changes in federal grazing policy would be much less than these figures might suggest.

Potential job and income loss associated with federal grazing reform can be expressed in terms of the time it would take for local western economies to replace jobs through the normal expansion of the economy. If state economic growth since 1980 is taken as the reference point, the loss of all federal grazing would cause income growth in the eleven western states to pause for six days. To make up for lost jobs, economic growth would pause for a week and a half. That is, in even the most extreme case where all grazing on federal land was eliminated, direct income and job losses would be made up in a matter of a few days by normal economic expansion. Obviously some communities would be harder hit than others given the uneven distribution of public grazing land across states. While the potential for local disruption should be analyzed and mitigated where necessary, it is still the case that economies of broad parts of the West would not significantly suffer from reduced grazing on public land.

The Hand That Feeds: The Increasing Reliance of Farm Families on the Nonfarm Economy

Cattle-raising operations are increasingly made financially feasible only because farm families have access to nonfarm employment and income. Nationally, almost 80 percent of the income received by beef-raising operations comes from nonfarm sources (table 8-3).[16] The Census of Agriculture does not provide a state-by-state breakdown of the importance of nonfarm income to cattle ranches, but it does provide such information for agriculture as a whole (table 8-4). For states like Utah, Nevada, and Oregon where the population is heavily concentrated in urban areas, off-farm income supplies 67 to 80 percent of farm family income. In other states the importance of off-farm income is not as great, but in general it represents the bulk of farm family income. In 1992, little more than a third (37 percent) of the total income received by farm operators nationwide was self-employment income associated with farm operations.[17]

TABLE 8-3.

The Importance of Off-Farm Income for Beef Cattle Raisers (except feedlots)

	Number of Farms	Income ($billion)
Farms with Farm-Related Income Only	626,366	4.2
Farms with Off-Farm Income	477,000	16.1
Nonfarm jobs		9.8
Self-employment		1.3
Retirement		1.9
Interest and dividends		1.6
	Percent of Total Income	
From the Farm	21	
From Off the Farm	79	

Source: U.S. Bureau of the Census, Census of Agriculture, 1987, Special Reports, Farm Economics.

TABLE 8-4.

The Importance of Off-Farm Income

	Net Cash Farm Income		Off-Farm Income		Off-Farm Income
	No. of Farms	$million	No. of Farms	$million	As % of On-Farm
Montana	22,989	244	15,313	329	135
Idaho	22,586	377	16,765	439	116
Wyoming	7,776	136	5,612	157	116
Colorado	22,737	339	18,114	560	165
New Mexico	11,969	668	8,509	263	39
Arizona	5,346	248	3,498	206	83
Utah	13,750	117	10,669	343	294
Nevada	3,098	40	2,188	96	237
Washington	27,834	868	20,996	594	68
Oregon	28,744	159	22,636	788	497
California	72,791	1,881	53,330	2,551	136
Aggregate					
Eleven States	239,620	5,076	177,630	6,325	125

Source: U.S. Bureau of the Census, Census of Agriculture, 1987, Special Reports, Farm Economics.

This belies the argument that urban economies depend on rural agriculture. On the contrary, agriculture increasingly depends on the vitality of urban and nonagricultural rural economies to provide the nonfarm income that keeps farm operations alive. That is, agriculture is a subsidiary activity supported by the vitality of the nonagricultural economy. Those concerned with the financial viability of agriculture need to address the nonfarm economy.

Agriculture's Special Status: A Socioeconomic Perspective

No matter what the economic statistics show about the role of agriculture in the overall economy, the treatment given to agriculture by both federal and state governments is a testament to the persistent, widely shared perception that there is something special about agriculture. One reason may be that many families farmed the land no more than a few generations ago. But there is more to this than a historical connection. People view agriculture not as just another type of commercial economic activity but rather as an honorable way of life, one that strengthens the social and political fabric of the nation and therefore deserves protection.

One of the most enduring articulations of this view is Thomas Jefferson's vision of a nation of yeoman farmers. To him, agriculture was the ideal economic structure for the United States not because of what it produced but because of the way it was organized. Farmers were independent producers. They worked for themselves using means of production they owned, and maintained largely self-sufficient households. Such independence reduced the likelihood that employers (or later, labor unions) would corrupt the political process by using their economic power to influence the way dependent employees voted. Economic independence was crucial to a responsible, functioning democratic society. Independence had ramifications beyond voting: it allowed households to take responsibility for themselves and for the development of their communities and public institutions, innovating, adapting, and creating. By contrast, urban wage earners were dependent on others for almost everything, jobs, income, subsistence goods. The assumption was that dependent individuals would not make responsible citizens. Hence the importance of keeping as large as possible a proportion of the population earning a living on the land.

Contemporary public support for agriculture has its roots in Jefferson's vision. Farming and ranching are seen as attractive ways of life rather than just commercial ventures pursuing profit. There is something wholesome about folks living on the land and harvesting its riches by the sweat of their own brow. Work and home life are integrated, and the farmer is a jack-of-all-trades, parent, mechanic, agronomist, veterinarian, businessperson, commodities speculator, weatherforecaster. Agriculture, as articulated by Wendell Berry in a modern restatement of the Jeffersonian vision, is a symbol of dignified economic activity.[18] Those who, by contrast, work in large bureaucracies have to take orders from a hierarchy of superiors. People specialize in narrow fields and produce no tangible product that they can claim as their own. Their work is far removed from home life and often in conflict with it.

Is it agriculture itself, or the autonomy, self-direction, and individual responsibility associated with it, that made Jefferson's vision and Berry's restatement of it attractive? During Jefferson's time slaves also worked the land, but their labor was not seen as any more ennobling than today's migrant farmers'. One could argue that almost any family-run business requires the same independence and responsibility that were once more exclusively the preserve of agriculture. Not only farmers and ranchers are self-employed, and not all agricultural workers are self-employed. The manufacturing and service sectors offer abundant examples of family-run business.

Our romantic vision of Jeffersonian yeoman agriculture ignores the role that slaves played in the development of the United States. Much of Southern agriculture, including Jefferson's plantation, was built not by independent farmers but on the backs of slaves, hardly a symbol of independence and responsibility. As time went on and farms grew larger and more specialized, they came to rely on a large migrant work force to help with the harvest. Today migrant workers harvest a large part of American fruit and vegetable crops, and they remain among the most exploited of workers: pay is low, living conditions can be atrocious, health and safety standards are not always maintained, workers receive no health insurance or retirement benefits. Of the major occupational groups, only domestic servants earn less by the week than hired farm workers.[19]

Consider the ultimate symbol of western ranch agriculture, the cowboy. The cowboy was not an independent businessperson responsibly managing his land, livestock, and buildings. He was a migrant worker employed by a ranch owner, working for meager wages and engaged in backbreaking labor. It was antisocial, this life of the single male who owned nothing but his saddle, a horse, and a change of clothes, and who had a reputation for barging into western towns disrupting them with his trigger-happy carousing.

Or take the rise of the corporate farm in the second half of the twentieth century. As a result of tax codes and the increasingly capital-intensive character of modern agriculture, more and more family farms are being replaced by corporate agricultural operations that hire managers and hands. Jefferson's yeoman has become a wage-earning employee just like his urban cousin.

The point is that only some of those employed in agriculture fit the image of the independent, self-employed businessperson. Just as important, there are independent, self-employed businesspeople in almost every field, not just agriculture. Nine out of every ten self-employed people in the United States work outside of agriculture. Over the last two decades this sector's percentage of proprietors has fallen from 23 to 10 percent and can be expected to fall further.[20] Given the declining percentage of population employed in agriculture, this would seem an unlikely industry to protect in the name of self-employment and family-operated business. The range of opportunity for self-employment is much broader outside of agriculture. In any case, it is not clear what the current justification is for supporting small businesses more generously in agriculture than in other fields of economic activity. It may be time to convert the historical accident of our agricultural support institutions to broader-based small-business extension services.

Harnessing Nature for Agriculture

Agriculture is popularly thought of as harvesting nature's bounty. But nature is not always coopera- tive. Land may be subject to drought or floods, pests may invade fields and eat plants, wildlife may threaten livestock. Because nature can be unruly, agriculture interests try to control it in order to boost production. Here we look at two particular ways of harnessing nature for agricultural purposes: the collection, storage, and distribution of water for irrigation, and the control of wild animals that threaten crops and livestock.

The economic logic of these efforts seems straightforward. Water can turn a desert into a vegetable garden, and control of wild animals can save lambs and calves. Agriculture becomes possible where other- wise it would fail or at least languish. Boosting agricultural productivity makes denser rural settlement possible and in turn supports agricul- tural economies.

But the actual economic logic of harnessing nature for agricultural purposes is anything but obvious. Policies intended to strengthen agri- culture often weaken it instead. In addition, manipulating nature often has negative environmental consequences. Such agricultural policies are doubly irrational: they damage the environment while harming the economic activity they seek to help.

Water in the Arid West: A Unique Resource?

In the inland West, limited rainfall combined with high temperatures during the summer have largely restricted agricultural activity to dispersed grazing. But residents and the politicians supporting them have not passively accepted the climate's limits. Meager rainfall can be supplemented by diverting and storing water for summer use. Water is seen as the precious life blood of the region and its communities, a special resource whose protection and use call for institutional backing. Like life itself, all economic activity ultimately depends on water.

The importance of scarce water in the West explains the heavy involvement by government, both federal and state, in the development and use of water resources. Special laws and courts govern the creation and transfer of water rights. Quasigovernmental organizations with the power to tax, irrigation districts or water conservation districts, supervise on-the-ground use of water. A federal agency, the U.S. Bureau of Reclamation, has spent billions upon billions of dollars on engineering marvels intended to supplement natural water supplies. Many state governments are heavily involved in developing supplemental water sources for agriculture.

The public perception of water as precious and scarce has led to policies that are sorely in need of an economic reality check, though they have been justified as central to the economic development of the West. Consider the obvious: if no price is attached to water, one can be almost certain that water will not always be used in high-value applications. Similarly, if one asks people how much water they need without placing a price tag on the water, the demand for water is likely to appear very large relative to the supply. Or if one assumes that all of the water that can be provided is needed no matter what the cost, it may be hard to market the water made available at a price that can pay for delivery. Water planning errors are not minor. If scarce public resources are committed in uneconomic ways to an irrigation infrastructure, for example, other rural public needs such as roads and schools and agricultural research may not be met.

Creating Water Scarcity

Of course, water is more readily available in some areas than in others. In some locations, natural rainfall is sufficient to support crop production in most years, and water does not have to be delivered by way of irrigation. In other locations, rainfall is not enough to grow crops. Some would restate this basic physical reality in economic terms: water supply is adequate in some areas while scarce in others. But this can be misleading. Agriculture uses water on a scale and with an intensity that dwarfs almost any other consumptive use of water. In the eleven western states, for instance, agriculture uses ten times more water than households, thirty-two times more than industry, and eight times more than all municipal and industrial activities.[1] Water supplies in many areas of the West are adequate for almost all residential and economic activities except irrigated agriculture. A shortage is created only when available water is assigned to water-intensive agricultural activities in arid areas. Agriculture's enormous appetite for water can easily deplete an otherwise adequate water supply.

Scarcity is a misleading economic characterization of water in the West—it's like saying that because bananas cannot grow outdoors in northern climates there is a scarcity of warmth there. Gigantic public projects could create heated domes in Minnesota to grow bananas, oranges, and cotton. That would solve the scarcity problem, but it would be outrageously uneconomic. The solution to scarcity is to adjust the mix of economic activities in a given location to its particular advantages or disadvantages. Trying to grow alfalfa in the desert with imported water when that can be done without irrigation in another location may create the appearance of scarcity, but it is not economic scarcity, it is politically contrived scarcity. In a market setting, as scarce resources are bought and sold they are systematically transferred to their highest valued use. A small amount of water can be diverted from agriculture to serve a large number of residential and other economic activities. Shifting water away from low-valued agricultural uses to higher-valued municipal and industrial uses would go a long way toward eliminating perceived water shortages. Legal barriers, however, often block such a shift.

Making the Desert Bloom: The Central Arizona Project

Although much of Arizona can be classified as desert, it has substantial surface and ground water resources. At the beginning of the century one of the first Bureau of Reclamation projects in the nation, the Salt River Project, harnessed water flowing from the mountains outside of Phoenix to reduce flooding and provide irrigation water to the surrounding area. With the advent of relatively cheap electricity in the

1950s, private landowners began pumping water from underground aquifers to support agricultural activities including fruit and nut orchards and cotton, alfalfa, and vegetable crops. Eventually groundwater levels fell and pumping costs rose. In addition, periodic floods in Phoenix's usually dry riverbeds isolated parts of the city and threatened its airport. Nature appeared to be playing games in Arizona.

As a result of a compromise brokered by the U.S. Supreme Court earlier in this century, Arizona had a legal right to divert to commercial use a substantial amount of Colorado River water flowing through the state. California, by default, was permitted to use any water not diverted by the other Colorado River states.[2] Arizona saw this source of water as a solution to its depleted groundwater. It also saw the facilities that would store the water as providing "free" flood control.

The engineering solution to Arizona's water problems, authorized in the later 1970s, was the Central Arizona Project (CAP). CAP would divert water from the Colorado River at Havasu Lake behind Parker Dam on the California–Arizona border, pump it over 2,000 vertical feet up and move it through a concrete-lined canal 25 feet deep and 130 feet wide. The water would then travel through 335 miles of aqueduct to the Phoenix and Tucson areas. To provide electricity for pumping the water uphill and to subsidize the project, the federal government would buy a share of the Navajo coal-fired generating station in northern Arizona. To assure a sufficient volume of water during peak summer periods, dams and reservoirs would have to be constructed in central Arizona, and to stabilize the flow of water in Arizona's rivers, four new dams would be built. Finally, because diverting water from the Colorado would increase the salinity of its remaining water above the level set by treaties with Mexico, a desalination plant would be built and operated on the Colorado just north of the Mexican border. This massive engineering effort, estimated to cost almost $5 billion in 1994 dollars, was seen as necessary to keep the Arizona economy afloat in the face of increasingly severe water shortages that were thought to be threatening its rapid economic growth.[3] The federal government was to be repaid at low or zero interest for part of the costs of CAP over a fifty-year period by those who used the water: irrigators, cities, and industries. Although federal taxes would provide a multibillion-dollar subsidy, Arizona residents would also face billions of dollars in costs.

Arizona residents would also bear the brunt of the environmental costs of CAP. The four planned reservoirs would have flooded thousands of acres of desert river habitat, the most productive wildlife habitat and recreation areas in the state, home to both the southern bald eagle and the peregrine falcon. Natural river fisheries would be replaced by reservoir fishing. Flood control from the dams would eliminate the rejuvenating natural water flow that supports cottonwood and other flood plain vegetation. Development of flood plains for commercial and residential use would have eliminated other natural systems. The huge aqueduct and other delivery canals would have fragmented wildlife habitat and blocked migration routes. CAP would have degraded significant elements of Arizona's natural environment.

Since the time of its original proposal, the project has been scaled back. Though the pumping stations and canal are now operating, the dams and flood-control facilities have largely been dropped. Meanwhile, the project has turned out to be quite different from what was originally envisioned. Many farmers CAP was supposed to rescue refuse to use the water because it is so costly. The desalination plant was built and operated sporadically for two years, but in 1993 it shut down. The City of Tucson has had to limit its delivery of CAP water to residents because of its unsafe mineral content. The State of Arizona is struggling over how to pay its share of the cost of the project without higher taxes and water charges, which could slow economic development. Arizona is asking Congress to postpone the beginning of the repayment period.

All of these problems had been predicted by CAP critics long before construction began. The analysis of how an economic plum became economic poison reveals the dangers inherent in uncritical efforts to harness nature for narrow commercial purposes.

The Water Development Game

The fatal flaw in the design of CAP was the assumption that additional water would have very high value to the state economy. Because Arizona is desert this assumption was accepted as intuitively obvious, except to economists. From the beginning Arizona's leading water economists, some of the nation's best water economists, disputed this.[4] Agriculture accounted for 90 percent of the state's water use, but most of that water was used to grow relatively low-valued crops. In addition, Arizona was no longer primarily an agricultural state. Only about 3 percent of the state's economic output was directly tied to agriculture. Over half of Arizona's water consumption went to agricultural uses of such low value that they were responsible for only 1.5 percent of total personal income. Those uses, including the irrigation of livestock forage and feed grain, contributed only one-thirtieth of 1 percent as much to personal income as manufacturing, trade, transportation, or services would have if they had consumed the same amount. That is, the water would have had a 3,000-fold larger impact on the economy if it had been used outside of agriculture. For livestock production, utilities, mining, and primary metals, water would have been 100 times more productive in supporting economic activity.[5]

Of course, most of the water being used in agriculture was not needed in these nonagricultural sectors. The point is that as the demand for water rose elsewhere in the Arizona economy, water could be switched from low-productivity uses in agriculture to much higher-productivity uses outside of agriculture with almost no negative impact on the Arizona economy.[6] Additional high-cost water sources were not needed to support ongoing growth of the state economy. Most of the water was simply being held in economically marginal uses until it was needed elsewhere in the economy. As elsewhere, however, agriculture was considered fundamental to the overall economic health of the state. A serious water shortage was sure to "strangle" development.[7]

Strangely enough for a desert state with a serious water shortage, per capita consumption of water was three times the average for the United States, making Arizona the seventh largest water user per capita in the nation.[8] The reason is clear: when a productive resource is made freely available or at a heavily subsidized price, demand always exceeds supply.

Another way of approaching the value of the additional water that CAP was planning to provide is to ask how much expected users would be willing to pay for it. After all, they should have a good idea of how additional water would allow them to increase returns from their operations. After comparing this value to the cost of the water that CAP was going to deliver, a judgment could be made about the economic and financial feasibility of the project. For most large-scale agriculture, the price that water users could afford to pay and remain profitable was between $10 and $20 per acre-foot.[9] But the cost of water from CAP ran to $100 per acre-foot. It was only through subsidies from federal and state taxpayers that CAP water would be made available to farms at much less than $100.[10] There were other substantial private costs associated with using CAP water. Many existing irrigators who were to switch from groundwater to CAP water would have to pay not only for the latter but also for distribution systems to carry the water from an aqueduct or irrigation district canal to their farms. The value of the additional water for use in agriculture was only a fraction of the cost of providing CAP water. Even with subsidies, farmers would not be able to afford it.

This was confirmed after the $5 billion had been invested and CAP completed. Irrigation districts originally tried to sell the water for more than $60 per acre-foot to farmers, the price necessary to cover Arizona's share of the cost of the project and of the distribution system. Few farmers were willing to buy. Less than half of the acreage that could have been irrigated by CAP water was contracted for that water. In irrigation districts that did contract for CAP water, purchases dropped by almost 50 percent between 1989 and 1991, before price-incentive programs were put in place. And those irrigation districts that borrowed money to build the delivery systems were driven to near or actual bankruptcy by the additional cost. Others have abandoned use of CAP water, transferring their CAP water rights to urban areas. As one Tucson area county supervisor said, "For the past 50 years, agricultural interests have dreamed of obtaining Colorado River water. And that dream is coming awfully close to becoming a nightmare for agriculture."[11]

To avoid the embarrassment of canals full of unsold water that has been moved hundreds of miles at the cost of billions of dollars, a variety of maneuvers are under way to shift more of the cost of the project to federal taxpayers. The federal government has been buying some of the water back and assigning it to Indian tribes to satisfy their water rights claims. But the tribes have little opportunity to use the water, and so may simply lease it back to white farmers at a price well below what the federal government paid to obtain the water rights.[12] Irrigation districts have been arguing that they cannot afford to pay more than $15 to $30 per acre-foot for CAP water.

Prices this low could be arranged if the state and cities were to purchase agricultural water rights at the high price and then lease the water back to farmers at a much lower price until it was needed elsewhere. Alternatively, irrigators who are now pumping groundwater could be allowed to trade some of that source for CAP water at about what it costs now to pump groundwater, the justification being that, indirectly, reduced pumping would help recharge the underground aquifer. In addition, some of the water that farmers cannot afford to use could be applied to urban golf courses, a much higher-valued use than agriculture. But the prices that potential agricultural users are willing to pay will still not generate the income to repay the $2 billion Arizona owes the federal government for building the project.[13] CAP water is not worth its production cost, even before any questions are raised about the environmental costs of diverting this water from the Colorado River and building hundreds of miles of canals across the Arizona desert.

The maneuvering by irrigators to shift the costs associated with the project serving them to someone else is a familiar strategy that one economist has called "the water development game.[14] When funding for construction of a project is being sought from the government, additional water is characterized as having fantastic power to transform an area's economy. Once the infrastructure is in place and costs are sunk, recipients of the water plead poverty and produce the same type of economic analysis that would have shown the project to be uneconomical to begin with, except that now the analysis is used to show that farmers cannot pay their share of the cost. Typically this ploy is successful.

What about the cost of desalted water produced at the Yuma plant so that Colorado River water crossing the border into Mexico could meet water-quality treaty obligations? That plant cost $256 million to build and about $30 million a year to operate. If it were to operate at peak capacity rather than the one-third capacity it averaged before shutting down in 1993, the annual cost of an acre-foot of water produced would be about $480, way above the $7 per acre-foot now charged by the Salt River Project to the City of Phoenix or the $17 per acre-foot that has been proposed by irrigation districts for CAP water.[15] Because this plant was partially built to allow the diversion of more CAP water out of the Colorado, it represents an additional cost for that water. The combined cost of the two efforts to supply additional water to central Arizona is astronomical. Water must indeed be priceless to justify incurring costs of this magnitude so that hay, barley, or cotton can be grown in the desert rather than in more suitable climates.

And the Costs Go on . . . and on . . . and on

When federal dollars are used to subsidize irrigation of crops such as cotton, feed grain, citrus fruit, and vegetables, it doesn't just increase Arizona agricultural production. Because there is a limited demand for food products, increased production in one area tends to decrease production elsewhere. To the extent that this is true, the benefit of expanded production in Arizona comes at a cost: the net gain from federally subsidized expansion of agriculture is much smaller than the irrigation project's gross output would suggest.

This is most obvious in programs where production is already surplus. Because of oversupply and low prices, the federal government often intervenes to support cotton, feed grain, and wheat prices and adopts programs to reduce these crops by paying farmers to take farmland out of production. In the late 1970s when CAP was authorized, 73 percent of Arizona's irrigated acreage was producing crops that were eligible for such federal subsidies.[16] The right hand was ignoring what the left hand was doing: one federal program boosted production of surplus agricultural products while another sought to reduce production of the same crops. The federal taxpayer was footing the bill two or three times, subsidizing irrigation projects, then making price-support payments, and finally paying other farmers to take their land out of production. In this context, it is hard to imagine that there is any benefit at all to subsidized expansion of irrigated agriculture.

Subsidized expansion of agriculture does not just have a negative impact on the U.S. taxpayer. It also systematically drives out of business farmers raising the same crops who have not benefited from an irrigation subsidy. When Idaho became a major producer of potatoes as a result of subsidized irrigation of the desertland along the Snake River plain, it drove potato prices down. Potato producers in Wisconsin, Maine, and elsewhere who had just barely survived commercially before the subsidized expansion of Idaho's potato crop were run out of business. The same can be said about expanded cotton production in the Southwest during the 1960s that was supported by federally subsidized irrigation—it coincided with a 50 percent decline in cotton acreage in the Southeast. Empirical analysis of the impact of federally subsidized expansion of agriculture in the West shows that it displaced 5 to 17 million acres of farmland in areas that did not qualify for federal "reclamation" support.[17] This is robbing Peter to pay Paul, with a perverse twist. Western states that were receiving subsidies were part of the fastest-growing areas of the nation, while rural areas being displaced elsewhere in the nation were already sliding into depression. The uneconomic and environmentally destructive nature of massive federal irrigation projects aside, their social costs are immense.

Shifting water from supporting agriculture to supporting urban expansion does not entirely solve the dilemma caused by CAP. CAP water, with high total dissolved solid (TDS) concentrations, has to be extensively treated before it can be used for household purposes. Even treated water, if it is used in metal plumbing that previously delivered groundwater, can corrode pipes and emerge from the household tap rusty and foul-smelling. It has to be softened for household use and requires more laundry detergent.[18]

This was especially a problem in the Tucson area where people were used to high-quality groundwater. Tucson's first delivery of CAP water unleashed a storm of complaints about costly damage. The city council initially voted to suspend use of CAP water until the problems could be worked out. But when the Arizona state government and congressional delegation put pressure on Tucson to keep using CAP water so that the state's debt could be paid off, Tucson compromised by switching only half of the residents being served with CAP water back to groundwater. For those left with CAP water, the city had to install filters, pay claims for broken pipes and damaged appliances, and reduce water bills in compensation for the increased flow necessary before tap water could be used. Moreover, Tucson will have to spend about $100 million to replace 200 miles of steel water mains being corroded by the CAP water. An additional treatment plant will have to be built to remove more of the corrosive elements from the water. Owners of older homes with metal plumbing face bills of $10,000 or more to replumb their homes. These costs are on top of the $250 million that Tucson had to invest to build the delivery system and initial treatment plant for CAP water.[19] All of these problems, too, were predicted before the project was built.[20] In 1995 the citizens of Tucson passed an initiative limiting the use of CAP water in the city water system. The initiative prohibits the use of CAP water for city homes for five years or until the water can be treated to match the quality of the city's groundwater. Either alternative will be costly to the city and state.

Clearly CAP is an economic catastrophe of major proportions, to the taxpayer, to the irrigation districts, to competing farmers, to urban residents, and to the environment. Water and agriculture were freed of normal market discipline because of their unique status as the assumed core of the Arizona economy, and one cannot escape the conclusion that massive economic and environmental waste were incurred for the pipe dream of blooming alfalfa fields in the desert. The agricultural exemption to economic logic is both costly and dangerous.

Killing Those That Kill:
Compound 1080 and Coyotes

In 1972 President Nixon surprised environmentalists as well as his more conservative allies in the West by banning the use of compound 1080 (sodium monofluoroacetate) for the control of livestock predators, primarily coyotes. Compound 1080 is an extremely toxic chemical: a teaspoon can kill up to a hundred human beings. The compound had been applied to beef carcasses used as bait to attract and kill coyotes. Unfortunately, more than coyotes fed on the poisoned bait, and of course other animals fed on the poisoned coyotes. Compound 1080 caused secondary poisoning of wildlife, some of which, like eagles and hawks, were threatened or endangered species. Stock-growing organizations and elected leaders from western states immediately began lobbying to lift the ban. In the early 1980s, the U.S. Environmental Protection Agency (EPA) began hearings on proposals to reauthorize the use of 1080 for controlling coyotes.

The basic argument for lifting the ban on 1080 was economic. Predation by coyotes, critics argued, was one of the chief threats to the viability of the U.S. sheep industry. In the absence of cheap and effective coyote control, the rising cost of raising sheep would throw American producers out of the competition with foreign producers. As evidence of the depth of the problem, advocates of 1080 pointed to the drastic decline in the number of sheep being raised in this country over the last thirty-five years. The ban, it was suggested, would be the coup de grace of the industry in the United States. And because the industry was concentrated in the rural West, it would represent a devastating blow to rural economies in that region.

There is a familiar ring to this. It assumes that agriculture lies at the heart of an economy. But as we have seen, today agriculture plays an increasingly smaller role in almost all state economies. Regardless of its quantitative size, agriculture is unlikely to be a source of economic vitality in America's local economies because it is largely a mature industry whose contribution to employment and income is bound to shrink further over time.

The Predator Market

It is true that sheep raising has declined precipitously over the past four decades: sheep herds in the early 1980s were only a fifth the size they were in the 1940s.[21] The decline is largely explained in terms of shifting consumer preferences. As a more uniform American diet replaced more specialized ethnic diets, per capita consumption of lamb declined by 60 percent between 1950 and 1980, while per capita beef consumption increased by 66 percent.[22] Similarly, the development of the synthetic fiber industry after World War II significantly undercut demand for wool. While per capita wool consumption declined 57 percent between 1955 and 1971, per capita synthetic fiber consumption rose 128 percent. With up to 40 percent of gross sheep-raising income derived from the sale of wool, this seriously affected the profitability of the sheep industry.[23]

There were other forces at work. As farm operators grew more and more dependent on off-farm work for their income, they had to adjust the type of agricultural activities in which they engaged. Farm activities that required continuous attention such as sheep raising were not as compatible with off-farm work as raising cattle or crops. Related to this was the problem of obtaining workers to help with sheep raising. The experienced, cheap immigrant sheepherders of previous decades were no longer available.

Shrinking demand and increasing costs associated with sheep raising led farmers and ranchers to make a rational adjustment in the mix of economic activities in which they engaged. Few sheep raisers had raised only sheep. Most had also raised cattle and crops.[24] Thus the shift away from sheep did not require that resources be abandoned. Land, capital, managerial effort, labor, and equipment were simply shifted from one type of economic activity to another, not a catastrophic loss but an adaptation to market forces.

Predation and Individual Sheep-Raising Operations

Not all sheep operators are seriously affected by predation, in fact, the majority of producers are not. Analysis of losses in western states after the ban on 1080 indicates that almost half of commercial producers lost no lambs and two-thirds lost no sheep to predation.[25] Only about a quarter of commercial producers lost more than 10 percent of their lambs. Three-quarters of all deaths of lambs and sheep are related not to predation but to birthing complications, old age, disease, parasites, bloat, theft, weather, and poisonous plants. Seen in this context, predation losses seem to have been exaggerated. Even ranches that do experience significant predation losses are not necessarily threatened financially by those losses. Analysis of the sustainable level of predation losses on well-managed ranches indicates a rate as high as 15 percent. Stated somewhat differently, a relatively high rate of predation does not result in a low financial return on sheep raising. If returns on sheep raising in those regions of the nation with the highest predation rates are compared with returns on sheep raising in regions with little or no predation, the returns are highest in the regions with the highest rates of predation. There is actually a significant positive correlation between high predation rates and net returns on sheep raising by region.[26]

Sheep management choice appears to be one of the primary determinants of the level of loss to predation. Obviously, operations that turn their livestock out into unfenced grazing land where they are largely unattended and where lambing takes place on the open range are likely to have high losses. Operations that closely supervise flocks, keeping lambs in enclosed sheds and controlling the movement of sheep, have much lower predation rates. Use of open federal grazing land reduces sheep-raising costs while increasing the risk of predation. Of course, close supervision is more costly in terms of labor, fencing, buildings, and grazing fees. Whether those additional costs are justified by lower predation rates is an economic calculation. Some sheep operators purposely adopt management strategies that increase their flocks' exposure to predators in order to reduce the cost of their operations. If they choose to do so, why should the public be expected to support predator-control programs, or why should wildlife be sacrificed? Risking predation to cut management costs is a voluntary business decision like any other. The manager making this choice should bear the costs associated with the risk. Otherwise there would be no incentive to make the responsible management decision.

Predation and the Industry of Sheep Raising

In a market setting, measures that benefit some individual producers, such as predator control, can actually harm producers as a whole. This is a widely recognized phenomenon in agricultural markets where demand is limited but the ability to produce is easily capable of expansion. In that situation, increased production puts downward pressure on the price suppliers can get. Increased production lowers total revenue earned, while reduced production raises it. This is why government farm-support programs seek to limit production and why private fruit-marketing groups often destroy part of a crop rather than market it. For individual producers, costless increases in production are always good, but such increases can leave producers as a group worse off because of the lower prices obtained.

In the lamb industry, what primarily determines whether increased production will have this overall negative impact is the sensitivity of prices to changes in the quantity placed on the market. If substantial additional marketing can be absorbed with little impact on price, the benefit of increased production will not be entirely offset by a decrease in price. On the other hand, if demand is limited and more marketing can be absorbed only with a considerable price reduction, increased production will make lamb producers as a group worse off.

This inverse relationship between market price and quantity is one of the most fundamental and widely recognized principles of economics. It tells us that we cannot calculate the economic impact of predation by simply multiplying the quantity of lambs lost by the market value of those lambs. As the quantity of lamb marketed changes, so does the price at which lamb is sold. This interaction has to be taken into account when predation is being discussed. By reducing the total amount of lamb marketed, predation may actually increase revenue received by sheep producers as a group.[27] Only an empirical analysis of price flexibility can tell us whether sheep raisers as a group gain or lose from predation, and by how much. If price flexibility is greater than one, meaning that a 10 percent increase in marketing would depress market prices by more than 10 percent, then increased production will be accompanied by decreased revenue.

Empirical analysis of the relationship between lamb marketing and the price received by sheep raisers for their lamb indicates a farm-level price flexibility in the 1.4 to 0.9 range.[28] Thus it is quite possible that increased predator control will reduce sheep-raising revenue by depressing prices more than enough to offset the revenue from increased sales of saved animals. Even if this is not the case, with price flexibility close to one, most of the gains from increased sales will be offset by the losses associated with decreased prices. Predator control will do little to assist sheep raisers as a group.

Because stock growers as a group do not necessarily benefit from predator control, their strong support for these programs in general and for 1080 in particular may seem puzzling. Ranchers and farmers tend to view the market from an individual perspective. For the individual stock grower, increased production represents the optimal response to the market situation he or she faces. If others are cutting back production, prices will rise and the individual who expands production will reap the benefits. If others are increasing production, not doing the same will not keep the prices an individual faces from falling. If a grower cuts production and faces declining prices, he or she is clearly worse off. This is a typical prisoners' dilemma. What is best for the individual is not best for the group, but it is difficult for the group to act in pursuit of their collective self-interest. Furthermore, those suffering directly from predators have a lot to gain from effective control, while the majority who may lose slightly as a result of reduced prices have a much more diffuse interest. As a result, those with a direct interest in predator control tend to be heard more clearly.

It makes a difference that most of the cost of predator control does not have to be paid by those who ask for the service. Federal and state governments carry the bulk, freeing stock growers from concern about the cost-effectiveness of the effort. Predator control, of course, goes far beyond the use of 1080 to poison coyotes. It also involves such methods and devices as aerial gunning, trapping, locating and destroying dens with cubs, and automated cyanide traps (M-44 "coyote getters"). If individual stock growers had to purchase the amount of predator control that they thought was cost effective for their operations, they might opt for a less intense approach or change management methods so that their flocks were not as vulnerable to predation. Other costs of predator control—the intended death of certain wildlife species and the unintended death of others—get shifted to the owners of that wildlife, the general public. That is, one of the resources consumed in predator control efforts is provided free to the stockgrowers.

Publicly funded predator control is just one of a broad range of public support programs for sheep raisers. Until the mid-1990s, the federal government made "wool incentive" payments, financed out of tariffs on imported wool and wool products, to supplement the income of sheep raisers. This gave double support to sheep raisers, providing supplemental income while discouraging foreign competition. In addition, many western sheep flocks graze on federal land for fees well below market value. As a result of this type of subsidy, sheep-raising operations that rely more heavily on public land for their feed have earned a much higher return on their investment.[29]

Some might find it hard to believe that coyotes are doing sheep raisers as a group a favor by devouring their lambs. But it is common for private and government agricultural marketing agencies to actively restrict or reduce supply in order to protect prices, for example, by destroying parts of a harvest or dumping surplus dairy products. This raises serious questions about federally subsidized predator control activities, one of the chief justifications for which is to make sheep raising more viable. Empirical evidence suggests that effective predator control does not accomplish its ultimate objective. Killing coyotes not only wastes tax dollars and public wildlife, it also hurts the very people it was intended to help.

What was the result of the EPA's hearings on proposals to reauthorize the use of 1080 for killing coyotes? In 1985 the agency approved the use of compound 1080 in special livestock collars designed to give coyotes a fatal dose if they attacked sheep. It rejected a return to the use of "bait stations," poisoned carcasses distributed in "problem" areas. That decision satisfied neither wildlife advocates nor stock growers. Those concerned with wildlife feared the reintroduction of this potent poison onto the range would lead to illegal use by ranchers and widespread poisoning, while stock growers saw the authorization of a specialized, experimental use as just a continuation of the ban. In 1994 the Texas Department of Agriculture requested a public-health exemption from the EPA ban to control the spread of gray fox rabies in forty-three counties. Wildlife groups interpreted this not as a rabies control program but as a return to earlier efforts to eliminate what agricultural interests say are pests and predators: the gray fox, red fox, coyote, bobcat, raccoon, striped skunk, and ringtail. In late 1994 the EPA denied the department's request on the grounds that 1080 would not be effective in controlling rabies and was not selective in the species it killed.[30]

Eliminating the Competition: Prairie Dogs and Strychnine

Prairie dog "towns" are common on grazing land in the West. Large expanses of tall forbs and grasses are stripped bare by the scurrying rodents, apparently reducing the cattle carrying capacity of the land and increasing feed costs for cattle ranchers. The solution preferred by stock growers is to eliminate the competition by poisoning prairie dogs with strychnine-laced grain. The problem with this solution is that it is not only prairie dogs that eat the poisoned grain. Birds do too, including bald eagles and golden eagles and peregrine falcons, which in the early 1980s were protected species. The nearly extinct black-footed ferret preys on prairie dogs and may be killed by the strychnine too. Because of such environmental problems, in 1983 the EPA proposed a ban on strychnine for this particular use. Stock growers objected vehemently that large portions of America's grazing lands would now be overtaken by prairie dogs. This, it was asserted, would have a costly impact on the U.S. cattle industry.

Advocates for the continued use of strychnine to control prairie dogs put forth questionable arguments. First, they depend on impressions rather than science in gauging the impact of prairie dogs on potential cattle forage. Second, they assume there is no alternative means of control available. Third, their usual method of estimating losses to stock growers seems to implicitly assume that prairie dogs eat cattle rather than grasses and forbs. Fourth, they assume that control efforts are effective and cost justified. Finally, they figure that there is an unlimited demand for beef. All of these assumptions are contradicted by empirical evidence. When they are abandoned, the economic "losses" to stock growers associated with banning strychnine as a prairie dog rodenticide disappear.

Appearance versus Scientific Reality

It is the appearance of prairie dog towns that leads stock growers to assume that prairie dogs alone are responsible for the land's reduced plant productivity and increased susceptibility to wind and water erosion. But scientific analysis of the actual role of prairie dogs does not support this. Cattle that graze on land colonized by prairie dogs show no less weight gain than those that graze adjacent uncolonized lands. Furthermore, plant production is not increased by the removal of prairie dogs. Indeed, prairie dogs may help some valuable grasses and forbs to grow by "clipping" tall plants, which can stimulate plant production, as well as by aerating and mixing soils through their activity. Prairie dogs increase species diversity in prairie ecosystems, making them biologically richer, and actually reduce erosion. Finally, because thick vegetation makes them too easy a target for their natural predators, prairie dogs tend to colonize areas that are already overgrazed. It may be that, contrary to what stock growers assert, prairie dogs move into areas that cattle have badly overgrazed. In that case it would be cattle grazing that causes the problem, not prairie dogs.[31] It is unclear from the scientific literature that prairie dogs are damaging the range and hurting the cattle raising industry. If they are not doing damage, obviously no loss is associated with restricting methods to control them.

Alternatives to Strychnine

If strychnine were the only effective tool against prairie dogs, then one could identify the damage done by prairie dogs that would have been controlled with strychnine as the cost associated with the restriction on strychnine. But if there are alternative methods available to control prairie dogs, then the only cost that can be assigned to restricting strychnine is the higher cost or lower effectiveness of the alternatives. In fact, there is an alternative available, zinc phosphide, which by the mid-1980s was already being used in 85 percent of efforts to control prairie dogs.[32] This substance, which is equally effective and costs about the same, drastically reduces or eliminates any cost associated with restricting strychnine. It might be argued that the remaining 15 percent of control efforts rely on strychnine because only it will work or because it is less expensive in those circumstances. But this may not be the case. Technological innovations that involve lower-cost production are not quickly and automatically adopted by all producers. That is one of the reasons that agricultural extension agencies have operated for more than half a century. Innovations in production spread slowly because producers have invested time and money in particular techniques and lack experience with new methods. Until there is no alternative but to change, familiarity tends to hold sway. This is likely the case with strychnine.

Carnivorous Prairie Dogs?

One common method of calculating losses associated with limiting strychnine is to estimate the reduced cattle-carrying capacity of a grazing allotment (that is, reduced cattle production) and multiply it by the value of the additional cattle that would have been raised in the absence of prairie dogs. This approach implicitly assumes that prairie dogs eat beef cattle, an amazing feat for a small rodent! At worst, prairie dogs reduce the forage available to stock growers. The value of needed replacement forage is what should be used to measure the cost associated with prairie dogs. Since grazing lands are regularly leased and forage and feed grains regularly bought and sold, we have the information to establish the value of any lost forage once we know how much, if any, the forage-producing capacity of the land has been reduced by prairie dogs. To use the value of cattle or the profits that could have been made by raising additional cattle to measure the losses caused by prairie dogs is to attribute to cattle feed the full value of the cattle-raising operation. If this were appropriate, we should value hay in the same way, that is, by asking how many cows a given amount of hay could feed and multiplying that by the value of the cows. This wouldn't make any sense, since it takes many inputs other than forage to raise cattle. Range and pasture costs represent only 5 to 10 percent of total cattle production costs in the West.[33] This tail cannot be used to wag the economic dog when analyzing the impact of prairie dogs. Forage is one of the low-cost inputs in cattle raising. It is the value of this low-cost input that may (questionably) be reduced by prairie dogs.

Prairie Dog Control: Cost Effective?

Most prairie dog colonies are not controlled because of the expense. It is only when public monies are made available that stock growers become enthusiastic about controlling prairie dogs. Control is not just a matter of spreading poisoned grain around and then going home. Prairie dog colonies scatter over considerable acreage. Each colony has to be visited once to spread the poison, then systematically revisited to prevent it from being recolonized by surviving prairie dogs. There are substantial administrative overhead costs associated with planning, management, and pre- and post-treatment monitoring. A 1985 survey of control costs found the full price to be at least $5 per acre of range ($7 in 1995 dollars).[34] At any rate, it takes time for grazing land to respond to changes in animal use. The elimination of prairie dogs does not immediately change the volume and character of vegetation. That can take many years. The cost of control is incurred now for uncertain benefits in the distant future. When that cost is compared with the value of forage, it becomes clear why ranchers do not readily pursue control on their own.

It takes several acres of grazing land to provide a month's worth of forage for a cow in the West, and stock growers are paying only a dollar or so an acre for the forage available on public land. Stock growers who lease public land insist that that is all its forage is worth. How, then, can spending $5 to $10 per acre to remove prairie dogs who may or may not eat some of the forage possibly be justified?[35] Private landowners know this. In general, they do not pursue the ambitious eradication programs the federal government conducts. Of the estimated 2 to 4 million acres of land populated by prairie dogs, control efforts are attempted on less than 500,000 acres. Between 75 and 90 percent of the colonized acres are left untreated.[36] Of course, if the costs of controlling prairie dogs are greater than the benefits of control, there is no economic loss in abandoning control efforts. In fact, trying to control prairie dogs in this situation is just a waste of resources.

Unlimited Demand for Beef?

Just as coyotes may be doing sheep growers as a group a favor by restricting the amount of lamb being placed on the market, prairie dogs, if they actually do reduce the total number of cattle being raised, are doing a favor for the cattle industry as a whole. Because forage obtained on open range is just one type of feed used in the production of beef cattle, it is not easy to state what the impact of a loss of a certain amount of this feed source would be. Even cattle raisers who depend largely on unimproved rangeland feed their cattle such supplements as hay, grain, crop residue, and protein. When one type of feed becomes less available or relatively more expensive, other types are substituted. The net impact of a reduction in one source would be an increase in the cost of producing cattle, in turn reducing the total number of cattle marketed and putting upward pressure on cattle prices. Whether higher prices would offset the decline in quantity and boost total revenue would depend on cattle price flexibility.[37] Studies over the last twenty-five years have consistently shown that price flexibility is between 1.5 and 2, meaning that a 10 percent decline in the quantity marketed will result in a 15 to 20 percent price increase. Thus, if prairie dogs reduce the number of cattle placed on the market, the revenue going to cattle raisers as a group will rise, not fall. Prairie dogs—if they damage forage—may help restrict the supply and boost the prices all stock growers get for their cattle.

The Incredible Shrinking Effect of Prairie Dogs

Is limiting strychnine use for prairie dog control the wrong course to take? Consider the cumulative impact of the following conservative assumptions:

- Prairie dogs do not completely destroy the forage value of land they colonize. We do not know whether the impact is even negative. Assume—contrary to empirical evidence—that half of the forage value is lost.
- In the absence of strychnine, prairie dogs can be controlled by agents of similar cost and effectiveness. At worst, just a small fraction of the areas where control is sought can only be controlled with strychnine. Assume that 10 percent can only be controlled with strychnine.
- Because of the expense, control efforts are targeted at only a small percentage of the total area inhabited by prairie dogs. Assume 15 percent of the colonized area is controlled (10 to 25 percent is typically controlled).
- Only a tiny percentage of total cattle feed sources are affected by prairie dogs. Assume that one-tenth of 1 percent of total cattle feed is associated with the land colonized by prairie dogs.[38]

These assumptions have a multiplicative impact: 0.5 x 0.1 x 0.15 x 0.001 = 0.0000075 or 7.5 per million. That is, based on conservative assumptions, the absence of strychnine to control prairie dogs would reduce cattle production by only 750 head out of the national inventory of about 100 million head. Moreover, this reduction would tend to increase the returns to cattle raisers as a group, not decrease them. There would be a net economic cost: although rising cattle prices and revenues are good for stock growers, they are not good for consumers, who would see food costs rise slightly. The economic question that needs to be answered is whether protecting other types of wildlife from strychnine poisoning is worth this small cost.

After issuing its notice of intent to cancel the registration of strychnine for control of prairie dogs in 1983, the EPA entered into negotiations with all parties that lasted over two years. Subsequently, all but two of the parties reached an agreement that allowed continued aboveground use of strychnine for control of prairie dogs if certain safeguards were implemented. The two environmental groups rejecting the settlement sued the EPA on the grounds, among other things, that continued registration of strychnine for this purpose violated the Endangered Species Act. Federal courts supported this claim and found that by registering strychnine for above-ground use for prairie dog control, the EPA was causing the illegal taking of endangered or threatened species. Effectively, this court decision banned the use of strychnine for controlling prairie dogs.

Marketing the Landscape: Tourism and the Local Economy

Extractive activities such as mining, timber, and agriculture are not the only natural resource—associated industries. In certain locations natural resources attract the nonextractive activities of tourism and commercial recreation. Visitors who purchase goods and services inject income into the local economy in the same way that the export of raw materials and manufactured goods does. In this sense, tourism is part of the economic base that provides employment and income to residents. But it is important to understand that it is not only through tourism that environmental amenities affect local economic well-being. In fact, in most communities the primary economic relationship between such amenities and the local economy is not likely to be tourism. As discussed earlier, the primary economic role of local environmental quality is its importance to current and potential local residents.

This is an important point, considering the potentially disruptive impact of high-volume tourism on local communities. Take, for example, the ski resort Big Mountain in Whitefish, Montana. Given the number of skiers who travel there, one might expect tourism to be the backbone of the local economy. But when the City of Whitefish studied its economy in preparation for an application to the Montana state government to levy a tourist-oriented "bed and board tax," it found that the impact of retirees settling in the area far exceeded that of tourists.[1] It was new permanent residents that lay behind the area's growth, not visitors. Of course, tourism often does have the potential to make a significant contribution to local economic vitality too.

The positive contribution that tourism can make to local economies

213

became clear during the 1980s. By the middle of the decade an unusual alignment of economic forces taking place in many nonmetropolitan areas of the United States caused traditional natural resource
industries—energy minerals, metal mining, lumber, and agriculture—
to slip into depression simultaneously. Only one natural resource industry continued to expand significantly, tourism and recreation, providing welcome support to many communities during hard times.
These changes—decline in the extractive sectors and expansion in the
tourist and recreation sectors—were actually part of an ongoing economic transformation of many of America's "natural resource–dependent" communities.

Travel and Recreation: Burgeoning Industries

Statistics on the travel industry are impressive. In the United States in
1990, over 10 million people were employed in tourist-related businesses, which took in over 330 billion dollars.[2] American travel industry
employment has been growing at over 4 percent per year, part of a
worldwide phenomenon. International travel, growing at 9 percent per
year, now accounts for 7 percent of total world exports and about 26
percent of international trade in services.[3] There is no indication that
this growth is likely to stop or even slow. The travel industry offers substantial new economic opportunity to individuals and communities.

In some ways, however, the statistics are misleading. It is difficult to
define exactly what the travel or tourist industry includes. People travel
for many different reasons and spend money on a broad range of businesses that primarily serve clients other than travelers. Unless we are
careful about what we are talking about and measuring, we may end up
counting as tourism economic activities that have nothing to do with
what most of us mean by that word, thereby exaggerating the economic
importance and potential of tourism.

To most people, tourism refers to travel for the pleasure and satisfaction of visiting certain sites. It does not refer to business-related
travel or travel to visit relatives or friends. A travel industry that serves
all travel is much broader than a tourist industry. About a quarter of
travel is undertaken for business purposes, another third to visit friends
and relatives. Only about a third is undertaken for "other pleasure."[4]
Moreover, it is hard to classify expenditures in restaurants, nightclubs,
gas stations, supermarkets, and shopping malls since these businesses,

though they receive half or more of tourist dollars, are not primarily travel-related.[5] The tourist industry is really a heterogeneous group of businesses most of which do not cater exclusively to tourists. To estimate the extent to which they are supported by tourist expenditure, we need to analyze the pattern of local tourist expenditure. Regularly reported business data do not measure the size of the tourist industry.

Simply because a sector is difficult to measure does not mean that it is any less real or important. If we scale back our measure of tourism from general travel to travel for pleasure, employment falls from 10 million to 6 million in the United States, but even this reduced work force earned almost $80 billion in the late 1980s.[6] Tourism represents a sizable and growing market into which communities can seek to tap.

Tourism: The Good and the Bad

As communities come to terms with the growing environmental sensitivity of their citizens, economic activities that damage the environment lose their allure and sometimes the political support needed to attract or retain them. Communities contemplating their economic development tend to search for clean industry, economic activities that will provide employment and income without environmental burdens. The old days of "smokestack chasing" have largely come to an end. Recreation and tourism may be attractive options. After all, they seek to capitalize on a region's natural beauty, and thus it is in their interest to preserve the landscape. Tourism is nonextractive. What the local community provides is the services that make access to the landscape and local culture possible. In fact, tourism's growth can be seen as just one part of the two-century-old shift in the economy from goods to services, which tend to be labor intensive rather than raw material or goods intensive.

Tourism is not exclusively a rural phenomenon. In fact, metropolitan tourism is growing as fast as or faster than tourism in our hinterlands. Nonetheless, tourist development in nonmetropolitan areas can help support more decentralized residential and economic patterns. For example, it is often after visiting an area as tourists that people decide to move their residence or business. Tourism is how both people and businesses "discover" places. In that sense, tourism is a recruiting device; the community puts its best face forward, attracting new permanent residents and revitalizing the economy.

Another advantage of a tourist industry is that its jobs are readily accessible to local residents, often requiring familiarity with the area. Unlike some industries imported from the outside and calling for specialized skills that the local population lacks, tourism offers many entry-level jobs. Because of the part-time and seasonal nature of many tourist jobs, they may also complement other pursuits such as farming, home-making, or school.

Finally, as mentioned above, the long-run trend in tourist employment and income is up, and there seems to be more of a future in tourism than in some traditional sectors of the economic base. Although one could argue that tourism is just another boom that will ultimately leave our communities bust, the length of tourism's cycle is much longer than timber or mining or agriculture's. Most leading tourist destinations in the United States have enjoyed expanding or at least stable markets for a long time. Florida, Washington, D.C., Yellowstone and Yosemite National Parks, Disneyland and Disney World, Nevada's gaming and entertainment industry—all appear to have long-term viability. Although some health spas have become ghost towns in the past, most modern-day ghost towns are the result of something other than collapsing tourism, for instance, lumber, mining, or agriculture.

Despite tourism's pluses, communities should carefully weigh their options before latching onto this industry as environmentally benign and economically promising. Only with its eyes wide open to all economic development proposals can a community mold economic development to its own ends. And there are a number of serious problems associated with tourism of which communities should be aware. First, employment tends to be low-income, unskilled, and dead end. Second, vacation homes and other tourist developments tend to drive up property values and the cost of living, driving out existing residents. Third, tourism brings in a flood of temporary visitors whose holiday mood and disregard for the local community can disrupt and permanently alter it. Fourth, tourists and recreationists put a lot of wear and tear on the natural landscape. Tourism isn't always, or even often, environmentally benign.

Tourism and the Quality of Employment

The average income associated with jobs in tourism is low. In 1986, for instance, the U.S. Travel Data Center reported that the industry generated 5.5 million jobs with an annual payroll of $70.3 billion—an average per-job income of $12,800 a year, 30 to 40 percent below average annual income in all jobs in the United States.[7] Because tourist jobs tend to be part-time and seasonal, these figures do not mean that the hourly pay in tourism is 30 to 40 percent below the hourly pay in all other industries. If the annual number of hours worked on these jobs were 30 to 40 percent below the average job, the hourly wage in tourism would be the same as the national average. Nonetheless, many tourist jobs are in sectors of the economy that do pay unusually low wages. Retail trade, for instance, pays an hourly wage a third below the average wage for all workers. And because many of these jobs are part-time, benefits are likely to be small or nonexistent. Not only do tourist jobs tend to be unskilled and entry level, but they also offer limited room for advancement. There is no occupational ladder leading up from cleaning toilets in a motel.[8]

This is a pretty bleak picture, probably too bleak. As pointed out above, low annual incomes associated with tourism are tied to the fact that many tourist jobs are part-time and/or seasonal. Moreover, the part-time and seasonal character of these jobs is not necessarily or even primarily a bad thing. They employ many people who don't want full-time work, including students, farmers, and women with young children, providing supplemental income and the freedom to pursue other activities. An economy is stronger for providing diverse employment opportunities that accommodate different lifestyles.

The low income associated with tourism may be misleading in another way. Tourist-serving businesses buy inputs for their operations from other local businesses, and the wages they pay get spent in other local businesses. These indirect and induced factors need to be taken into account if one wants to describe accurately the full impact of tourist activity on the local economy.[9] Moreover, the total set of jobs directly and indirectly connected to tourism resembles a cross-section of employment in the overall economy. Tourist expenditures ultimately support construction, public administration, professional, medical, and educational services jobs, none of which tend to be low paying. The point here is not to deny that income per job is unusually low in tourism, but to note that the local impact of tourism encompasses much more than that initial income.[10]

Finally, income data on some tourist-related jobs is inaccurately reported. The most obvious example is bar and restaurant servers, who rely on gratuities for most of their income. Most professional guides and recreational instructors also receive a significant part of their income as unreported tips. Given the prevalence of personal service activity in tourism, data for this industry may seriously understate actual income.

Paying for Tourists: Housing, Cost of Living, and Taxes

Space is needed to lodge, feed, entertain, and supply tourists. When tourism grows, so does the demand for land and housing. If supplies are limited, land and building prices will rise. Because land and buildings are necessary to almost all other local economic activity, the cost of doing business in the area will also rise along with prices for locally produced goods and services. Large-scale tourism also requires public services such as roads, police and fire protection, and recreational facilities. Rising property values along with rising demand for public services will almost certainly lead to higher taxes. In short, a large tourist industry is likely to send the local cost of living up.

The impact on existing residents can be quite disruptive. In effect, temporary visitors are competing with local residents to take possession of their homes, stores, streets, and parks. Those who consider their residences, either rented or owned, as homes rather than investments will find it increasingly costly to remain in the community. Rising property taxes alone are enough to push property owners out, rising rents to push renters out. Residents may be squeezed out to the periphery of town, from which they will have to commute to work or they may be displaced altogether, moving to other areas.

Many resort towns have experienced this syndrome. One is Jackson, Wyoming, a major summer and winter resort adjacent to Grand Teton and Yellowstone National Parks. During the 1970s and 1980s Jackson's population grew 4 percent per year while jobs expanded over 6 percent per year. Total income tripled in real terms. But rising demand for limited land led the cost of living during the 1980s to rise at twice the rate for the State of Wyoming as a whole. This, combined with relatively low wages paid in tourist-oriented businesses, led average real income per job to decline by 30 percent—taking into account only the national rate of inflation. When Jackson's specific cost of living was accounted for, real earnings per job fell by 50 percent. As a report commissioned by the Jackson Main Street Association put it, "The price paid by the average worker to live in paradise was to see the purchasing power of the earned dollar almost halved in ten years."[11] To escape this squeeze, most of the work force moved out of Jackson across Teton Pass and into small towns on the Idaho side of the border.

Although this phenomenon characterizes successful resort towns, one has to be careful about how to interpret it. Clearly tourism is not unique in changing land values and raising the cost of living. The metropolitan areas of Boston, New York, Washington, D.C., San Diego, Los Angeles, and San Francisco contain 55 million people who have to cope regularly with very high costs of living. America's tourist towns taken together probably do not contain 5 percent of this number of people. In general, in an area with limited land resources, any type of rapid economic growth that causes population growth will raise land values and the cost of living. To the extent that recreation and tourism are more land intensive than other economic activities, they may trigger cost-of-living increases more quickly. Given the demand for second homes in recreation areas and the limited economic stimulus that occasional residence provides to the local economy, it may be that recreational development is unusually land intensive. But in considering the impact of tourism on local economic well-being, a community has to be clear about alternatives. If it is comparing tourist development with some other type of development that provides the same number of jobs and income, the impact on the local cost of living may be similar. If, however, it is considering the impact of tourist development with no alternative prospect for development, then the issue is not so much tourism as it is the local benefits, if any, of economic growth in general. It may be that those concerned about the impact of tourism are really objecting to population and economic growth in general.

One other aspect of increased cost of living has to be considered. Although renters are clearly harmed by rising land and rental values, the impact on home owners is mixed. As land values and the cost of living rise, home owners experience a windfall in the value of their assets. Their net worth increases. When and if they are forced out, they will pocket a fairly sizable amount of money in compensation for their loss. For those only slightly attached to the community this will be a net gain, but home owners with strong ties may consider themselves worse off. At any rate, the fact that the rising cost of living also increases the net wealth of community members who own property complicates the evaluation of who gains and who loses from development. It would be simplistic to claim that a community is better off because rising property values have increased its "wealth," just as it would be incomplete to conclude that rising property values made residents worse off.

Swallowed Up and Transformed by Tourism

Large-scale tourism brings a constant flow of strangers through a community. A flow of thousands can engulf cities with populations of 10,000 to 50,000 and obliterate small rural towns, replacing the residents with entirely new populations. Communities pursuing tourism are effectively inviting hordes of strangers to share their streets, public facilities, and commercial businesses. Very large tourist developments commonly attract outside workers to the community.[12] The net result is a major increase in the number of transients residing in the community at any given time, people who may care little about its history, culture, and values. Those who are on vacation may behave in ways they wouldn't consider appropriate in their own communities. High-rolling big spenders desperately trying to squeeze as much fun as possible into their limited vacation time can encourage a local lifestyle that no community would openly ask for. Tourism can threaten a community's most closely held values.

Resort towns such as Aspen, Colorado, and Jackson, Wyoming, have almost completely transformed and swallowed up their "original" communities, as have Nevada and New Jersey's gambling centers or Florida and Hawaii's beach cities. Large-scale tourism is not just another economic activity, with it can come cultural change and the physical transformation of a community.

To repeat, not all of these impacts are unique to tourism. Ongoing industrialization of a region can have a similar impact, swallowing up a former way of life and, as the example of coal once showed, physically transforming a community. Economic development necessarily involves a certain amount of change. There is, however, a difference with tourism. Rather than permanent new residents it brings temporary visitors into the community, and this can have a corrosive effect that is not characteristic of all economic development.

The Environmental Downside

Herds of tourists can degrade the very landscape or culture to which they are drawn. America's national parks are a good example of this phenomenon. To cope with crowds, roads, trails, lodgings, and services can lead to water and air pollution as well as disrupt the landscape and its wildlife. When resort towns take off, surrounding open space tends to get swallowed up by condominium developments, "trophy" homes, golf courses, shopping malls, and trailer parks. All of these come at a

cost to the natural and cultural environment. Wildlife habitat is fragmented. The flow of effluents into the environment rises. The landscape that once drew people to the area gets loved to death. Some natural areas are very fragile ecosystems that can tolerate only limited
human use. Tourist development may quickly overstep the boundaries.

While acknowledging that tourism has an environmental impact, it
is important to ask, Compared to what? Backpackers and hunters may
be so numerous that they start to damage the land and wildlife in a particular area, but they will probably never have as disruptive an impact
as clear-cutting millions of acres of forest has had. Although whitewater rafters and other recreationists can have various environmental
effects on rivers, it is hard to imagine any recreational use having as
great an impact on America's rivers as large-scale dams, flood control
channelization, irrigation diversion, and agricultural chemical runoff.
Or consider backpacking and mountain biking in deserts and canyon
country. It is certainly true that these will cause some damage, but
nothing approaching what a century of uncontrolled grazing has done
to grassland and riparian areas. Modern chemical mining moves
mountains to produce a few ounces of gold. Mountaineering, no
matter how concentrated, could never have the same impact.

Tourism, recreation, and vacation-home developments definitely
have environmental impacts that should be avoided where possible. But
one has to look at other urban or industrial uses to which land may well
be put before concluding that tourism is the threat rather than economic growth in general. It is not usually helpful to compare a nonvi-
able, ideal land use to a proposed new use in making a judgment about
how to proceed. Doing so may leave the community with a worse set of
default land uses that bear no resemblance to the ideal. To protect environmental quality, it is best to entertain viable alternatives in natural
resource use, and be explicit about what those alternatives are.

Industrial-Grade Tourism:
Three Sisters and the Bow Corridor

In the Town of Canmore, Alberta, we have a case study of tourism
threatening to disrupt rather than enhance a community's well-being.
This shift of attention from local economies in the United States to a
community in Canada is not intended to blur or ignore the significant

differences in the two countries' economic and environmental policies, or the different legal and regulatory tools they have at their disposal for implementing such policies. The object here is merely to evaluate the possible impact of tourism at the local level, and Canmore is a good example because its breathtaking natural beauty recently attracted the attention of developers interested in building a world-class resort.

Canmore lies just outside the eastern gate of Banff National Park, which not only protects and provides public access to some of the most spectacular alpine scenery and "charismatic mega-fauna" (grizzly bear, wolf, elk, and bighorn sheep) in North America, but also serves as a world-class destination ski area. The park is the centerpiece of Alberta's tourist industry, a significant and growing "natural resource industry" in the province. Canmore is a service center for the recreation and tourist activities in and adjacent to the park. The town sits in the spectacular Bow Corridor, the narrow mountain canyon of the Bow River.

As a matter of policy, Banff National Park is trying to limit further expansion of economic activity within the park and the Town of Banff by steering development outside of the park boundaries. This has made Canmore the likely location for future development. The town is growing rapidly. Several international chains have built or plan to build luxury hotels in Canmore, and condominium developments are sprouting up.

In the early 1990s a proposal was made to build a destination resort along the Bow River adjacent to the Town of Canmore. The proposed Three Sisters Resort, named after the triple mountain buttresses that dominate the view from Canmore, would have included hotels, convention facilities, golf courses, a retail shopping complex, and hundreds of residential housing units. The hotels and convention center would have been located in the largely isolated Wind Valley, while the golf course and housing would have been interspersed along the Bow River. The proposed project, as the size of the land resource committed to it would suggest, was huge. Proponents projected that it would support a four- to sixfold increase in population in the Bow Corridor over the coming twenty years, bringing multiple benefits to existing residents and the Town of Canmore. But many local residents, the town itself, and the Canadian Park Service had doubts about the wisdom of the project as proposed. The Alberta Natural Resources Conservation Board was charged with holding hearings on the resort proposal and then deciding whether the development was "in the public interest" given its social, economic, and environmental effects.[13]

Measuring Community Costs and Benefits

The socioeconomic analysis presented by the resort developers labeled the golf courses and all of the additional jobs and income to be realized by the project as benefits to the local population. This claim put the cart before the horse. Whether something is a benefit and just how valuable a benefit it is should be determined by the potential beneficiaries, not the business producing the good or service. Expertly crafted widgits produced at enormous cost are not valuable goods unless the public wants them. The same is true of nonmarketed goods and services. In the case of the proposed Three Sisters Resort the residents of Canmore, whom the resort would affect, were the ones to be consulted.

Canmore had gone through several planning exercises in the years just before the Three Sisters Proposal to determine the type of community that residents wanted to see develop. In 1991 the town launched a public process to develop a vision for the community and a statement of goals for attaining that vision. Vision 2020, as the program was called, drafted a tourist plan based on two "implementation principles":

- Effort should be geared to consolidating and strengthening community assets rather than attracting major resort developments, and this requires supporting local ventures and utilizing local resources.
- To distinguish itself from the tourism development model followed by Banff, the Town [of Canmore] should prefer low-impact, smaller-scale, dispersed developments which fit into the existing settlement and are owner-operated so that revenues stay in the community.[14]

The town also commissioned a professional survey of the values of Canmore residents, to which two-thirds of Canmore's 2,100 households responded.[15] When asked to cite the main reasons they lived in Canmore, the majority of residents mentioned the setting, quality of life, and recreation. Job opportunity was mentioned by only one in six. That is, environmental reasons far outweighed economic reasons. When asked to mention the single most important feature of Canmore, 38 percent cited the small town atmosphere, 26 percent quality of life,

29 percent the natural setting, and 5 percent recreational opportunities. Expanded tourism was an acceptable form of economic development for all but 10 percent of residents. However, tourism ranked sixth in a list of activities appropriate for development. When asked what type of tourist-related developments to encourage, respondents emphasized dispersed/low-density recreation such as adventure recreation and cross-country skiing. Festivals and heritage/cultural programs out-ranked golf and resorts.

The Three Sisters Resort developers themselves commissioned a survey as part of their effort to put together a "socioeconomic profile" of the area.[16] That survey indicated that over half (53 percent) of the population thought that the pace of tourist and commercial development should be slowed. About 25 percent felt that the current pace was fine. Only about 15 percent thought that the pace should be accelerated. When asked if they were interested in the Bow Corridor being developed as an international resort, 47 percent indicated that they were "not at all" interested, 7 percent "not interested." Only 9 percent said that they were "very interested." When asked about how an increase in tourism and commercial development would benefit them, 44 percent responded that they would not benefit while only 11 percent cited higher employment or more business. The overwhelming majority thought that further tourist and commercial development would have the following consequences: higher land prices, more expensive municipal services, more transients, more crime, deteriorating water and air quality, and decreased wildlife populations.

Obviously, if one were to judge the impacts of Three Sisters by using the preferences of Canmore residents, most of those impacts could not be called benefits because they would not be considered improvements by the majority of the population.

When Are More Jobs Not a Benefit?

The Three Sisters developers listed employment as one of the major advantages that their project would bring to Canmore: "The positive economic impacts will be significant . . . . 8700 jobs over 20 years will help sustain economic growth in Canmore."

Three Sisters analysts realized that because almost all of Canmore's work force was already employed, the new jobs would not be taken by existing residents but either by nonresidents who commuted to work in Canmore or by inmigrants who came to live there. With the unemployment rate in Canmore at 2.8 percent (compared with 7 percent in Alberta and 8 percent in Canada), clearly the population was almost fully employed. One can use Canmore labor market statistics to estimate the additional work force that would have been available to staff the resort. The number of unemployed residents at the time was 125, of homemakers outside the work force 329, and of part-time and seasonal workers 531. If half of the homemakers and seasonal and part-time workers held their employment status only because of limited job opportunities in Canmore *and* the unemployment rate among Canmore residents could be reduced to 0, about 550 Canmore residents would be available to work on the resort. But these assumptions are unrealistic: the demand for workers in Canmore has been quite high for many years, which is why the unemployment rate was unusually low. Thus almost all of those residents who wished to work full-time outside the home were probably already doing so. That means that 550 workers among Canmore residents is an extreme upper limit to the population in Canmore available to staff the resort.

Three Sisters analysts estimated that the peak employment increase in the Bow Corridor during construction of the resort would be about 11,000 above the current level, that is, twenty times the maximum that could be served by Bow Corridor residents. Put somewhat differently, 95 percent or more of the jobs generated by the resort would be of no benefit to Bow Corridor residents. Those jobs would go instead to inmigrants or commuters, while existing Bow Corridor residents would have to cope with the changes in their community that accompanied a massive increase in population and economic activity.

Besides the fact that almost all of the new employment would have to be filled by inmigrants, there was the issue of job quality. Most of the jobs associated with the resort would be in the hospitality and food sectors where wages tend to be low, jobs seasonal and part-time, and job tenure short. Three Sisters admitted that the average household income generated by these jobs would be considerably lower than that of the average existing household in Canmore. The massive boost in employment offered by the resort would actually reduce average household income in the Bow Corridor while increasing the demand for municipal services to accommodate the influx of new residents.

Finally, the impact of a large, unskilled, low-paid, transient work force on the Canmore community had to be considered. Canmore has a heterogeneous population drawn to the area primarily for its mountain landscape. The economy is reasonably diverse, with professional tourist services existing alongside family-run lodging and food and drinking establishments, components of the Canadian National Park Service, and business firms serving Calgary and the rest of Alberta. Canmore has a definite community feel. The flow of thousands of transient workers into and out of the community could change that considerably. One trend in Banff gave reason to pause. A Royal Canadian Mounted Police analysis of the work force in that nearby resort town found that 72 percent of employed males over the age of twenty-five had been convicted of some criminal violation. As the Town of Banff itself concluded with respect to the impact of tourism, "Social problems associated with alcohol, personal and family stress, drugs, suicide, and sexual assault all tend to be higher than would be expected in a community of 7,000.[17] High-volume tourism can transform communities in ugly ways.

Ignoring Local Concerns for the Sake of the Larger Economy

Some might reject the preferences of Canmore residents as too parochial. The local area might not reap benefits, but the province as a whole would. Indeed, this was the emphasis of the Three Sisters developers: almost all of the jobs and income generated by the resort would go to Alberta residents. There are three important errors in this simple assertion. First, it implicitly assumes that if the Bow Corridor land at issue was not used by the Three Sisters Resort, it would be used for nothing else. Second, it assumes that all of the money spent at the resort would come from the pockets of visitors from outside of Alberta. Third, it assumes that all of the resources that might be employed at Three Sisters would otherwise be permanently unemployed. None of these assumptions is tenable.

Consider the first, implicit assumption: that if the Three Sisters Resort were not built, the 2,600 acres of land that are now part of the Town of Canmore would be used for no other purpose of economic consequence to the province. This assumption, of course, is preposterous. The only thing lost if Three Sisters were not approved would be the advantage it had, if any, over the best alternative use to which the land could be put. Since it is not clear that the proposed project is the best possible economic use, it may have no advantage and there may be no loss at all to the province associated with rejecting Three Sisters. If it is the superior project, then the loss to the province would only be its advantage over the next best alternative. That would likely be only a fraction of the value associated with the overall project.

As for the second assumption, it is simply not true that all the people who would use the resort would come from outside of Alberta, or that the money spent at the resort would all be money that otherwise would not be spent in Alberta. Three-quarters of Banff area skiers are Albertans, and two-thirds of the projected market for the additional golf that Three Sisters would provide would be Albertan. In other words, most of the customers would be Albertans spending discretionary income at this location rather than at some other location in the same province. Most of the resort spending would not stimulate the Alberta economy. Only a small part of the spending at Three Sisters would be spending that otherwise would not occur in Alberta.

The third assumption, that all of the economic activity associated with Three Sisters would put otherwise idle Alberta resources (such as labor and capital) to work is a misrepresentation of how a market economy works. One user of resources bids resources away from other potential users so that resources flow to their most productive use. When one project does not proceed, the resources that would have been used in that project are employed elsewhere. Only a tiny fraction of the economic activity stimulated by Three Sisters would be supported by resources that otherwise would be permanently unemployed.

Simple arithmetic demonstrates how these assumptions grossly exaggerate the benefits of Three Sisters Resort to the provincial economy. Suppose, conservatively, that the proposed Three Sisters Resort would be twice as productive as any alternative use of the 2,600 acres in the Bow Corridor. Using data on current and projected recreational use of the Bow Corridor, assume that only one-third of the resort spending would come from non-Albertans, and that two-thirds of the non-Albertan spending would occur only if Three Sisters was built. Finally, make the wild hypothesis that a third of the additional economic activity was supported by what would otherwise be permanently unemployed labor and capital resources. These assumptions would reduce the estimated provincial benefits of the Three Sisters Resort by 96 percent:

$$0.5 \times 0.33 \times 0.67 \times 0.33 = 0.0365 \text{ or about 4 percent.}$$

Put slightly differently, the assumption that all of the jobs and income associated with Three Sisters would be economic benefits to the province is off by a factor of 25! With net provincial benefits this much lower, one might wonder whether the gain to the province would be worth the loss to the local area.

Sacrificing That Which Is Unique for That Which Is Common

Banff National Park is already the mainstay of Alberta's tourist industry, as the Town of Canmore makes clear in an investment plan it drew up for tourism infrastructure in the Bow Corridor:

> The Banff–Lake Louise area has been the centerpiece of Alberta's tourism industry for several decades. The area has provided the foundation for the province's international travel image and reputation and arguably is the core tourism generator upon which so much of the province's external tourism rests. Banff National Park continues to account for more than two-thirds of the combined visitation to all national parks in the province and attracts more than four million visitors per year, three-fifths of whom stay overnight. Banff National Park and the adjoining region which extends to and includes Calgary now account for roughly two-fifths of the Alberta tourism industry.[18]

What the Three Sisters Resort involves is further specialization of Alberta's tourist industry on the Banff National Park base. It would put more of Alberta's economic eggs in an already full basket rather than diversifying the tourist base so that it is less reliant on an already heavily utilized landscape resource. Moreover, Alberta already has ample facilities for golfing and skiing. In both senses, the Three Sisters Resort represents specialization, not diversification.

Given the pressure that is already threatening Banff National Park, further development may end up weakening the goose that lays the golden egg. Overdeveloping the park would be no different from overharvesting forestland or withdrawing gas and oil from reservoirs at uneconomic rates: it would damage the resource upon which jobs and income depend. Moreover, Three Sisters would commit the tourist industry to a couple of recreational trends that may not be reliable. The Alberta skiing market has been flat for two reasons: recent expanded capacity, which spread a fixed number of skiers over a larger number of resorts, and competition with the Whistler-Blackcomb ski areas. As for golf courses, construction has expanded rapidly in Alberta in recent years and dozens of new courses have been proposed. The long-term viability of unlimited expansion has to be questioned.

One can expect that recreation/tourist markets will change substantially over the next ten years. That has to be kept in mind in evaluating more intensive exploitation of the landscape in and around Banff National Park. The proposed destination resort with its "upscale" or "luxury" hotel, golf courses, recreation, and shopping facilities follows the pattern of tourist development already established at Banff–Lake Louise. The developers seek to create a familiar and luxurious setting in the midst of some of the most spectacular wild landscape in the world. Visitors would be "protected" from the wild landscape inside plush hotels and on the artificial turf of golf courses largely indistinguishable from facilities found in any major metropolitan area or world-class resort.

It is not clear that future discretionary spending will flow in such a direction. The fastest-growing part of the market is in adventure recreation, ecotourism, and cultural tourism.[19] More and more, travelers want to make direct contact with the landscapes, communities, and cultures they visit. Facilities that move large volumes of passive tourists through a familiar and unchallenging artificial landscape may not be what the traveler of the future is looking for. Tourist facilities that undermine that which is unique about an area may well be destroying their own market.

What the Three Sisters developers proposed was to commit a large part of a relatively scarce resource, the Bow Corridor landscape, to relatively common recreational activities that could be pursued elsewhere in Alberta. The commitment of scarce and breathtaking land to provide an artificial landscape for such a commonplace activity as golf would be more than a little incongruous; it would be completely out of sync with the natural and social environment of the Bow Corridor.

In late 1992 the Alberta Natural Resources Conservation Board rejected the bulk of the Three Sisters proposal. In particular, it refused to allow the construction of hotels, a convention center, a shopping center, and a golf course in the Wind Valley. The board believed that the environmental effects of the Wind Valley development on vegetation and wildlife would be longlasting. It did offer to allow a golf course and housing development on the land along the Bow River, subject to restrictions. The Town of Canmore was given control over the timing and nature of this development. The board's decision, aimed at protecting the natural and social environment of the area, effectively killed the resort proposal.

A Different Type of Tourism: Far from the Madding Crowd

Most resort towns and recreational meccas in North America represent "industrial-grade" tourism, that is, a large-scale, high-volume industry that inundates communities and almost replaces them. But tourism does not have to take place on this scale or in this manner. There is an alternative type of tourism that protects what is unique in an area by limiting and dispersing the impact of visitors.

Any community seeking to maintain its own identity is likely to hesitate before embracing tourism as a means of economic development. This is especially true of Native American communities. Reservations tend to be located in relatively isolated natural landscapes with a lot of potential for tourism or recreation. Even where this is not the case, reservations can be turned into gambling havens. Are tribal traditions compatible with tourism, or is it a corrosive element that will undermine the culture the reservation is supposed in part to preserve?

Tribes and Tourism

It is natural for anyone serving a stream of tourists to regard them as strangers in a hurry who don't care to know the community or its people. Not uncommonly, tourist-industry employees are surly and hostile toward visitors, who react with pushy insensitivity. Add to this situation cultural or racial tensions and it may be tinder waiting to ignite. There are a number of reasons Native Americans might want to think twice before turning their reservations over to a traditional tourist trade.

Tourists tend to be affluent folks whose vacation lifestyle has an element of unreality to it: lots of discretionary income, fancy meals, drinking, gambling, casual sex. This version of the good life may not be exactly what Native American tribes want their young people to yearn for.

Furthermore, turning the entire reservation into a community museum and developing watch-the-wildlife programs may send tourists streaming into every nook and cranny of the reservation, raising tension with invasion of privacy, congestion, and confusion. The disadvantages of dispersing transient strangers to all corners of the reservation have to be weighed against the advantages.

Most high-amenity rural areas are discovered by potential new residents while they are traveling as tourists. That is how the desert Southwest and Florida got launched as centers of Sunbelt development. In many situations, new residents and the economic activity they bring may be preferred to tourists. But this is not necessarily the case on the reservation. Gaining new residents as a result of tourism could threaten to boost the non–Native American population disproportionately and erode tribal control and sovereignty.

Another problem is that tourism can cost tribes more money than it's worth. Interpretive signs, visitor centers, cultural and environmental guides, and museums do not usually generate much if any revenue, yet producing and maintaining them require a lot of money and volunteer labor. Such tourist infrastructure may get the tribe's "message" out, but it is unlikely to be profit making, and even if it holds tourists in the area longer the benefits may well go to non-Indian enterprises.

Alternative Tourism

Tourism on the nation's reservations usually consists of a stream of visitors who just happen by on the way to some other destination. They have little interest in or knowledge of tribes and their reservations. Hurried, transient tourists rushing between national parks or monuments may not be a productive market for cash-strapped reservations to tap. But what about an altogether different type of visitor, someone who came specifically to see the reservation and who would spend several days in intensive exploration, employing the unique skills and knowledge of tribal members? Most reservations have a diverse set of natural, recreational, and cultural resources that certain people would enjoy seeing. Tribal members could act as guides, dispensing information about resources and at the same time protecting them from harm. For example, a tribe could attract a small number of people to its reservation for a skilled labor–intensive, relatively costly program lasting anywhere from three days to two weeks.

Such specialized tourism is not far-fetched. "Ecotourism," adventure tourism, educational travel, and cultural tourism—together these represent the fastest-growing part of the tourist industry. Affluent travelers with limited time are looking for something other than casual touring where most time is spent either in the car or in a resort hotel indistinguishable from any other resort hotel. Indian reservations are an ideal site for this market.

Tribal wildlife programs could conceivably nurture wildlife populations large enough to support guided "trophy hunting." Tribes could charge a very high permit fee to hunters (thousands of dollars per animal) while members acted as guides. This might require that some areas be closed to general tribal hunting, a potentially controversial development that might be resolved by successful game management programs throughout the reservation and enforcement of aboriginal rights to hunt on and off the reservation. Some western tribes have already started such hunting programs.

Or Native American spiritual leaders might consider following the example of religious traditions that have supported their own leaders and healers by running programs such as retreats and workshops that in no way cheapen their beliefs or way of life. Catholic monasteries take in small groups and individuals who want to experience life in a religious order, and various Buddhist communities invite serious people for extended visits.

Besides opening up employment and business opportunities to the tribe, programs providing guided access to selected resources could realize other substantial benefits. Programs that tapped unique tribal knowledge and skills would be an incentive to develop, maintain, and pass them on to young people. Evidence that outsiders appreciated tribal culture and lands would confirm their value. Of course, only a minority would become guides, but many more would gain the incentive to master knowledge of the tribe's culture and history and of the reservation's ecology. This would strengthen the sense of tribal identity. Specialized tourism would also develop entrepreneurial skills that could be transferred to other economic activities. In all of this tribal schools and colleges would play an important role, passing on cultural traditions and teaching business skills. Tribes would have to consider how to support collective marketing efforts as well as how to guide and regulate this type of activity. It takes time and patient planning to develop a market and the businesses serving it.

Native American homelands are a particularly sensitive example of regions with potential for the development of noninvasive tourism. But the general principles are applicable to any community looking for opportunities to diversify its economy and generate business and employment without selling its soul in the process. Small-scale, dispersed activities that give visitors access to local recreation or culture can employ skilled local labor and take place without disrupting the community or trampling the landscape. Recreational businesses have existed for a long time in the form of professional outfitters who guide hunting, fishing, and rafting trips. Traditional dude ranches are another familiar model. Such business opportunities are expanding as travelers prove that they are willing to spend money in exchange for an authentic experience off the beaten track. A growing segment of the travel market is dismissing "tourist traps" as not worth the cost in either time or money. For communities to tap into this selective market, they have to focus on the quality of the experience, not the quantity of visitors. They need to make sure that tourists do not displace local residents and that the attractions that draw visitors remain valued amenities to local residents, for what threatens the community's cultural and natural environment also threatens a potentially lucrative tourist market. Control and management are as important as promotion, for without them, the community has nothing to market.

Tourism As Economic Development

To keep tourism from swamping a local community, the industry has to be maintained at an appropriate scale. For most communities this means that it should never represent more than a small part of overall economic activity. It is important to remember that nobody loves a tourist. In fact, most of us have such a strong distaste for the species that we rarely, if ever, consider ourselves part of it. Our aversion to the word *tourist* underlines the incompatibility of conventional mass tourism and local communities. It is also a warning about the political viability of offering tourism as an environmentally benign alternative to extractive activities.

This is not to say that there is no viable economic alternative to extractive activities. As discussed earlier in the book, the primary economic contribution of protected landscapes and communities is attracting not tourists but rather permanent residents and businesses, which stimulate and support diverse economic activity. But tourism can be part of the economic mix without poisoning it. Two key elements in determining which direction the industry goes in a particular community are the community's confidence in itself and its level of entrepreneurial energy. If a community adopts a helpless beggars-can't-be-choosers attitude and passively accepts any and all tourist proposals, tourism may well someday consume it. But if the community cherishes its amenities and has the confidence to protect them, it can lay the foundation for local entrepreneurs to develop compatible, dispersed tourist businesses that help vitalize the local economy.

11

The Gift of Nature: Extraction, the Environment, and Local Vitality

This book has focused on the distortions created by thinking about the local economy primarily in terms of the extractive and export-oriented commercial activities that are commonly identified as its economic base and often closely associated with local history. While such activities are part of an economic dynamic that may be important, especially in the short run, they distract us from the total economy, the full set of forces that determines the community's economic well-being. By spotlighting mature industries in relative or absolute decline both locally and nationally, the economic base approach creates fatalism about the future that does more than just demoralize people; that perspective tends to urge the community into adopting policies to save declining industries rather than supporting new, dynamic sources of economic vitality. The emphasis on extraction, heavy industry, and exports may keep us from seeing what is actually happening in our communities and from taking measures to support emerging economic forces that are positive.

The positive changes that tend to be overlooked include the following:

- The creation of many new jobs in relatively small businesses;
- The shift of jobs from goods production to services production;
- Overall, a substantial expansion in employment opportunity that has provided jobs to an increasing percentage of the adult population;
- The decentralization of economic activity toward areas where people choose to live;

- Improvements in transportation and communication that have reduced the isolation and costs associated with living away from large urban centers;
- The shift in public values toward environmental quality;
- The increased role of residential choice in determining the geographic distribution of economic activity;
- The rising importance of environmental amenities in determining where people live and where firms migrate;
- The increased importance of nonemployment income and the locational choices of retired individuals in stabilizing local economies and determining the location of economic activity; and
- The growing role of nonmarket, noncommercial goods and services flowing from the natural environment, the local community, the nonprofit sector, and government agencies in determining local economic well-being.

There are broad-ranging economic forces afoot that are more than offsetting job losses in extractive and heavy industries and that offer our families new sources of well-being and our communities new sources of vitality. These changes are largely invisible when the local economy is viewed from the economic base perspective. We won't see what is actually happening to us unless we turn away from the rearview mirror and abandon certain entrenched elements of folk economics. And unless we see what is actually happening, we can't shape viable or even safe public economic policy.

The Changing Role of
Natural Resources in the Local Economy

Some may interpret the basic analysis in this book as indicating that natural resources are becoming less and less important in determining our economic well-being. That is not the conclusion being developed here. It is not that natural resources are becoming economically less important, but, rather, that the role of natural resources in determining well-being is changing. Commercial, extractive use of the natural landscape is declining in relative importance, while noncommercial, nonconsumptive landscape values are rising in importance.

The natural landscape is not only a "warehouse" of commercial resources waiting to be extracted by various industries. The landscape is also the source of a broad range of largely noncommercial goods and services that include clean air and water, wildlife and biodiversity, scenic beauty, recreational opportunities, and cultural, historical, and spiritual values.

Some may be tempted to dismiss environmental goods and services as of relatively minor importance compared with the commercial potential associated with the extraction of commodities. But that is not an accurate gauge of competing values. Most extractive activities produce relatively uniform commodities that are readily available from other sources. Oversupply is the reason agricultural, fuel, metal, and fiber prices are so low and the reason these industries are in relative decline. Modest increases in their production will add relatively little economic value because of limited demand for the product. By contrast, to most Americans, clean air, safe water, endangered wildlife, intact ecosystems, and scenic beauty are in dangerously short supply.[1] One would expect, as a result, that the value associated with protected landscapes would be high. There is nothing economically trivial about the flow of goods and services from the natural world. They continue to play a central role in determining our individual and collective economic well-being. The relative importance of the goods and services that the natural world offers has simply shifted away from the commercial and extractive to the environmental.

A Sense of Place

As we have seen, people care where they live and, given the choice, gravitate toward more desirable residential areas. Economic activity tends to follow them. Thus it cannot be said that environmental quality is only an aesthetic concern to be pursued if a community feels prosperous enough to afford it. Environmental quality has become a central element of local economic bases and a central determinant of local economic vitality. A community won't show much vitality, economic or social, if no one wants to live there. Where most people are just putting in time until they can afford to move away, investment will be depressed and economic infrastructure, both private and public, will be underdeveloped. The economy will slavishly follow fluctuations in distant commodity markets, and the community, populated by people uncommitted to place, will contain a disproportionate number of transients or commuters.

Commitment to place is important to local economic development, and thus the qualities that instill commitment have economic importance in addition to whatever social, biological, or cultural importance they have. One quality that has always instilled a sense of place is a desirable natural landscape. Another is an attractive social environment. Efforts to protect the landscape and enhance the social environment have to be looked at as integral to any economic development strategy. They are not just social or aesthetic concerns. As local citizens organize themselves to promote continued economic vitality in their community, the qualities that make it an attractive place to live, work, and do business should be of central concern.

A Resilient Economy: Transformation, Not Decline

For a variety of reasons, some historical, some cultural, we tend to think about economic activity primarily in terms of the production of material goods. Economic concerns are characterized as fundamentally materialist, and economic activities such as farming, ranching, mining, forestry, and fishing that require human labor to extract the gifts of nature are categorized as primary production. Because these activities historically provided the food, clothing, shelter, and tools necessary to survival as well as to all other types of economic activity, and because our culture has tended to romanticize such activities, this characterization is understandable. The drama of the individual matching wits with nature in a primeval contest is alluring. But a society can keep historical and cultural traditions alive without allowing them to dictate current and future economic policy. Basing contemporary economic policy on folklore is a distraction: there is no longer anything primary about extractive, natural resource–based activities. They represent a tiny and declining part of our overall economic efforts. Since this pattern has been under way for over a century, not just in the United States but worldwide, there is no reason to believe the trend will change. Extractive activity is not only not the source of economic vitality, it is often a source of economic instability and depression. Local communities should be cautious when considering whether to tie their future to increased reliance on extractive industries.

Our extractive industries as well as a good part of our heavy industry (steel, automobiles, equipment manufacturing, chemicals) have recently declined as sources of employment and income. Because, historically, these industries led American industrialization and were associated with good (high-paying, high-benefits) jobs, their decline has been interpreted as a sign of economic decline. We are, some insist, losing the very "industrial base" responsible for America's past prosperity and economic dominance. There is a sense of economic insecurity in the air. Good economic policy is rarely made in the context of fear. When livelihoods appear threatened by forces over which people can exercise no control, they tend to react with unfocused and uninformed anger and frustration. This frame of mind can be especially destructive when it comes to efforts to protect the natural environment. If economic decline is making beggars out of us, clearly we cannot afford to be choosers in environmental matters. We have to be thankful for whatever economic activity we have, and not burden it with high-cost environmental regulations. The threat of economic decline makes environmental protection appear unaffordable.

But economies are almost always in motion, shifting and transforming themselves. What is important is not whether some activities are in decline—some *always* are—but whether they are being replaced by economic activities that will continue to use our workers' skills productively. Economic development is about exactly such changes: less productive or valued activities decline in absolute or relative terms and release the resources they once used to more productive or valued activities. If 85 percent of us were still employed in extractive activities in rural areas—the case in the early 1800s—our standard of living would be dramatically lower than it is today. Economic development *requires* decline in some economic activities so that resources can shift to other activities. The rearview mirror makes development appear to be decline—clearly, a dangerous distortion. For almost two centuries, our extractive economic base has been in relative decline so that today it represents just a tiny fraction of the entire economy. The manufacturing and service sector grew substantially to displace declining extractive sectors; beginning in the second half of the twentieth century, manufacturing also began a slow decline while services continued to expand (figure 11-1). The decline in the extractive and then the manufacturing "industrial base" did not lead to an overall decline in national prosperity; rather, this two-century-long process is what provided Americans with one of the highest standards of living in the world.

It is not true that the economy has been generating a larger group of permanently unemployed workers and permanently unemployed resources. Overall, jobs are not being lost. Unless we are futilely seeking to freeze our economy at some point in the past, transformation should not be condemned simply because it involves declining employment in some sectors. The full set of adjustments in the economy has to be studied, expanding sectors as well as contracting, before we can make any judgment about the impact of the entire set of changes. Such studies have been done, and they reveal a much more positive pattern than the current mood of apprehension and insecurity would suggest.[2]

From Dis-Services to Services: Setting the Record Straight

Despite the current economic transformation that is successfully shifting human resources from one use to another, some observers are still concerned about our economic well-being. If the shift moves people from good, well-paid, and attractive jobs to jobs with low pay, miserable working conditions, and no hope of advancement, our prosperity could still be threatened. But the truth is, the shift in our economy away from extractive and heavy industry is not impoverishing us. The service activities that are replacing goods production have many advantages. These include the following:

- Wages in services are as high as or higher than those in goods production;
- The skill level of service jobs is significantly higher, the educational level of employees is higher, and the rewards for that education are higher;
- The potential for advancement is higher in services than in goods production; service wages rise faster and end up higher;
- More flexible working hours in services allow workers to combine other economic and nonmarket activities with their service industry employment;
- Job security is significantly greater in service jobs; and

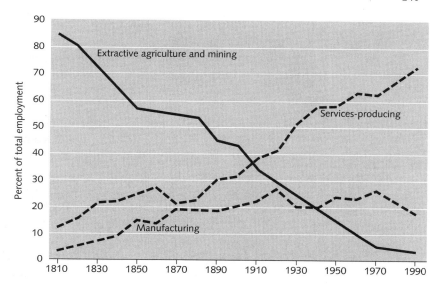

FIGURE 11-1. Changes in the relative economic importance of extraction, manufacturing, and services in the American economy since 1810. The rise in services and the decline in extractive activity is not a recent trend; it has coincided with the transformation of the American economy into a modern, affluent society. (*Data sources:* U.S. Bureau of the Census *Historical Statistics of the United States,* and BEA REIS.)

- Over the last two decades, while real wages in goods production have been declining, real wages in narrow services have been increasing.

This is not to say that there are not disadvantages associated with the shift toward services. Among them are a decline in employer support for medical insurance and retirement and an increase in involuntary part-time work. In addition, because blue-collar jobs that are being lost required little formal education, workers who held them have difficulty shifting into service jobs, which require more education and skill overall. Thus some experienced workers are facing a significant decline in pay and being pushed out of their middle-class lifestyle. This is a serious problem that calls for both public and private efforts to facilitate the transition, but it should not be used to characterize the transition as a whole. We are not creating too many unskilled jobs. The problem, if there is one, is that we are creating too many skilled jobs, which displaced workers are having trouble obtaining.

It is also true that growth in the standard of living in this country has been slowed dramatically, but by forces that have nothing to do with the decline in extractive and heavy industry and the rise in services. Wages in all industries are being pressed down. The reasons for this are complex and beyond the scope of this book. It is important, however, not to lay blame at the wrong doorstep. Worldwide competition arising from the globalization of the economy is having a profound impact on the U.S. economy. In addition, fundamental political and social changes have eroded belief in the "social minimum wage" and dramatically widened income inequality. For a variety of reasons, Americans have abandoned social structures put in place in the first half of this century that sought to boost wages and living conditions at the lower end of the economic spectrum. The floor has fallen out from under a significant part of our population. These changes are worrisome, and our analysis should not be interpreted as minimizing or dismissing them. Rather, we have tried to focus on which of them, if any, can be attributed to efforts to protect the natural environment and the environments in which we live. By answering, Almost none! we are not suggesting that there is not a real problem, only that it has other causes. All of us need to be concerned with what appears to be a growing impoverished underclass in our cities and nonmetropolitan areas. But efforts to protect the environment have not spawned it. Those concerned with the environment have a direct interest in helping find solutions to this and other economic problems not because environmental policy created them but because good environmental policy cannot be made in the context of economic desperation.

What You See Isn't Always What You Get

Local politicians and economic development agencies are inclined to mislead us about what local economic development actually looks like. They claim responsibility for all the good that happens in the local economy while shrugging off any responsibility for the bad, which is attributed to national or international economic forces, or to local political opponents. There is political hay to be made from dramatic changes, both positive and negative, and not surprisingly the stories we are told about how local economies develop or flounder center on large-scale changes: Toyota builds a sprawling new plant employing thousands of people in the countryside; the federal government closes a shipyard; Citibank opens a "back office" in a rural state; ASARCO closes a mine; the federal government builds a new research facility; Champion International sells off its timberland and mills; . . . Economic development apparently rests on the locational decisions made by large corporations and the federal government. This view is closely associated with the business-recruiting mind-set that until recently dominated local economic development strategies.[3]

Such changes, no matter how dramatic, have little to do with economic development. Economic development is an ongoing process of many small, almost invisible changes that slowly transform the local economy. Dramatic change in the wake of relocation of large facilities can be a shock or disruption that may or may not contribute to local economic development, depending on how residents respond. If they adopt a passive approach to their economic well-being, waiting for a fairy godmother or white knight to appear on the scene and instantly transform the economy, little development is likely to take place.

Consider the history of company towns, communities dependent on a single employer. Economic dominance is likely to lead to political and social dominance as well. Company towns are rarely dynamic, constantly improving communities. They have no future except for that of the company on which they depend, a future fraught with uncertainty. And often such communities are run-down, despite the high wages paid, because people are not willing to risk investment in a single-company town. This, and the suppression of entrepreneurial initiative, sends high wages flowing out of town to other, more economically diverse communities.

Entrepreneurial energy is what fuels development, local economic actors—individuals, private businesses, nonprofit organizations, and government agencies—aggressively pursuing opportunities and generating thousands of small changes. No single change is likely to be dramatic or even visible. But together the changes slowly and systematically transform the local economy. Hundreds of small businesses adding a few employees here and there can generate thousands of new jobs, and as a result, though no one such business decision will be newsworthy, change as large as that associated with a huge new industrial facility may take place without anyone noticing. Over a fairly short period of time a local economy can be invisibly transformed. We may deny that the change took place or, when the signs are all around us, see it as unreliable or peripheral. At best, we think, it is a baffling anomaly, not part of a pattern indicating where our community is now and what the future holds.

We need to broaden our view of what economic development is all about, embracing the crucial role played by the collective entrepreneurial energy of the community. Economic development may be invisible to people with their gaze fixed on the rearview mirror, but a close look usually reveals signs of the ongoing transformation. Public economic policy needs to focus on these signs, either to encourage the positive aspects of transformation or to mitigate the damage from the negative or to redirect it and thereby protect local values.

Extractive Industry: An Environmental Boon?

One objection raised to the economic transformation that is shifting our economic activities away from extractive and export-oriented sectors toward service and residential sectors is that it threatens the natural landscape and communities. More of our land base, the thinking goes, will be committed to residential use. Subdivisions, grids of rectangular ranchettes, the trophy homes of the well-to-do, condominium complexes, all seem to be sprouting everywhere across the previously agricultural landscape. Open space is closing, wildlife habitat is fragmented, recreational pressure in sensitive ecosystems is building. We are loving the land to death. Meanwhile, our communities are changing. Traditional means of livelihood are being displaced or swamped by new economic activities that have no social or cultural roots in the area. Newcomers bring with them different values that clash with those of long-time residents. In short, the transformation of the landscape from extractive to residential use is seen by some as going from the frying pan into the fire.

Many, maybe most, of us resist change. We are comfortable with the familiar, having invested in learning to cope productively with a certain environment. Change adds uncertainty and threatens our competence. This is a natural human inclination and may be a useful social control. But wholesale rejection of all change and blanket defense of the status quo is unlikely to be productive or meaningful. We need to focus on actual threats to important values, not just express our preference for the familiar.

The primary environmental objection to expanded residential activity is that residential subdivisions and urbanization damage the landscape in a variety of ways. This no doubt is true if residential subdivisions are compared with, say, protecting land as a wildlife preserve or as classified wilderness. But that is rarely the alternative use to which the land would be put. The more common use is agriculture. The appropriate comparison, then, is between the environmental impact of agricultural activity and that of residential use. We must put our agrarian sympathies aside: agriculture does not step lightly on the land. Modern agriculture involves heavy use of pesticides and herbicides that find their way into our water. Most planting techniques lead to the extensive loss of topsoil. The diversion and impoundment of water for irrigation severely strain arid water systems. Extensive overgrazing of western lands has radically modified arid ecosystems and led to the destruction of riparian areas. The systematic elimination of wildlife that competes with agriculture has been a "successful" publicly subsidized project. The introduction of acre upon acre of monoculture has drastically reduced biodiversity. The list goes on.

Residential settlement can actually reduce the demand for water, reduce the quantity of chemicals introduced into the environment, and create a more diverse habitat—trees, shrubs, parks with wetlands—to replace field crops.[4] Just as important, subdivisions are never likely to affect as much of the landscape as, say, agriculture, logging, and mining. Consider one of our most urbanized states, California. Only about 3.4 million acres are affected by urbanization (housing tracts, commercial areas, roads and highways) while 29.4 million acres are still in agricultural use and 35 million acres are private or public forestland. Only 3 to 4 percent of California's landscape is urbanized.[5] In the Pacific Northwest, one need only compare massive clear-cuts that scar almost all of the forested landscape with the size of suburban or exurban subdivisions to judge which type of activity disturbs more of the landscape. Or one need only visit the gold-mining areas of Nevada and South Dakota, the coal fields of Appalachia and the northern Great Plains, and the uranium and copper pit mines scattered across the West to determine the extent and scope of the damage done by modern strip mining compared with residential development.

Those who decry the environmental impact that expanded residential settlement has in rural areas appear to offer extractive industry as an economic alternative to settlement. That stance assumes that there is a tradeoff or choice to be made between expanded residential settlement and extractive industry, which is unlikely. The residential development that has taken place in many nonmetropolitan areas did not cause the negative trajectory that extractive industry is on. Expanded settlement and the economic vitality accompanying it are part of a new economy that is growing up beside the declining historic base. Nor is the extractive decline, in general, a prerequisite for the emergence of new sectors. Where there is a tradeoff between extractive activity and residential growth, it is because the extractive activity is so destructive that it discourages residential location.

This is not a defense of unregulated residential and commercial sprawl, which does do environmental damage, though some of that is avoidable. The issue is really whether residential development, when it replaces extractive activity in the normal process of economic development, puts more stress on the environment. It seems unlikely that the claim can be sustained.

Quality, Not Quantity

The economy is almost always characterized in quantitative terms—the level of income, number of jobs, rate of growth of output, size of the population, rate of inflation or unemployment. Market exchanges and commercial business play an important role in our economy, and accordingly, we track the economy the way a business owner would track her business, carefully studying costs, revenues, material flows, production rates. Although quantitative analysis is central to a well-operating business, and usually business success can be accurately judged in such terms, they cannot be used to measure the health of the local economy. In fact, familiar quantitative measures of local economic health such as average money income are perversely misleading.

Recall the problems with average income as a measure of local economic well-being discussed in Chapter 3. When an area has a high cost of living, congestion, and other dominant urban disamenities, average income will usually be high to compensate for the damage to local well-being. Or when residents make choices that they think improve their well-being but involve nonmarket activities such as having and raising children, average income declines. Similarly, if an area is attractive to people because of its social and/or natural environment, a surplus labor supply will put downward pressure on wages not because there is something wrong with the economy but because there is something right about the quality of life. In none of these examples does average income reflect the degree of local economic well-being. The same is true of most other measures of local economic health. Consider growth in employment. If additional jobs are created but they primarily go to inmigrants, what is the benefit to the local economy? The problems of those in the local economy who were having difficulty finding and holding jobs have not been solved. Population growth is no better an indicator. In what way is the well-being of existing residents improved because there are now more human beings living in their vicinity? There is no economic principle that says living in the presence of more people improves your well-being. If that were true, the tens of millions living in the rapidly growing shanty towns of the developing world would be much better off than they are. The most commonly used indicators of local economic well-being do not accurately measure well-being.

Part of the problem is simply that the objectives of a community are more complex than those of a business operating in a commercial market. A business focuses on the bottom line, net profit; communities have no overriding single objective. That is why it is important in discussions of local economic development to begin with direct and detailed statements of what it is that residents want from their community. When this is done, it becomes quickly apparent that most of their wishes are qualitative, not to be attained by quantitative growth alone. That is why it is better to describe the dynamism and diversity of opportunity we seek on the local economic level in terms of the qualitative term *vitality* rather than the quantitative term *growth*.

Citizens involved in the development of public economic policy should not feel constrained in insisting that qualitative objectives are not only legitimate but dominant.[6] Increasingly in private economic activity it is discretionary quality that we seek—not more and larger cars or more television sets but rather better cars and higher-quality "entertainment centers." A similar point can be made about the primary inputs into our economy: the quality of the work force, its skill, knowledge, and values, is what determines the productivity of the economy, not the quantity of workers or machines or the number of hours they put in. If qualities are the primary productive input to our economy and the primary output we seek from it, it is obviously appropriate to insist that our qualitative goals guide our community direct local economic development policy.

Public Economic Policy: Beyond the Commercial Sector

One of the more distorting shortcuts taken in public discussions of local economic well-being is to equate the local economy with local commercial businesses and to gauge economic health by means of their profitability. As useful as this is to businesses that want to pursue their self-interest in the name of the public interest, only bad economic policy can flow from this confusion of economics with private commercial concerns.

As we wrestle with the issues surrounding regulation of extractive industry and protection of natural landscape, it is crucial that we face the fact that what we seek through both extractive industry and environmental protection are economic goods and services. Both involve the use of scarce natural resources to produce valued goods and services on which the well-being of the population depends. Both are economic ventures. Both represent problems in natural resource economics. The fact that one is pursued by commercial businesses while the other may be pursued by noncommercial organizations does not make one economic and the other noneconomic. As the global population expands and the urbanization of society continues, intensifying stress on the environment and increasing our mutual interdependency, well-being will depend more and more on the quality of our social and natural environments and less and less on the private goods we purchase.

In thinking about local economic well-being and development policy, it is important to take a total view of the economy. If we focus only on the commercial sector, we end up ignoring the impact that part of our economic activity has on other sources of well-being. Extractive activity that gives us more copper or paper pulp may damage our health, wildlife, scenic beauty, water quality, or recreation. Or take the example of increased work outside of the home. It has reduced the amount of time available for home-based production—preparing meals, raising children, repairing homes. All of the increase in income does not represent an increase in well-being, since much of the additional income goes to pay for services we used to provide ourselves—services whose quality may be inferior.

What about the growing tendency of firms to require overtime of full-time employees? Because there are fixed costs associated with hiring new employees, firms often find it cheaper to pay existing workers a higher wage for overtime. Full-time workers may be required to work fifty hours a week instead of forty. This could boost workers' gross pay by as much as a third, and a narrow commercial analysis might conclude that they were blessed with unusual prosperity. Then why have workers been known to object to and even go on strike to eliminate this practice? And why do employers require extra hours rather than asking for volunteers? Clearly, to workers, this is not a pure economic blessing. The increased income comes at the cost of reduced family and free time and, for many, it is not worth that price. To many people, there is no more important task than the raising of children. Yet certain changes in our late-twentieth-century economy have made it more difficult for us to focus our energy on that task. Many parents have not been able to cope with the conflicting demands placed on them, and their children have suffered. This is no trivial matter. The point is that noncommercial home-based activity cannot be ignored in evaluations of well-being.

It is not just environmental goods and services and home-based production that are overlooked by an exclusive focus on the commercial sector. What about other major sources of productivity and well-being—schools and universities, hospitals and research institutions? And what about the diverse set of organizations and institutions we label government? Even the most vehement antigovernment advocates must recognize the critical economic services rendered by government: public streets and highways, a judicial system to enforce contracts and property rights, public health and safety, a stable monetary system, military defense and public order . . . . Government organizations, along with the not-for-profit sector, establish the context without which commercial activity as we know it would be impossible. The bandit capitalism of the drug trade in the United States and in the countries that supply it are graphic evidence of what type of society private enterprise can generate in the absence of effective public institutions. The rise of the Russian Mafia in the former Soviet Union is another chilling example.

In contemplating the economic transformation that has overtaken many of our communities and the choices we have to make about how we are going to treat our natural landscapes, it is important not to focus on one or a few commercial activities as if they were the sole foundation of the local economy. Our sources of well-being stretch far beyond the extractive industries we may have been told are our economic base, and our communities have far more stability and resilience than a "mono-industry" mind-set would suggest. This is not to say certain industries are not important or that they are not sources of well-being. Rather, it is to insist that they be put in the context of the total economy before choices are made about how our natural landscapes can best contribute to our well-being.

Jobs and Income

The dominant public economic policy objective of the second half of the twentieth century can be summarized in the commonplace mantra, jobs and income. Neither jobs nor income by itself represents a reasonable public policy objective. "Jobs" suggests that our objective should be to scrape together as many wage-paying positions as possible, regardless of their quality. "Income" suggests that money can buy happiness, though we have abundant empirical evidence to the contrary.

The emphasis on jobs is understandable, if misguided. Socially productive, satisfying work is central to most adults' sense of self-worth and identity in the community. Satisfaction with work contributes more to an individual's well-being than income earned or goods purchased with that income. The social need is for productive work, not just a "job" or "employment" regardless of the quality of work or its social meaning—that is, passive acceptance of someone else's power over us. The character of work does indeed matter, and most workers do want to take initiative and bear responsibility. The quality of work is a central "output" of the economy because of what it contributes to individual welfare.[7]

When we think of employment in our society, we tend to imagine people going to work full-time for a relatively large private business. It might surprise some to find out that of 178 million adults in 1990, only about 31 million, or one-sixth, held a full-time job working for a relatively large (100+ employees) private business (table 11-1). Twenty-two million adult Americans work part-time, not full time, three-quarters voluntarily. Ten million are self-employed. Another 9 million full-time adult workers are employed by government, not private business. About 6 million adults work full-time for nonprofit organizations. About 23 million between the ages of twenty and fifty-four are not in the labor force at all, their work effort being focused outside of the commercial economy. Thirty-four million adults fifty-five years old or older have withdrawn from the labor force. About 18 million full-time adult workers are employed in enterprises with fewer than twenty employees. Another 20 million work in firms that employ between twenty and

TABLE 11-1.

Work Status of American Adults, 1990

	Number (millions)	% of Adult Population
Adult Population age 20+	178.0	100%
Age 55+ out of Labor Force	33.6	18.8
Age 20–54 out of Labor Force	23.2	13.0
Part-Time Age 20+ Wage and Salary Worker	17.4	9.8
Self-Employed	10.0	5.6
Nonprofit, Private	6.1	3.4
Government Employee (full time)	9.0	5.1
Small Firm, Full Time (<20 workers)	18.1	10.2
Medium Firm, Full Time (20–99 workers)	20.4	11.5
Military and Institutions	3.8	2.1
Unemployed, Age >19	5.8	3.3
Large Private Business	30.60	17.2

Source: Statistical Abstract of the United States, 1993.

ninety-nine workers. There are also the unemployed who are seeking work and in the meantime, no doubt, engaging in other productive activities.

In other words, the simple label "jobs" does not adequately reflect the diverse choices Americans have made in their work or the opportunities they face. Most adults who are not employed full time by a large business are not inactive or unproductive or unfulfilled. Reality is more complex than the "nine-to-five" corporate ladder. In fact, that work pattern is in decline as larger corporations downsize, turning more and more to small businesses and independent contractors to provide them with services. In thinking about providing our citizens with opportunities for productive and satisfying work, the total economy has to be kept in mind. Self-employment, small business, home-based production, volunteer work, the not-for-profit sector, public institutions, the activities of retired and semiretired citizens—all these have to be taken into consideration. After all, they represent how most of us are productively engaged.

In some ways, recent trends are a return to past patterns of economic activity. Employment in the sense of working for some large commercial business was a phenomenon that developed during the industrial revolution and reached its pinnacle in the period of big business, big labor, and big government in the third quarter of the twentieth century. It has been in substantial decline since. A much less structured and more varied work pattern has been developing as the century draws to a close, even within large corporations.[8] The flexibility this provides people and the productivity it adds to the overall economy are positive developments. The changes may also represent a return to a scale of organization with which most of us are more comfortable and better able to cope. The decline in protective oversight by both unions and government, however, could prove to be a serious drawback, turning the clock back to the days of exploitation and limited or no medical and retirement benefits. The public policy challenge today is to maintain the positive aspects of change in the workplace while striving to build new institutional support structures.

Our public economic goal should be meaningful and satisfying work for all adults, not just more jobs. We aren't served by a narrow quantitative goal that assumes adults are helpless and need to be rescued by some large commercial or government organization. We are served by a qualitative objective that recognizes the preferences and initiative of adults as well as the variety of productive work situations. Economic development that seeks expanded work opportunity only through large corporate operations implicitly ignores local entrepreneurial energy, the way work contributes to well-being, and the reality of today's workplace.

What about the other half of the economic mantra, income? Rare are the people who do not think that they could use more money. The widespread wish for more, along with the singleminded pursuit of profit on the part of commercial business, easily translates into a public policy goal. But public institutions are not intended to be mere extensions of private interest. If more income were unambiguously associated with a higher level of overall well-being, one might view the emphasis in public economic policy on boosting income as reflecting concern for the entire population's welfare. But studies indicate that higher income does not generally improve well-being except for those living in poverty.[9] Well-being, of course, is a slippery term. We use it here to refer to a feeling of satisfaction with life as a whole, the overall judgment by individuals about how well their lives are going.

Studies have shown that, as far as the external circumstances of people's lives are concerned, the dominant sources of well-being in order of importance are family life, friendship, work satisfaction, and leisure activities. None of these is a market commodity directly linked to level of income. Although one might hypothesize that work satisfaction and the quality of leisure activities improve with income, empirical research contradicts that. As for internal sources of well-being, they are primarily self-esteem and a sense of effectiveness, or the belief that one has met life's challenges. Again, money income does not play a direct role.[10]

If we shift away from well-being to the daily pleasures of life, the role of money income does not gain much. A survey on what gives the most personal satisfaction or enjoyment day in and day out indicates that family activities again rank first, followed in declining order of importance by television, friends, music, books and newspapers, house or apartment, work, meals, car, sports, and clothes.[11] Although a minimum level of income is required for most of these pleasures, they are available to all but the most poverty stricken. Where income is likely to matter the most in this list, the satisfaction is tied to comparative achievement, not the absolute level of achievement—how, for example, your clothes, car, and living quarters stack up against those of the people you are judging yourself against. Emphasis on income and purchased commodities puts us in a rat race that few of us can win and which directly contributes little either to overall sense of well-being or the daily sense of pleasure and satisfaction. To repeat, it is primarily family, friendship, and work that contribute to our well-being, none of which can be purchased in commercial markets.

Enlightened public economic policy would address families and family life, community, and the quality of the work experience, not just the commercial sector. These true sources of well-being are all only distantly associated with material flows. Public economic policy that worked harder to improve real well-being would be less of a threat to the local environments that support us than current policy, obsessed as it is with more jobs and more income.

Sacrificing the Precious and Scarce for the Cheap and Common

Several centuries of European settlement and development of North America have made the United States one of the richest nations on the planet. In the pursuit of commercial wealth, we have cleared land of natural vegetation and planted monoculture crops, dammed and diverted most of our major water courses, moved mountains to extract mineral wealth, replaced native wildlife with imported domestic animals, unleashed a toxic brew of complex organic chemicals into our ground and surface water, air, and food supplies. We have been intrepid in our experiments with nature, making radical changes without knowing the full consequences, hoping that whatever they are, we will be able to cope and still reap some benefit. However we think of ourselves politically, we have been anything but conservative. We are among the most radical people in the history of civilization.

The legacy of our economic adventure is a radically modified, fragmented landscape. Intact ecosystems are rare islands surrounded by the "econo-tech" culture of the late twentieth century. What natural landscapes remain are shriveled vestiges of the original gift of nature Europeans found on this continent. Their value lies in their fragile, irreplaceable biodiversity. Intact ecosystems are increasingly scarce and unique. We are down to the last, and what we lose now we cannot regain.

Ultimately, it is in this context that the demands of extractive industry must be considered. Extractive industries are mature; they produce standardized products that are sold in worldwide markets. There is nothing unique or special about a barrel of oil from Texas. It is interchangeable with a barrel from Alaska, Nigeria, Venezuela, or Saudi Arabia. The same can be said of bushels of wheat from the United States, Canada, Russia, or New Zealand, the copper in electric wiring from Utah, Chile, or Zaire, the natural gas in pipelines, which comes from any of thousands of sources and is delivered indiscriminately to users throughout the world. Such commodities are not only uniform, they are abundant, and oversupply regularly plagues their markets. In most years, extractive industries struggle to cope with depressed commodity prices by boosting productivity to cut per-unit costs. But increased productivity, which all producers pursue, serves only to maintain the downward pressure on price, and low prices render much extractive activity economically marginal. If some of it did not take place, little net value would be lost because cost is so close to revenue and because there are readily available alternative sources of supply.

Contrast the two sets of economic values associated with natural landscape, the environmental and the extractive. Commodities are cheap and easily replaced, and additional increments produce little net economic value. Remnant natural landscapes are scarce, relatively unique, irreplaceable assets. In many cases, if we opt for extractive activity to keep the local economy afloat, we will be sacrificing what is scarce and unique for what is common and cheap. With the twenty-first century looming, we as a people can no longer afford such irrational waste. Neither can the planet.

Glossary

Many terms that have both ordinary language and technical meanings are frequently used throughout the book. To help the reader understand the meaning of those terms in the context of this book, the following brief glossary is provided.

agglomerative: An economic context or environment created by the concentration of certain types, or a certain range, of economic activities in a particular location, for instance, the location of a large number of software or computer design firms in an area.

amenity: A site-specific quality of the living environment in a particular location that impacts individuals' well-being, for instance, comfortable climate or scenic beauty.

basic: In the context of the economic base model, those economic activities that cause income to flow into a particular area. Within that model, these activities are seen as the primary causal force in the local economy.

community stability: The idea that a local area's economic health can be protected or enhanced by protecting or enhancing the flow of raw materials from the surrounding natural landscape. The U.S. Forest Service has used this concept in the past as an important objective of its management of National Forest lands.

compensating wage differentials: Differences in payments to workers to compensate them for negative aspects of their work situation, which can include risks to health and life, discomfort, higher cost of living, or degraded social and natural environments. Since these higher money payments simply compensate the worker for losses, they do not, on net, represent improvements in economic well-being.

cost of living: The different cost of obtaining a standard market-basket of goods and services in one location as opposed to another or at one time as opposed to another.

derivative: Within the context of the economic base model, locally oriented economic activities that depend upon the circulation of income injected into the local economy by basic activities. Derivative activities are viewed as the passive effects of more fundamental changes elsewhere in the economy.

direct impacts: The income generated, or the employment provided, by an economic activity before any linkages between that activity and others are taken into account.

economic: An activity, institution, or thing has an economic aspect if it relies upon
    scarce resources that have alternative uses in satisfying the diverse preferences
    of the population. Monetary or commercial characteristics are not necessary for
    something to have an economic aspect.
economic activity: All human activities that protect or develop scarce resources,
    transform them into useful goods and services, or distribute them in ways that sat-
    isfy peoples' diverse needs. These activities need not be commercially oriented.
economic base: A hypothesized kernel or core of the economy that is thought
    to be the causal force that drives the rest of the economy. This theoretical
    conceptualization of the economy assumes that some economic activities
    are more important than others and that economic analysis should focus upon
    those key economic activities.
economic value: The capacity of an economic good or service to make a positive
    difference in people's lives. Its measure is the sacrifice individuals are willing to
    make of other valuable things they possess to obtain this particular good or ser-
    vices. Money flows and commercial businesses need not be involved. The state-
    ment of an economic value can be in barter or money terms.
economic vitality: The capacity of a local economy to sufficiently satisfy the eco-
    nomic needs and desires of its residents in an ongoing way so that continued res-
    idence there remains attractive.
economic well-being: That part of human well-being that is influenced by the use
    of scarce resources. This definition is not limited to the monetary and commer-
    cial aspects of our lives.
economy: That part of our social organization that protects or develops scarce re-
    sources, transforms them into useful goods and services, and distributes them to
    satisfy the diverse preferences of the population. It includes noncommercial and
    nonmonetary institutions.
expected value: The average value of an uncertain outcome if the event were re-
    peated an unlimited number of times. The sum of all of the possible mutually
    exclusive outcomes weighted by the probability of each occurring.
export oriented: Economic activities that focus on producing a good or service for
    nonlocal use.
extractive: Activities that physically remove resources from their original natural
    environment for consumption within the economy.
folk economics: The set of popular cultural beliefs about the economy that may or
    may not have any empirical or theoretical basis.
footloose: Economic activity that is not tied to a particular location but can move to
    locations attractive to the economic agent. Income that is not tied to economic
    activities in a particular location but moves with the person who receives that in-
    come.
goods: Material products of economic activity, including the output of agriculture,
    mining, construction, and manufacturing.
import substitution: Expansion of the local economy through the local production
    of goods and services that had previously been imported. In the context of the
    export base model, this reduces the leakage and increases the multiplier.
income injection: Income that flows into the local economy from the larger external
    economy. These flows can be associated with the export of economic goods and
    services, nonlocal government spending, tourism, property and retirement in-
    come, etc.

indirect impacts: Within the context of the economic base model, the impacts associated with the linkages between one type of economic activity and others. An example would be the impact of expanded output in one industry on other businesses that provide inputs to that industry.

inmigration: The movement of people into a particular area or community. It usually refers to the internal migration of citizens within the country.

landscape: The physical environment on or near the surface of the earth, including the topographic character, the biological communities, the microclimates, the physical resources present, the visual appearance, etc.

leakage: In the context of the economic base model, the flow of money out of the local economy. These outflows include payments for imports, investments outside the local economy, payment of nonlocal taxes, etc.

metropolitan area: A federal classification of larger urban areas based upon the size of the central city as well as the population in the built up area surrounding the central city. Small urban areas are not metropolitan areas by this definition and metropolitan areas so defined may contain rural areas within them.

multiplier: In the context of the economic base model, a summary of the impact that changes in the economic base have on the rest of the economy. An income multiplier or employment multiplier of three would imply that one additional dollar of income or one additional job in the economic base would cause total income or employment to expand by three dollars or three jobs.

nonemployment income: Personal income received from sources not associated with current employment in the workforce. The primary sources are retirement income, property income (dividends, rent, and interest), and transfers from the government.

qualities: The subjectively evaluated aspects of economic resources, goods, and services.

real value: An economic value expressed in dollar terms that has been adjusted to remove the effects of inflation.

residentiary: Related to residential location and habitation. In particular, the local economic activities that support the needs and desires of residents.

retail trade: The sale of goods to final customers. Supermarkets, shopping malls, and restaurants are examples. Retail trade is not a "service" industry although it is sometimes included in the large category of "services-producing" industries.

royalty, gross: A payment to the owner of mineral rights for the right to take ownership of and remove those minerals. A gross royalty is based upon the market value of the mineral in the form it is in as it leaves the mineral property. No consideration is given to the costs associated with extraction or on-site concentration or enhancement.

services: This term has two meanings, one broad, the other narrow. In its broadest meaning it refers to a residual: all non-goods production including retail and wholesale trade, transportation and public utilities, government, finance, insurance, and real estate. In its narrow meaning it refers to the production of a type of economic value that has to be produced on demand because it is not easily stored. This includes medical, business, personal, repair, management, engineering, educational, etc. services.

transfer payments: Income flows that are not related to or a reward for current economic productivity. Government income support and retirement programs as well as gifts and grants from private organizations are examples.

Notes

Introduction

1. See, for instance, Yaffee. For a discussion of the jobs issue, see Sample and Le Master 1992.

2. See chapter 5 in Wilkinson 1992. For discussions of early indigenous and Anglo fisheries on the Columbia River, see Smith 1979. For a discussion of both the early fishery and the causes of its decline, see Scholz et al. 1985.

3. See, for instance, Helvarg 1994.

Chapter 1

1. The application of the economic base model to the analysis of local economies goes back to at least the early 1920s (Aurousseau 1921). It was popularized in the United States because of a widely read monograph by Charles Tiebout (1962). An earlier academic debate between Tiebout and economic historian Douglas North attracted attention to the limits of the economic base model as a way of thinking about regional economic growth (Tiebout 1956 and North 1956). Environmental laws requiring "economic impact" analysis for almost all significant projects created a demand for easily manipulated models of the local economy. During the 1980s, this and the development of PC-based input-output models invested economic base modeling with new life (see Klosterman et al. 1993).

2. Persky et al. 1993.

3. See Krannich and Luloff 1991.

4. Many studies of local economies do take nonemployment income flow into account, especially for areas where retirement income is already recognized as an important part of the economic base. More often than not, however, analyses of the local economy are conducted in terms of earnings (wages, salaries, and self-employment income) from various industries. Sometimes this is because of the difficulty of determining the size of nonemployment income

flows, other times because earnings are believed to have a more substantial and reliable impact on the local economy than nonemployment income. In either case, this source of income is often ignored.

5. Ullman 1954.

6. Deavers 1989.

7. U.S. Department of Agriculture, Economic Research Service, 1994.

8. See Broadway 1994.

9. Borts and Stein 1964.

10. Richardson 1985. For a more recent review that came to the same conclusion, see Krikelas 1992.

11. Power 1988a, chapter 8.

12. Meyer 1992.

13. Templet and Farber 1994. The Pearson correlation coefficients between toxic releases per job and the unemployment rate, poverty rate, and disposable per capita income are +0.57, +0.26, and –0.29, respectively, which are statistically different from 0 at the 0.01, 0.10, and 0.05 levels. Also see the results of analyzing the impact of the location of waste-disposal sites on property values in Been 1994. These results may appear to conflict with the compensating wage differential analysis indicating that people have to be compensated with higher income or expanded economic opportunity in order to accept environmental degradation. Unequal distribution of income, economic opportunity, and political power may explain why toxic facilities are located where they are, near the least powerful or in neighborhoods abandoned by those who could afford to flee. Poor living environments may be inherited by those who are desperate and have less choice.

14. Power 1988a, chapters 2 and 3.

15. Denison 1967, 1974, 1985, and 1962. Also see Fukuyama 1995 and Sowell 1980.

16. In this example, the United States, Japan, and Western Europe have been used to represent the affluent countries, Africa, Asia (except for Japan), and South America to represent the rest of the world's population. In 1990 the population of the affluent countries was 687 million or 13 percent of the world's 5.3 billion. The average gross domestic product per capita in the affluent countries was $22,222, while for the poorer countries it was only $769. If these GDP figures are taken to reflect population and consumption differences, the affluent countries are consuming at about thirty times the rate of the poorer countries. If through population growth and economic expansion the affluent countries expanded at a rate of 2 percent per year, poorer countries would have to grow by a factor of 64 to boost per capita consumption to the same level as consumption in affluent countries $[(1.02)^{40}] * 29$. The impact on overall resource use would "only" be a fourteen-fold expansion because the poor countries begin with an aggregate consumption level that is only a quarter

that of the aggregate of the affluent countries. (World Resources Institute 1994, tables 15.1 and 16.1).

17. U.S. Bureau of Labor Statistics 1988.

18. U.S. Congressional Budget Office 1993, p. 50.

19. U.S. Bureau of the Census 1994, table 631.

20. Maguire 1991. Data is for January 1991.

Chapter 2

1. Douglas North would dispute this statement (see North 1966). During the period preceding the American Civil War, he concluded, cotton exports from the South drove and financed a complex specialization of production and trade within the United States that was the primary engine of American growth. Even if one accepts the important role of exports in American economic development, it is true that the U.S. economy focused on expanding internal markets rather than international trade.

2. For an analysis of the use of local currencies within a national economy, see Greco 1994.

3. See Schmenner 1982, Isard 1956, or Hoover 1948.

4. Duffy 1994. Also see Greenwood 1981, pp. 39–42.

5. Polzin 1976.

6. Berry and Parr 1989, pp. 33–34, and Moore and Jacobsen 1984. Also see the discussion of the variability of multipliers for cities of similar size in Joseph Persky et al. 1993, p. 19.

7. Kendall and Pigozzi 1994; Mulligan 1987; and Mulligan and Gibson 1984.

8. Greenwood 1981, cited in Sastry 1992, p. 61; and Sastry 1992, p. 63.

9. See Longino and Crown 1990, and the citations provided there.

10. Glasgow 1988.

11. U.S. Department of Agriculture, Economic Research Service, 1994, p. 15. Population growth rate in retirement counties was twice the average for all nonmetro counties and a third larger than the growth rate in metro counties for 1990–1992. For the performance of these counties during the 1980s, see Deavers 1989.

12. Borts and Stein (1964) first presented a systematic analysis for long-run local employment adjusting to the labor supply within a particular region. Numerous empirical analyses based on the assumption of mutual causality between migration and job creation have lent support to their hypothesis. See Greenwood 1980, p. 39, and Sastry 1992, pp. 60–62, for a summary. Studies of firm-location decisions also confirm the importance of labor supply. See Calzonetti and Walker 1991; Kieschnick 1981; Braden and Rideout 1978, pp. 111–113; and Schmenner 1981.

13. This position was initially argued by Muth (1971), who was wrestling with the chicken-and-egg problem. Greenwood's more recent empirical work

confirms this proposition (Greenwood and Hunt 1984; Greenwood et al. 1986; and Greenwood 1981).

14. Gottlieb 1992, Amenities as an Economic Development Tool, and 1992, Amenity-Oriented Firm Location.

15. See, for instance, Shankland 1988; Ross and Usher 1986; Robertson 1985; and Kahne 1985.

16. *The Monthly Magazine,* London, 1811, cited by Kendall and Pigozzi 1994, p. 52.

17. Bell 1973, p. 173.

18. Ullman 1954.

19. See Smilor, Gibson, and Kozmetsky 1988; and Brett et al. 1991.

20. Tiebout 1956. For a general discussion of this point see Power 1988. Also see, for instance, Blomquist et al. 1988; Roback 1988; Greenwood et al. 1991. The general approach taken by analysts is to study the variation in earnings in a geographic cross-section of the nation and relate the variation not only to various measures of labor supply and demand but also to measures of local conditions (air pollution, crime, climate, etc.) and cost of living. The coefficients on the amenity variables are taken as a measure of the impact of local conditions on local earnings, all other earning determinants being constant.

21. Blomquist et al. 1988 estimated the aggregate value of the amenity package; they measured it as $5,146 per year higher in the best compared to the worst urban areas in 1980. The value was adjusted to 1994 dollars using the consumer price index.

22. Gyourko and Tracy 1991, table 2, adjusted from 1979 to 1994 dollars.

23. See, for instance, Hannon 1994 and Clark 1992. Also see the results of the analysis of the impact of the location of waste-disposal sites on property values in Been 1994.

24. Deavers 1989.

25. U.S. Department of Agriculture, Economic Research Service, 1994.

26. Johnson and Rasker 1993.

27. The data, for 1992, are based on the Regional Economic Information system (REIS) data on personal income. This point has been made in connection with the 1980s by Mills and Chodes (1988).

28. See endnote number 13. Also Steinnes 1978 and 1982; Cooke 1978; and Muth 1971.

29. For a conventional discussion of the role of amenities in shifting the location of economic activity, see Coppack 1988. For the earliest formulation of this mechanism, see Tiebout 1956.

30. The REIS, Bureau of Economic Analysis, provides county-level data on these categories of nonemployment income: dividends, rent, and interest and transfer payments. Also see Kendall and Pigozzi 1994.

31. Some analysts, however, have simply assumed that nonemployment income is basic income. See, for instance, Bender 1987. Many other researchers

have pointed out the need to include nonemployment income as part of basic income.

32. Kendall and Pigozzi 1994. Summers and Hirschl 1985 also found high-income multipliers for retirement income.

33. Mulligan 1987.

34. Bain (1984) found the impact of transfer income to be three times larger than the impact of earned income. Hirschl and Summers (1982) found that transfer payments were the most efficient generator of nonbasic employment growth. McNulty (1977) found multipliers of 2 to 3 for nonemployment income. Harmston (1979) found that retirement cash transfers had a multiplier effect greater than 2.0. Eldon Smith et al. (1982) found that transfer payments had the largest impact on employment compared with all other sources of income.

35. Sastry 1992.

36. Smith 1986.

37. U.S. Bureau of the Census 1992, table 144 (the data is for 1990). The average senior household was approximated at 1.75 persons (table 59).

38. The REIS, Bureau of Economic Analysis, data on earnings and total employment indicate an average earning per job of $26,500 in 1992. Those 60 years old and older made up 16.7 percent of the population in 1991 (U.S. Bureau of the Census 1992, table 12). Total population divided by total employment for those under 65 was 1.79 people per job in 1990 (U.S. Bureau of the Census 1992, tables 12 and 623). Actual migration of seniors represents only a small percentage of total migration between counties in the United States. In 1990 migrants 55 and over represented 8 percent of total migrants. Migrants 65 and over represented 4.5 percent of intercounty migrants (U.S. Bureau of the Census 1992, table 22). Retirees, however, do not have to move to an area in order to have an impact; if they choose to stay at a location, the income associated with their retirement has the same impact on the local economy as that of an inmigrating retiree.

39. Sastry 1992, p. 55.

40. Greenwood 1981, p. 42.

41. Persky and Wiewel 1992.

42. REIS, Bureau of Economic Analysis, CD-ROM, personal income, 1969–92.

43. Moore and Jacobsen 1984, figure 2.

44. Persky and Wiewel 1992.

45. Such population growth would also tend to increase the range of economic activity that was viable at that location. The impact is discussed later as part of the impact of inmigration on the tendency to spend locally.

46. See, for instance, Stabler and Olfert 1994, table 1. The authors of this article do not come to this conclusion, but their data on population and business growth in small cities supports it.

47. For such a change in the average propensity to purchase locally to be triggered solely by increased local population, population growth would have to be quite high, 5 to 6 percent per year sustained over a ten-year period, or a ten-year change of over 80 percent. This would approach "boom" conditions. Less rapid growth of, say, 3 percent per year would, over a decade, lead the average propensity to consume locally to increase by about 2 percentage points, not 4. In addition, the scale of the local economy is likely to be critical. Very small towns and villages located in primarily agricultural areas are likely to see declining economic activity, not expansion. See Moore and Jacobsen 1984, p. 223, and Fuguitt 1994.

48. Jobes 1988, p. 282.

49. Meyers 1989.

50. A third of total personal income is assumed to be nonemployment income. If a third of this is assumed to not enter the local economy at all and the income multiplier is assumed to be three, the impact would be 10% * (0.333)* (0.667) * (3.0) = 6.67%.

51. See the text above for a discussion of the logic of this calculation. The arithmetic involves the following: {[$17,500 * 3) – $17,500)/$26,500] * 1.8 +1} * (10/6) = 5.6.

52. The assumption made here is that there are two sources of the increase in the fraction of local income spent locally (and, therefore, the increase in the income multiplier): (1) a national trend that leads this fraction to increase by 0.6 percent per year, and (2) the local impact of increased population. If we are focused on a five-year period during which inmigration adds 10 percent to the population, the national trend will increase the propensity to spend locally by 3 percent, which will lead the multiplier and the economy to expand by 4.6 percent. Thus about half of the inmigration would be absorbed simply by this expansion in the economy. The propensity to spend locally also grows as the population expands. The relationship used here comes from Craig L. Moore and Marilyn Jacobsen, "Minimum Requirements and Regional Economics," *Economic Geography* 60:215–224, p. 233: Propensity to Spend Locally (%) = –30.4 + 15.58 * Log (Population). A 10 percent increase in population would result in a change in the propensity to spend locally of 0.645 of a percentage point. If that were 60 percent to begin with, this would be a 1.07 percent increase. The impact on the multiplier and total income would be about 1.6 percent. The combination of these two impacts of the increasing propensity to spend locally would be an expansion of the local economy of 6.2 percent.

53. The assumption is that one in six of the inmigrants gets added to the surplus labor force, which in turn attracts additional export-oriented (or import-substitution) economic activity at about average wages. If the income multiplier is three, then each of these bring two additional jobs into existence and a total of three find employment: 10/6 * 3 = 5, or 50% of the ten inmigrants.

54. Residential investment in housing comes to about 12 percent of total personal outlays, which in turn are about 84 percent of personal income. If we assume that newcomers invest at about this level, residential investment per permanent new inmigrant would be about 10 percent of per capita income. If, in addition, there are at least two persons who try to settle in the area for each that succeeds and the failing effort covers one month of residence during which expenditures match the average for residents, then the expenditures from this would be one-sixth of per capita income. If a multiplier of 2.5 were to be applied to these expenditures, the impact would be: $2.5 * (0.10 + 1/6) * $ Avg. Income = $0.667 *$ Avg. Income.

55. Wilkinson 1992, chapter 1.

Chapter 3

1. See for instance, Bluestone and Harrison 1986.

2. U.S. Bureau of the Census 1992, table 667. Services refers to narrowly defined services such as business, medical, educational, social, repair, personal, and engineering services. The decline in average wages refers only to production and nonsupervisory workers. This is important because there has been a shift in employment away from production workers and toward professional-technical and supervisory employment. When total earnings of all workers are taken into account, real earnings per job have not declined. When the increased prevalence of part-time jobs is accounted for, real earnings per hour have increased.

3. If 1970 employment shares are used to weight 1992 average wages by industry, average wages in private, nonagricultural employment decline by 5.2 percent. If 1992 employment weights are used for 1992 wages, the decline is 6.2 percent. The difference can be attributed to the shift toward service-producing industries over that period.

4. Howell 1994, p. 31.

5. Ibid.

6. REIS, Bureau of Economic Analysis, CD-ROM 1969–1992.

7. This broad statement is based on average earnings for a variety of skills in goods and services production. Such simple comparison of average earnings allows only one variable, sex, to be held constant. Although that is the way public discussion of this topic is usually conducted, it does not reliably isolate the effects of the various determinants of earnings. Multiple regression analysis allows simultaneous consideration of several different determinants of earnings levels as well as a study of the impact of each while all the others are held constant. In this type of more detailed analysis, employment in services-producing industries *does* appear to reduce earnings if one also holds skill and occupation constant. The discussion in the next paragraph documents this: For the same occupation/skill level, both male and female workers get paid less in services than in goods production. This is an important empirical characteristic of ser-

vice jobs that is not positive. However, it does not contradict the point made here and in the following paragraph. Because of the higher skill levels associated with service jobs, when the sex of the worker is accounted for, wages in services are as high as or higher than wages in goods production.

8. One way of stating this would be that the return to labor of any given skill is lower in services than it is in goods production. The focus of the discussion in this section has been on whether earnings in services, averaged across skill levels, is lower than in goods production—the claim usually made about services employment. The claim is wrong, although the more narrow claim that the return to labor of a given skill level is lower in services may be true. This combination of characteristics is *not* typical of service jobs, even though they may reward occupational level less than goods production does. The difference is the higher skill that characterizes service jobs. The analysis provided here purposely combines industry and occupational characteristics rather than holding occupation/skill constant because the different occupational characteristics of service jobs are a critical consideration in responding to the concern that the economy is primarily creating poor jobs.

9. Bednarzik 1987. The time period of the analysis was 1973–85.

10. To say that the percentage of jobs in high- or low-wage sectors has increased or decreased requires that these sectors be defined. There are two possibilities. One is to take the current period and divide narrow industries according to their relative pay, putting, for instance, the lowest third in the low-wage category. This classification of industries would then be applied to the comparison period, and one would track the shift in employment among the industries so characterized. This assumes that low-wage industries remain low wage. Alternatively, on could categorize all jobs in the sample according to their real earnings and divide them into, say, the top, middle, and bottom third. The structure of high, middle, and low real wages could then be applied to the comparison period. This allows industries to shift between categories but assumes that the structure of earnings remains the same (see Bednarzik 1987). These two approaches both indicate the same thing with respect to female workers: a shift toward higher-wage sectors over time. For male workers the first approach indicates a shift to lower-paying jobs, but the second approach indicates increases in high-wage jobs as well as low-wage jobs. The latter result is confirmed by the "middle-class squeeze" literature. See McMahon and Tschetter 1986, and Horrigan and Haugen 1988.

11. Blank 1990, p. 125.

12. See chapter 8, particularly tables 8-3 and 8-4. Also see U.S. Department of Agriculture, Economic Research Service, 1993.

13. Blank 1990, table 1.

14. Eberts and Groshen 1990, p. 6.

15. The U.S. Department of Labor measures the unemployment rate for workers in a given industry by associating each unemployed person with the industry in which that person last held a full-time job. Such "industry"

unemployment rates measure the rate at which employees in a particular industry lose jobs. Since workers can move between industries, the association of unemployment with a particular industry can be misleading.

16. Eberts and Groshen 1990, p. 7.

17. U.S. Bureau of the Census 1992, table 677.

18. Blackburn et al. 1990, pp. 45–47, and 1990, pp. 129–33.

19. Bednarzik 1987.

20. For two overlapping sets of essays dealing with this problem, see Burtless 1990, and Kosters 1991.

21. Horrigan and Haugen 1988.

22. Howell 1994.

23. Thurow 1989, p. 7.

24. Kassab 1992.

25. Ibid., pp. 105–6.

26. The following discussion is partially based on Power 1994, chapter 6.

27. McMahon 1988.

28. American Chamber of Commerce Researchers Association quarterly, ACCRA Inter-City Cost of Living Index, Louisville, Kentucky.

29. Gilford 1981.

30. Sahling and Smith 1983; Roback 1988; Farber and Newman 1987; and Dickie and Gerking 1987.

31. For the development of the equilibrium approach to regional variation in earnings, see Rosen 1979; Roback 1982 and 1988; and Dickie and Gerking 1987.

32. Ed Whitelaw coined this phrase. See, for instance, Niemi and Whitelaw 1995, p. 12.

33. U.S. Bureau of the Census 1993, tables 69 and 626. The years referred to are 1990 for dependents and 1992 for labor-force participation rate.

34. Ibid., table 661.

35. See, for example, Kahne 1985.

36. Niemi and Whitelaw 1995, p. 12.

37. For a discussion as well as a critique of the equilibrium wage-differential approach, see Beeson 1991; Evans 1990; and Hunt 1992.

38. See Hoch 1978, and Power 1981. As discussed in chapter 3, there are cultural amenities in larger cities as well as a greater range of commercial opportunity. The assumption being made does not contradict this aspect of urban size, it is simply being assumed that the net effect of the urban-size amenity is negative.

39. Hoch et al. 1983, p. 35.

Chapter 4

1. U.S. Bureau of the Census 1991, table 674.

2. This characterization is accurate based on the pre-mining and mining pe-

riods and/or changes in the number of jobs. If one looks at the percentage change in employment, the slowest growth was during the post-mining period, 1980–90. The same number of jobs was created in 1973–80 and 1980–90, but the latter period is longer and the base level of employment is higher. So the rate of growth of employment was slower after the mine closed. There was no decline in employment, but it could be argued that local economic expansion slowed.

3. See Peoples 1989, pp. 69–71.

4. Wyoming, having a significant positive relationship between changes in mining employment and changes in other employment, was an exception to this pattern. Simple regression analysis of this type, where only one or two explanatory variables are used, is not very convincing. Regional economies are much more complicated than this primitive modeling assumes. The mining industry, in its attack on any reform of the 1872 Hardrock Mining Act during the early 1990s, used simple regression analysis of this type to argue that mining was still the "industrial base" of western states with high "multiplier" effects on the rest of the economy (Evans 1993, pp. 20–21).

5. The huge disparity in these two employment numbers, with seventy nonmining jobs being added for each mining job lost, also partially answers the concern about the wage levels with new jobs. Many new service jobs are in relatively high-paid industries (figure 4-4). Although most of the jobs being added do not pay wages similar to those that had been paid in mining, if only 10 percent of the new jobs were relatively high-paid, seven times as many high-paying jobs would have been added for each high-paying job lost.

6. The employment data used for this analysis is that of the REIS, Bureau of Economic Analysis, CA27 full- and part-time wage and salary employment. By counting part-time jobs as if they were full time, it tends to overstate employment, but since it ignores self-employed miners it also tends to underestimate employment. The REIS CA27 data is the highest of the alternative sources available. The Bureau of Census County Business Patterns' employment data, as well as employment data from the Department of Labor's Mine Safety and Health Administration, Division of Mining Information Systems, indicate significantly smaller employment levels.

7. U.S. General Accounting Office 1992.

8. Crude petroleum and natural gas prices (average value at the point of production) are from U.S. Bureau of the Census 1991, table 1221.

9. Copper and gold commodity prices are from the annual *Mineral Commodity Summaries*, Bureau of Mines, U.S. Department of Interior.

10. Daniel 1992, p. 84.

11. U.S. Bureau of Labor Statistics 1993. Evans Economics, Inc., reported metal-mining productivity rising at 10.8 percent per year over the last decade "far more than any other basic industry" (M. K. Evans 1993).

12. For an example of employment analysis that accounts for these types of uncertainty, see Power 1987, pp. 20–25.

13. Park 1993, chapter 15.

14. See Power 1987, pp. 20–25, and Shaffer and Vatne 1984. The Montana Department of State Lands collects information on the inmigration of population associated with new metal mines. For one report based on this data, see Montana Department of Health and Environmental Sciences 1992, p. 92. Also see the Electric Power Research Institutes model in inmigration to generation sites contained in Stauffer 1994.

15. Such indirect employment can be treated as a benefit only if it can be shown that the workers who fill the jobs would otherwise have remained indefinitely unemployed. The Water Resources Council, a federal interagency organization, published first "Principles and Standards for Planning Water and Related Land Resources" (December 1971) and then the "Manual of Procedures for Evaluating Benefits and Costs of Federal Water Resources Projects" (May 1979). In the early 1980s President Reagan abolished the Water Resources Council, but the principles of project evaluation continued to be used.

Chapter 5

1. For clarity, this discussion is set in the context of another source of supply for the same mineral. When a mine is shut down or not allowed to begin production, the resources that would otherwise have been committed to it are shifted to other productive activities, in mining or elsewhere. The loss to the economy is any productive advantage the original mining activity had over the alternatives to which the resources would flow.

2. Fickett et al. 1990, and Lovins et al. 1982.

3. See Figure 5-1 for a demonstration of the range of gold production that would be marginal at various levels of gold commodity prices. Because there are few restrictions on entry into mining, mining operations tend to be undertaken whenever a competitive return on the mine operation is supported by current metal prices. At those prices, some operations are profitable. Others are marginal, just breaking even, or losing money.

4. This statement is based on several simplified assumptions, for example, that the decisionmaker neither is risk-adverse nor enjoys the risk involved. The incentives and opportunities created by the taxation of mines and mining property may change the evaluation of the risk. Each company is likely to operate with somewhat different investment criteria. The point remains, however, that an uncertain return of a certain amount is not identical to the certain return of the same amount.

5. For a more formal presentation of this type of analysis, see Power 1990 and 1988.

6. This assumes that delaying extraction creates no intertemporal allocation problem. Some worry that current generations will leave future generations with a smaller endowment of resources than the current generation has enjoyed. Others have argued that with ongoing economic development, future

generations will be better off and that conservation simply shifts resources from the less well-to-do to the more well-to-do. Because inflation-adjusted monetary measures of well-being have been constant or declining for two decades, and measures of well-being that include changes in the quality of the social and natural environments indicate declining levels of well-being, this may not be an accurate characterization of the relative position of present and future generations. See Cobb and Cobb 1994. In addition, that consideration does not appear to reduce efforts by parents to provide for their children and grandchildren, or of one generation to care about the quality of the endowment they are passing on to other generations. The "rational" rate of extraction of a nonrenewable resource will depend, among other things, on a comparison of the expected growth in the annual "profit" (gross value less costs) associated with mining the resource and the rate of return that can be earned on investment made in other parts of the economy. See Randall 1981, pp. 218–19.

7. For a more complete development, see Power 1988.

8. Krutilla 1967; Fisher et al. 1972; Krutilla and Fisher 1975.

9. John Krutilla (1967, and Krutilla and Fisher 1975) appears to be the first economist to have made this point and developed its economic implications. There has been little empirical research seeking to verify the relative importance of the natural characteristics of the landscape to users and others who value environmental preservation. Certain characteristics such as lakes, clear air and water, wildlife, and biological diversity, have been shown to increase the value assigned to landscape. The impact of deviations from "pristine" status on the valuation of natural landscape, however, has not been extensively studied.

10. For a development of the techniques that can be used for this purpose, see Krutilla and Fisher 1975, pp. 128–35. In the simplest cases, where no carrying capacity or congestion constraints have been reached, the growth rate can be approximated by the sum of the growth rates in usage and in real average income.

11. Mineral Policy Center 1993.

12. Walsh 1984, and Otis 1977.

13. Mineral Policy Center 1993.

14. See, for instance, Clark 1992, and Templet and Farber 1994. The Pearson correlation coefficients between toxic releases per job and unemployment rate, poverty rate, and disposable per capita income are +0.57, +0.26, and –0.29, respectively, statistically different from 0 at the 0.01, 0.10, and 0.05 levels. Also see the results of the analysis of the impact of the location of waste-disposal sites on property values in Been 1994, and consult Meyer 1992 and 1993.

15. Mineral Policy Center 1993, p. 31.

16. Alfers and Graff 1992, p. 41.

17. Evans 1993, p. 20.

18. Dobra 1993, p. 12.

19. Alfers 1993, pp. 6 and 10. The job loss is greater than total employment in metal mining because indirect impacts of job loss in metal mining are included in the calculation.

20. Some have argued that there is indeed an important difference between private gross royalties and the proposed federal royalty: private mineral estate owners negotiate a royalty rate that is likely to vary with the expected profitability of the mine, while the proposed federal law would impose a standard rate on all mines regardless of profitability. This is not quite true. The proposed legislation sets a minimum royalty but would allow the federal government to negotiate a higher royalty if it could. This is the same approach taken to oil, gas, and coal leasing on federal lands as well as for hard-rock minerals on acquired federal land. There is no sign it has had catastrophic, or even, negative, consequences in those mineral development fields. Similarly, state governments often levy taxes on mineral operations. In the thirty-seven states levying special mineral extraction taxes, only six have chosen to base the tax on net proceeds (Schenck 1984). Typically, the tax does not vary with the profitability of the mining operation. It is not clear, either, that these state taxes have had significant negative consequences on mining.

21. Guzzardi 1982, p. 48.

22. Excluding Alaska, about 48 percent of land in the eleven western states is federally owned. Including Alaska, about 55 percent of land in the twelve western states is federally owned (Public Land Statistics 1990, and U.S. Bureau of the Census 1991).

23. If mines developed on federal land before the passage of mining law reform limiting the patenting of federal mining claims continue to have a legal right to proceed with the patenting of their claims, the percentage of hard-rock mining on federal land could continue to decline through this decade.

24. Dobra and Thomas 1992, p. 18.

25. U.S. General Accounting Office 1992.

26. Danielson and McNamara 1994.

Chapter 6

1. Hoidal 1980.
2. Morison 1942, p. 232.
3. Cox et al. 1985, p. 3.
4. Ibid., p. 8.
5. Ibid., chapter 9.
6. Shands and Healy 1977.
7. Cox et al. 1985, pp. 76–76, and Fortman et al. 1989, p. 45.
8. Cox et al. 1985, pp. 154–55.
9. For a discussion of the changes in the Pacific Northwest timber industry and their impact on the regional economy, see Anderson and Olson 1991.

10. While private industrial land in the Pacific Northwest has been harvested at a rate that is not sustainable, federal land managers insist that they have been managing federal land to supply a "nondeclining even flow" of logs. While this *may* be true in terms of a comparison of fiber harvested compared with annual growth in fiber, it is not true in terms of the environmental impact associated with that harvest. The damage done to other forest resources in the process of harvesting federal timber is the dominant constraint on timber harvests now. This real physical constraint partially determines what level of harvest is sustainable.

11. If one measures instability in terms of the percentage *decline* in real earnings by two-digit industry, instability in wood products is 50 percent higher than the unweighted average of the decline in other two-digit industries for the years 1969–92. Primary metals (partially related to mining) and automotive production were two manufacturing industries that were more unstable than wood products.Use of declines in real earnings to measure instability will mix ongoing long-term declines with downward fluctuations. Ideally, one would measure fluctuations alone. However, upward or downward trends would have to be removed, adding a layer of modeling assumptions that may not make things clearer. Since it is *negative* impacts of the wood products industry on the local economy that are at issue, mixing long-term decline with downward fluctuation should not confuse the analysis.

12. The R-square for a regression of the sum of the annual percentage decline in personal income on the percentage of total income derived from wood products was 0.90 in western Montana and 0.55 in western Oregon. Only those counties with a significant share of total income from wood products were included. The greater this dependence was, the larger the periodic negative changes in personal income were.

13. Flaim and Sehgal 1985, and Horvath 1987.

14. Gorte and Gorte 1989, p. 163.

15. Heberlein 1994.

16. U.S. Bureau of Labor Statistics 1993, p. 30. Cubbage (1987) calculated that improvements in productivity led to a 1.2 percent annual decline in forest products employment in southeastern forests over an extended period.

17. Drielsma 1984. The study area included New England and mid-Atlantic states.

18. Migration activity is primarily influenced by the demographic characteristics of the population. Young adults with above-average education who have moved before or come from families who have moved in the recent past are much more likely to move away from their current location. Since areas gaining population have a large number of such people, areas with a high *in*migration rate also tend to have a high *out*migration rate. This, of course, confounds statistical analysis. When the population's "propensity" to move (as indicated by demographic characteristics) is taken into account, some outmigration can be explained by local economic conditions. On inmigration and

outmigration rates being correlated, see Schachter and Althaus 1989. For a discussion of the larger issue of creating jobs to keep children in the community, see Power 1988, pp. 159–60.

19. Maguire 1993, p. 53.

20. Ibid.

21. Although the previous comparison of the median length of tenure for a particular employer between wood products and services is probably reliable, comparing tenure within a particular industry may not be. Service jobs, even narrowly defined, include a broad variety of industries: repair, business, health, educational, engineering, personal. People shifting among these may be classified as continuing to be in the same industry, services, even though there has been a significant job change. Of course, there are many different jobs within wood products, too. The accuracy of comparisons of tenure on the job depends on how narrowly the job is defined. The main point, however, is that there is not evidence of long job tenure in wood products.

22. Rufolo, Strathman, and Bronfman 1988, pp. 25–26.

23. See Shepard et al. 1992, figures A8d and A8e.

24. Power 1988, p. 159.

25. Pendleton 1975, and Paulozzi 1987.

26. Fortman et al. 1989, p. 44. Also see the U.S. Bureau of Labor Statistics, U.S. Department of Labor data series, *Occupational Injuries and Illnesses in the United States by Industry,* an annual report.

27. Whitelaw 1992, p. 3.

28. Guidelines for Economic and Social Analysis, *Federal Regulations,* 47, 17942, April 26, 1982.

29. San Juan and Grand Mesa–Uncompahgre–Gunnison National Forests during 1983–1985. See *Forest Planning* 4 (9): 2, and *High Country News,* August 19, 1985, p. 3.

Chapter 7

1. In the 103d Congress, the Forest Biodiversity and Clearcutting Prohibition Act (HR 1164) was introduced by John Bryant of Texas. It would have prohibited roaded logging in roadless areas. The Northern Rockies Ecosystem Protection Act, also introduced in that Congress (HR 2636), focused a similar ban on a six-state region in the northern Rockies. The Native Forest Council (Eugene, Oregon) proposed a zero cut on federal forestland (Miller 1995).

2. Shands and Healy 1977, chapter 1.

3. See table 7-1 and the discussion later of the employment impact of the Northern Rockies Ecosystem Protection Act, as well as Power 1992.

4. Power 1978, Alternative W.

5. The Multiple-Use Sustained-Yield Act of 1960 requires that the Forest Service "give equal consideration" to all renewable resources of the national forests. The Forest Service's continued emphasis on timber harvest at the ap-

parent expense of other forest values led to the passage of the National Forest Management Act (NFMA) of 1976, which seeks specific standards for increased protection of nontimber resources. The NFMA calls for the protection of fisheries and watersheds and the preservation of biological diversity. It also seeks to limit the use of clear-cutting and to restrict logging to areas that are economically and physically suited for intensive management (see section 6(k), 16 U.S.C.1604K).

6. U.S. Bureau of the Census 1992, table 1133.

7. Haynes 1992.

8. Adams 1977.

9. This discussion does not deal with the impact of such supply reductions on the price of wood products. If the supply adjustments also involve large price increases, the price of wood products may rise significantly. That could have a disruptive impact on wood-intensive industries such as housing construction. In that sense, even when there is a significant supply response, the economic impact might not be small if demand is not very sensitive to price and it takes large price increases to trigger supply responses. Economic modeling of such responses to supply curtailment, however, does not indicate that large price changes would be required. See Adams 1977; U.S. Department of Commerce 1976; and Buchwalter 1978.

10. Gorte 1990, table 18.

11. U.S. Forest Service 1990, 1: 19, 27, 55.

12. Tourism tends to be an urban-based activity. For that reason, its overall impact is not to redistribute income from urban to rural areas but the reverse. Still, rural-based tourist activity can counter this tendency.

13. Bell 1988, p. 2..

14. Florence Williams, "Sheep Putting Town on Fast Track," *Los Angeles Times,* November 11, 1993, p. A5.

15. Manning 1992, p. 28.

16. Murdock 1991.

17. Ibid.

18. Ibid.

19. Ibid., and J. Murdock, personal communication with the author, December 1993. Income estimates for the Dubois area were based on input-output modeling using primary data developed through Professor Murdock's research.

20. The earliest official warning that the rate of harvest of old growth in the Pacific Northwest was not sustainable came in U.S. Forest Service 1963. For a statement of the problems created by overcutting old growth on public and private land, see U.S. Forest Service 1969. Also see Haynes 1992.

21. See O'Toole 1993 and O'Toole 1988, chapter 2.

22. Beuter (1990) estimated that 147,000 jobs would be lost to implementation of the spotted owl conservation strategy and modification of forest plains. See also Sample and LeMaster 1992.

23. Flowers et al. 1993, p. 18.
24. Egan 1994.
25. Ibid.
26. Hatcher 1993, p. 13.
27. Power 1992.
28. Ibid., Executive Summary, table 1.
29. Ibid., Executive Summary, pp. 4–6.

Chapter 8

1. In this early economic modeling, other types of economic activity were seen as sterile in the sense of contributing no surplus over the value of inputs to production. Most agriculture obviously produced a surplus; that was the source of the rent claimed by owners who were not involved in the management or operation of their farms. No similar surplus was seen as regularly available in the small-scale economic activities outside of primary production. See, for instance, Blaug 1985, pp. 24–28.

2. Ibid.

3. The reforestation of the eastern states is a good example of marginal agriculture yielding to forests. During the eighteenth and nineteenth centuries much of the land in the region was stripped of trees and converted to crops and grazing. With the opening of the Midwest to agriculture, the East could not compete and much of its agricultural land was abandoned. Over time the land has been reforested simply as a result of natural processes. See McKibben 1995.

4. For world trends through 1992, see World Resources Institute 1994.

5. The higher output of both rich and poor countries has come from what may well be nonsustainable commitments of resources. Much farming has become heavily reliant on petroleum-based chemicals and fuels and methods that lead to soil erosion and increased salinity (from irrigation). Some international resource-conservation groups see the world's food supply as tenuous at best, despite surpluses and low commodity prices. See Worldwatch Institute 1994 and Brown 1989. A food crisis does not necessarily contradict the idea that a declining percentage of our economic activity will be committed to agriculture in the future. Physical shortages of food among the desperately poor do not represent an economic demand for food to which farmers could profitably respond. That is, the starving, who have no money to purchase food, do not represent a market demand. Governments or NGOs would have to create the market demand for hungry but poverty stricken populations.

6. Between 1950 and 1960 agricultural employment in the San Jose metropolitan area fell by almost a third. When food processing was combined with agriculture, the contribution of food production to total employment declined from about 18 percent to 3 percent between 1950 and 1980. In real earnings,

in Santa Clara County between 1969 and 1992 agriculture and food processing declined by a third and their relative contribution to total income declined by two-thirds. The extractive economic base was clearly in absolute and relative decline. The 165,000 jobs added in machinery manufacturing (including electronic hardware) no doubt cushioned the blow of a declining agricultural base. While real earnings in agriculture and food processing declined by $200 million, real earnings in computer-related production increased by $6 *billion* (U.S. Census of the Population, 1950 and 1980, tables 79 and 122. REIS, Bureau of Economic Analysis, CD-ROM).

7. McKibben 1995.

8. This is not meant to imply that all of the changes that have taken place in American agriculture are ideal or efficient, for example, the heavy use of pesticides to maintain an extensive monoculture, which has yet to be proved biologically viable in the long run.

9. Snyder and Lewis 1989.

10. U.S. Department of Agriculture, Economic Research Service, 1987. See also Snyder and Lewis 1989, p. 19.

11. The percent of cattle feed coming from federal land was taken from table 5 in Godfrey and Pope 1990. The data is for the year 1988. The percent of feed from federal land given by Godfrey and Pope is significantly lower than that estimated in a recent New Mexico study (table 6 in Torell et al. 1992). Most of this difference can be explained by the failure of the New Mexico study to include all of the cattle inventory in its analysis. When the full cattle inventory is included and their feed needs are weighted following the Forest Service's analysis of the range forage situation in the United States, (Joyce 1989), the Godfrey and Pope results for 1985 can be largely reproduced for 1989.

12. U.S. Department of Agriculture, Forest Service, et al. 1992, p. 2. Note the distinction between forage and feed requirements. Forage includes pasture, rangeland, and crop aftermath. Total feed, however, is likely to include fed hay and grain as well as forage. Because the cattle herd depends on all sources of feed for survival and weight gain, other sources of feed should not be ignored in calculating the dependence of cattle herds on federal grazing land.

13. New Mexico State University College of Agriculture 1992.

14. The employment, income, and agricultural sales data came from REIS, Bureau of Economic Analysis, CD-ROM. It was assumed that the percentage of total agricultural income and employment associated with livestock operations was directly proportional to the share of total agricultural marketings that was livestock. This probably overstates the relative importance of livestock operations. In calculating the relative importance of federal grazing as a source of income, income data was deflated using the consumer price index and the average relative importance of agriculture for the period 1980–91 was used. The 1991 data was used for employment since agricultural employment fluctuates much less than agricultural income.

15. U.S. Census of Agriculture 1987.

16. Ibid.

17. Current population survey data reported in U.S. Department of Agriculture, Economic Research Service, 1993. Farm operators include those who identify their occupation as farm operator or manager as well as those who report farm self-employment income. Some farm operators are employees who receive no farm self-employment income but who do receive farm-related wage and salary income.

18. Berry 1977.

19. U.S. Department of Agriculture, Economic Research Service, 1993.

20. REIS, Bureau of Economic Analysis, 1969–91.

Chapter 9

1. U.S. Bureau of the Census 1992, table 348.

2. Barr and Pingry 1977, p. 1, and Wilson 1992, pp. 1–3.

3. U.S. Bureau of Reclamation 1977, p. 4, lists the total project cost as $1.8 billion. This has been converted to 1994 dollars using the consumer price index. With the bulk of the project now completed, the estimated cost is $4.7 billion (*Denver Post*, February 6, 1994, p. 27A).

4. Young and Martin 1967; Kelso et al. 1973; Power 1978, *An Economic Analysis*.

5. Young and Martin 1967, p. 10.

6. CAP, in fact, was probably designed primarily as a way of providing additional water for municipal and industrial uses in Arizona's rapidly growing urban economy. Agricultural use of CAP water was probably seen as simply a temporary arrangement until rising urban needs claimed that water. An agricultural "cover" for the project, however, was politically necessary. The western states are not alone in wrestling with developing adequate water supplies for urban areas. Older cities in the East face similar problems. It is not clear that Congress would be willing to subsidize urban water supplies in the West while refusing such assistance elsewhere in the nation. Framing CAP as a project that was needed to save Arizona agriculture and allow the ongoing settlement of a harsh landscape made it more salable to Congress than if it were simply presented as a federally subsidized urban water system.

7. Another consideration added to the urgency of supplementing water supplies. The state's heavy per capita water consumption was supported primarily by drafting underground water supplies. Withdrawals far exceeded the recharge of aquifers, and water levels were falling. Continuing the withdrawals would have incurred higher and higher pumping costs. CAP was partly intended to mitigate this problem. The overuse of underground water is not surprising because the only price water users had to pay was the cost of drilling and pumping. When that cost was low, quite predictably consumption was high.

8. Young and Martin 1967, p. 10.

9. There are specialty crops whose value would support a much higher price for water. These include cotton, vegetables, citrus and other fruits, and nuts. The income per acre-foot of water committed to such crops is six times as high as that associated with feed grains and four times as high as forage crops. These higher valued crops use, however, less than 40 percent of Arizona's water (Young and Martin 1967, pp. 10 and 11).

10. See Power 1978, *An Economic Analysis,* pp. 7–9; Young and Martin 1967, pp. 13–16; Kelso et al. p. 42. All of these dollar values are for the early 1970s, when CAP funding was being debated. Put in 1994 dollars, they would have to be multiplied by 2.5.

11. *The Arizona Republic,* "Lagging CAP Sales Are Strapping Irrigation Districts," Phoenix, September 26, 1992, pp. CL40. For a discussion of the precarious financial conditions in irrigation districts resulting from CAP, see Wilson 1992.

12. The federal government, for instance, bought the CAP allocation of the Harquahala Valley Irrigation District and gave it to the Fort McDowell Mohave-Apache Indians. The federal government paid $1,050 per acre-foot for those water rights (Van der Werf, "Irrigation District Sells CAP Allotment," *Arizona Republic,* August 13, 1993, p. B1).

13. *The Denver Post,* February 6, 1994, p. 27A.

14. Martin et al. 1982, and Martin 1988.

15. The capital cost of the plant was amortized over twenty-five years at 7 percent, and this was added to the annual operating costs. The capital and operating costs were obtained from *High Country News,* February 21, 1994, p. 11.

16. See Power 1978, *An Economic Analysis,* figure 9. This figure is for 1977 and Arizona's primary irrigated counties, Maricopa, Pinal, and Pima.

17. Howe and Easter 1971, pp. 148–54 and 173.

18. Power 1978, *An Economic Analysis,* p. 22.

19. M. Davidson, "Tucson to Vote on Water Issue," May 16, p. B1, "Governor, Tucson Council to Huddle on CAP Vote," October 6, p. B1, and "Tucson Deluged with Water Problems," September 14, p. B1, *Arizona Republic* (Phoenix); A. Rotstein, "Tucson Panel Rejects Governor's Plea," *Arizona Republic,* October 7, 1993, p. A20; M. J. Pitzil, "Tucson Alters Stand," *Arizona Republic,* October 13, 1993, p. B1; and Davidson 1993.

20. Power 1978, *An Economic Analysis,* p. 22.

21. T. Power, Testimony on the Economics of the Sheep Industry, before the U.S. Environmental Protection Agency, re: Reregistration of 1080, on behalf of the Defenders of Wildlife et al., September 1982, figure 1.

22. Ibid., p. 10.

23. Ibid., p. 13.

24. Gee and Magleby 1976, pp. 8 and 13.

25. Gee et al. 1977; Power 1982.

26. Gee and Magleby 1976, pp. 39–48.

27. Of course, as a practical matter, the impact of predation on the amount of lamb marketed in the United States is so small that it is unlikely that the impact on prices could be directly measured. The discussion here applies standard economic relationships to the impact of predation, without suggesting that predation has a significant impact on lamb prices.

28. Magleby 1976, pp. 30–36.

29. Ibid., pp. 63–64.

30. *Wildlife Damage Review* (Spring 1995), p. 7.

31. Power 1985, pp. 7–13. Also see Collins et al. 1984; Uresk 1985; Uresk and Bjugstad 1981; and Halvorson 1988.

32. Power 1985, pp. 13–19.

33. Ibid., pp. 21–24.

34. Ibid., pp. 24–31.

35. Ibid., pp. 31–40.

36. Ibid., p. 35.

37. Although economists usually describe the relationship between price and demand in terms of price elasticity, agricultural analysts often speak in terms of price flexibility. Price flexibility measures the impact of a change in the quantity marketed on the price at which the product will sell. Price elasticity measures the impact of a change in price on the quantity that can be sold.

38. If 2 million acres are colonized and the average productivity of the land is a very high 15 acres per animal-unit-year, these lands could provide the feed for 133,000 cattle. If the cattle inventory is 100 million head, the colonized acres could support about one-tenth of 1 percent of the total inventory.

Chapter 10

1. Brooks 1994.

2. U.S. Bureau of the Census 1993, table 422.

3. World Tourism Organization as cited in Winterbottom 1991, table 425.

4. U.S. Bureau of the Census 1993, table 419.

5. Mathieson and Wall 1982, p. 75. Travel and lodging costs make up 40 to 50 percent of tourist expenditures, but some of the travel costs are expenditures on automobile fuel and repair.

6. Winterbottom 1991, p. 10.

7. Ibid., REIS, Bureau of Economic Analysis, total earnings divided by total employment.

8. For a description of the impact of tourist development in rural counties in twelve southeastern states, see Smith 1989. For a description of tourist-related jobs in Montana, see Barrett 1987.

9. This "indirect" impact of tourist employment and income on the rest of the economy is the impact usually described in economic base modeling in

terms of the multiplier process. The expansion of economic activity at a particular location does indeed have indirect and induced impacts. Whether a description of these exclusively in terms of a multiplier is accurate or useful is a different question. It is not being suggested that indirect employment and income be treated as the economic benefits that justify public investment. The point here is much more limited: when the total impact of tourism on the local economy is analyzed, these additional impacts should be taken into account.

10. Kubursi 1992.

11. Schechter 1990.

12. Robbins 1991.

13. This section is based on materials prepared by various parties for presentation to the Alberta Natural Resources Conservation Board. It summarizes "The Socio-Economic Impact of the Proposed Three Sisters Resort, Canmore, Alberta," a 1991 report submitted to the board by the author on behalf of BowCORD, a Canmore citizens' organization opposing the Three Sisters Resort.

14. Town of Canmore, no date, Vision 2020/goals for Canmore, with Alberta Municipal Affairs, p. 39.

15. Town of Canmore, September 1991, Economic Development Committee, Canmore Economic Development Survey Results, vol. 1, main report, Praxis, Calgary, Alberta.

16. Three Sisters Golf Resorts, Technical Report 9.9a, Socio-Economics, Environmental Impact Assessment, UMA engineering.

17. Town of Banff, "Not Really A Small Town," April 1992, Banff, Alberta.

18. Town of Canmore, "An Investment Plan for Tourism Infrastructure in the Bow Corridor," October 1991, p. 2.

19. J. Mara Dellipriscoli, "F-2: Fun with a Focus," Travel Leisure Consulting, Arlington, Virginia, 1992. For a description of trends in tourism, see Tarlow and Muehsam 1992. For a discussion of threats to the environment from rapidly growing ecotourism, see Norris 1994.

Chapter 11

1. See, for instance, Dunlap 1991; Dunlap and Scarce 1991; Donaton and Fitzgerald 1992, and Pope 1992. On attitudes toward natural landscape preservation, see Sonner 1995; the Lee Newspaper poll reported in the *Billings Gazette*, (Montana) June 1, 1994, p. 1; Howell and Laska 1992; Krause 1993; and the *Billings Gazette*, Billings, Montana, June 1994, p. 1.

2. There are, of course, areas where the work force regularly goes unemployed, even for long periods. Our center cities and Indian reservations are the two most dramatic examples. The arguments in this book have not sought to deny the reality of such economic problems. It is important to understand, however, that chronic unemployment has roots other than those discussed in

this book. It was not environmental regulations that created problem, nor was it the decline in the extractive industry. "Liberating" mining, logging, and publicly subsidized agriculture from public regulation would not solve these serious socioeconomic problems.

3. There has been a shift away from the business-recruitment approach to local economic development over the last decade. At the national level, the Corporation for Enterprise Development (CED) has worked actively to get communities and states to think more broadly about their economies and their well-being. See Corporation for Enterprise Development 1986, 1988, 1991 and 1994. For a good example of the broader approach implemented in state economic planning, see Oregon 1989 and Oregon 1990.

4. Wuerthner 1994; and Sodhi 1992.

5. Wuerthner 1994, p. 906, and U.S. Bureau of the Census 1994, table 355.

6. See Power 1988.

7. Lane 1993. For earlier explorations of this issue, see Easterlin 1973, and Easterlin 1974.

8. See, for instance, Shankland 1988; Robertson 1985; Kahne 1985; and Appelbaum and Batt 1994.

9. Lane 1993.

10. Ibid.

11. Ibid.

References

Adams, D. M. 1977. Effects of National Forest Timber Harvest on Softwood Stumpage, Timber, and Plywood Markets. *Oregon State University School of Forestry Research Bulletin* 15.

Alfers, S. D., and R. P. Graff. 1992. Economic Impact of Mining Law Reform. A report prepared for the American Mining Congress, Washington, D.C. Davis, Graham and Stubbs and Coopers and Lybrand. January 28.

American Chamber of Commerce Researchers Association 1988. Inter-City Cost of Living Index, Louisville, Kentucky.

Anderson, H. M., and J. T. Olson. 1991. *Federal Forests and the Economic Base of the Pacific Northwest.* Washington, D.C.: The Wilderness Society.

Appelbaum, E., and R. Batt. 1994. *The New American Workplace: Transforming Work Systems in the United States.* Ithaca, N.Y.: ILR Press.

Aurousseau, M. 1921. The Distribution of Population: A Constructive Problem. *Geographical Review* 11 (4): 563–82.

Bain, J. S. 1984. Transfer Payment Impacts on Rural Retail Markets: A Regression Analysis. *Regional Science Perspectives* 14 (1): 3–17.

Barr, J. M., and D. E. Pingry. 1977. The Central Arizona Project: An Inquiry into Its Potential Impacts. *Arizona Review* 26 (4): 1–49.

Barrett, R. N. 1987. Tourism Employment in Montana: Quality versus Quantity? *Western Wildlands* 13 (2): 18–21.

———. 1990. Trends in Earnings Inequality in the Pacific Northwest. Proceedings of the 24th Annual Pacific Northwest Regional Economic Conference, April 26–28, at the Northwest Policy Center, Seattle.

Bednarzik, R. W. 1987. The "Quality" of U.S. Jobs. Economic Discussion Paper 25, Office of International Economic Affairs, U.S. Department of Labor.

Been, V. 1994. Locally Undesirable Land Uses in Minority Neighborhoods: Disproportionate Siting or Market Dynamics? *Yale Law Journal* 103: 1383.

Beeson, P. E. 1991. Amenities and Regional Differences in Returns to Worker Characteristics. *Journal of Urban Economics* 30 (2): 224–41.

Bell, D. 1973. *The Coming of Post-Industrial Society.* New York: Basic Books.

Bell, T. Tourism Beats Logging in Wyoming. *High Country News,* October 10, 1988.

Bender, L. D. 1987. The Role of Services in Rural Development Policies. *Land Economics* 63 (1): 62–71.

Berry, B. J. L., and J. B. Parr. 1989. *Market Centers and Retail Location: Theory and Applications.* Englewood Cliffs, N.J.: Prentice Hall.

Berry, W. 1977. *The Unsettling of America: Culture and Agriculture.* San Francisco: Sierra Club Books.

Beuter, J. H. 1990. *Social and Economic Impacts of the Spotted Owl Conservation Strategy.* Washington, D.C.: American Forest Resources Alliance.

Blackburn, M. L., et al. 1990. The Declining Economic Position of Less Skilled American Men. In *A Future of Lousy Jobs? The Changing Structure of U.S. Wages,* ed. G. Burtless. Washington, D.C.: Brookings Institution.

Blank, R. M. 1990. Are Part-Time Jobs Bad Jobs? In *A Future of Lousy Jobs? The Changing Structure of U.S. Wages,* ed. G. Burtless. Washington, D.C.: The Brookings Institution.

Blaug, M. 1985. *Economic Theory in Retrospect.* 4th ed. Cambridge: Cambridge University Press.

Blomquist, G. C., et al. 1988. New Estimates of Quality of Life in Urban Areas. *American Economic Review* 78 (1): 89–108.

Bluestone, B., and B. Harrison. 1986. *The Great American Job Machine: The Proliferation of Low-Wage Employment in the U.S. Economy.* A study prepared for the Joint Economic Committee of the U.S. Congress. Washington, D.C.: GPO.

Borts, G. H., and J. L. Stein. 1964. *Economic Growth in a Free Market.* New York: Columbia University Press.

Braden, P. A., and S. R. Rideout. 1978. *Location Decision-Making in Export-Oriented Business and Industry.* Ann Arbor: Division of Research, Graduate School of Business Administration, University of Michigan.

Brett, A., et al. 1991. *University Spin-Off Companies: Economic Development, Faculty Entrepreneurs, and Technology Transfer.* Savage, Md.: Rowman and Littlefield.

Broadway, M. J. 1994. Hogtowns and Rural Development. *Rural Development Perspectives* 9 (1): 40–46.

Brooks, P. 1994. Whitefish Resort Community Report. Prepared for the City of Whitefish, Montana.

Brown, L. R. 1989. Feeding Six Billion. *Worldwatch* 2 (5): 32–40.

Burtless, G., ed. 1990. *A Future of Lousy Jobs? The Changing Structure of U.S. Wages.* Washington, D.C.: The Brookings Institution.

Calzonetti, F. J., and R. T. Walker. 1991. Factors Affecting Industrial Location Decisions: A Survey Approach, in *Industry Location and Public Policy,* ed. H. W. Herzog, Jr., and A. M. Schlottmann. Knoxville: University of Tennessee Press.

Center for the New West. 1992. *Measuring Distress: Economic Indicators and the Great Plains.* Denver: Center for the New West.

Clark, D. E. 1992. Do Noxious Facilities Influence Migration Rates? Evidence from a Countywide Model. Paper presented at the Annual Meeting of the Regional Science Association International, November 13–15, Chicago.

Cobb, C. W., and J. B. Cobb, Jr. 1994. *The Green National Product: A Proposed Index of Sustainable Economic Welfare.* New York: University Press of America.

Collins, A. R., et al. 1984. An Economic Analysis of Black-Tailed Prairie Dog Control. *Journal of Range Management* 37 (4): 466–68.

Cooke, T. W. 1978. Causality Reconsidered: A Note. *Journal of Urban Economics* 5 (4): 538–42.

Coppack, P. M. 1988. Reflections on the Role of Amenity in the Evolution of the Urban Field. *Geografiska Annaler* 70B (3): 353–61.

Corporation for Enterprise Development. 1986. *Taken for Granted: How Grant Thornton's Business Climate Index Leads States Astray.* Washington, D.C.: Corporation for Enterprise Development.

———. 1988. *Making the Grade: The 1988 Development Report Card for the States.* Washington, D.C.: Corporation for Enterprise Development.

———. 1991. *The 1991 Development Report Card for the States.* Washington, D.C.: Corporation for Enterprise Development.

———. 1994. *Bidding for Business: Are Cities and States Selling Themselves Short?* Washington, D.C.: Corporation for Enterprise Development.

Cox, T. R., et al. 1985. *This Well-Wooded Land: Americans and Their Forests from Colonial Times to the Present.* Lincoln: University of Nebraska Press.

Cubbage, F. W. 1987. *Assessing Methodologies to Estimate Trends in Southern Forest Products Industry Employment, Wages, and Regional Multipliers.* Athens: School of Forestry, University of Georgia.

Daly, H. E. 1991. *Steady-State Economics.* 2d ed. Washington, D.C.: Island Press.

Daniel, P. 1992. Economic Policy in Mineral-Exporting Countries: What Have We Learned? In *Mineral Wealth and Economic Development,* ed. J. E. Tilton. Washington, D.C.: Resources for the Future.

Danielson, L., and A. McNamara. 1994. The Summitville Saga. *Clementine* (Winter): 7–9. Washington, D.C.: Mineral Policy Center.

Deavers, K. 1989. The Reversal of the Rural Renaissance: A Recent Historical Perspective. *Entrepreneurial Economy Review* 3–5.

Denison, E. F. 1962. *The Sources of Economic Growth in the United States and the Alternatives before Us.* Washington, D.C.: Brookings Institution.

———. 1967. *Why Growth Rates Differ: Postwar Experiences in Nine Western Countries.* Washington, D.C.: Brookings Institution.

———. 1974. *Accounting for U.S. Economic Growth, 1929–82.* Washington, D.C.: Brookings Institution.

———. 1985. *Trends in American Economic Growth, 1929–82.* Washington, D.C.: Brookings Institution.

Dickie, M., and S. Gerking. 1987. Interregional Wage Differentials: An Equilibrium Perspective. *Journal of Regional Science* 27 (4): 571–85.

Dobra, J. L. Testimony presented before the Subcommittee on Mineral Resources Development and Production of the U.S. Senate Committee on Energy and Natural Resources. 103d Cong., 1st sess., May 4, 1993.

Dobra, J. L., and P. R. Thomas. 1992. The U.S. Gold Industry 1992. *Nevada Bureau of Mines and Geology Special Publication* 14.

Donaton, S., and K. Fitzgerald. 1992. Polls Show Ecological Concern Is Strong. *Advertising Age* 63 (24): 49.

Drielsma, J. H. 1984. The Influence of Forest-Based Industries on Rural Communities. Ph.D. diss., School of Forestry and Environmental Studies, Yale University, New Haven.

Duffy, N. E. 1994. The Determinants of State Manufacturing Growth Rates: A Two-Digit Analysis. *Journal of Regional Science* 34 (2): 137–62.

Dunlap, R. E. 1991. Trends in Public Opinion towards Environmental Issues: 1965–90. *Society and Natural Resources* 4: 285–312.

Dunlap, R. E., and R. Scarce. 1991. The Polls—A Report: Environmental Problems and Protection. *Public Opinion Quarterly* 55: 713–34.

Easterlin, R. A. 1973. Does Money Buy Happiness? *The Public Interest* 113 (Fall): 320.

———. 1974. Does Economic Growth Improve the Human Lot? Some Empirical Evidence. In *Nations and Households in Economic Growth,* eds. P. A. David and M. W. Reder. New York: Academic Press.

Eberts, R. W., and E. L. Groshen. 1990. Service Jobs versus Manufacturing Jobs. *Economic Development Commentary* 14 (2): 4–10.

Egan, T. Oregon, Failing Forecasters, Thrives As It Protects Owls. *The New York Times,* October 11, 1994.

Evans, A. W. 1990. The Assumption of Equilibrium in the Analysis of Migration and Inter-regional Differences: A Review of Some Recent Literature. *Journal of Regional Science* 30 (4): 515–31.

Evans, M. K. Testimony presented before the Subcommittee on Mineral Resources Development and Production of the U.S. Senate Committee on Energy and Natural Resources. 103d Cong., 1st sess., 1993.

Farber, S. C., and R. J. Newman. 1987. Accounting for South/Non-South Real Wage Differentials and for Changes in Those Differentials over Time. *Review of Economics and Statistics* 69 (2): 215–23.

Farling, B. Butte Comes out of the Pit. *High Country News,* November 29, 1993.

Fickett, A. R., et al. 1990. Efficient Use of Electricity. *Scientific American* 263 (3): 54–109.

Fisher, A. C., et al. 1972. The Economics of Environmental Preservation: A

Theoretical and Empirical Analysis. *American Economic Review* 62 (4): 605–19.

Flaim, P. O., and E. Sehgal. 1985. Displaced Workers of 1979–83: How Well Have They Fared? *Monthly Labor Review* 5 (108): 3–16.

Flowers, P. J., et al. 1993. An Assessment of Montana's Timber Situation. *Miscellaneous Publication* 53. Montana Forest and Conservation Experiment Station, School of Forestry University of Montana, Missoula.

Fortman, L. P., et al. 1989. Community Stability: The Foresters' Fig Leaf. In *Community Stability in Forest-Based Economies,* eds. D. C. LeMaster and J. H. Beuter. Portland, Oregon: Timber Press.

Fukuyama, F. 1995. *Trust: The Social Virtues and the Creation of Prosperity.* Riverside, N.J.: The Free Press.

Gee, K. C., and R. S. Magleby. 1976. Characteristics of Sheep Production in the Western United States. Agricultural Economic Report No. 345, Economic Research Service, U.S. Department of Agriculture.

Gee, K. C., et al. 1977. Sheep and Lamb Losses to Predators and Other Causes in the Western United States. Agricultural Economic Report No. 369, Economic Research Service, U.S. Department of Agriculture.

Gerking, S., and M. Dickie. 1987. Interregional Wage Differentials: An Equilibrium Perspective. *Journal of Regional Science* 27 (4): 571–85.

Gilford, D. M. 1981. Statistics for Rural Development Policy. U.S. Office of Management and Budget *Statistical Reporter* 82-2.

Glasgow, N. 1988. The Nonmetro Elderly: Economic and Demographic Status. RDRR-70, Economic Research Service, U.S. Department of Agriculture.

Godfrey, E. B., and C. A. Pope. 1990. The Trouble with Livestock Grazing on Public Lands. In *Current Issues in Rangeland Resource Economics.* Corvallis: Oregon State University Extension Service.

Godwin, P. 1991. *Sherwood.* New York: William Morrow.

———. 1993. *Robin and the King.* New York: William Morrow.

Gorte, J. F., and R. W. Gorte. 1989. Employment and Community Stability in the Forest Products Industries. In *Community Stability in Forest-Based Economies,* eds. D. C. LeMaster and J. H. Beuter. Portland, Ore.: Timber Press.

Gorte, R. W. 1990. The Economic Impacts of Enacting Alternative Wilderness Proposals for the National Forest in Montana. Report of the Congressional Research Service, Library of Congress.

Gottlieb, P. D. 1992. Amenities As an Economic Development Tool: Is There Enough Evidence? Paper presented at the 39th Annual Meeting of the Association of Collegiate Schools of Planning, Columbus, Ohio, October 30.

———. 1992. Amenity-Oriented Firm Location: Theoretical and Empirical Issues. Paper presented at the Annual Meeting of the Regional Science Association International, November 13–15, Chicago.

Greco, T. H. 1994. *New Money for Healthy Communities*. Tucson, Ariz.: Greco Press.

Greenwood, M. J. 1981. *Migration and Economic Growth in the United States: National, Regional, and Metropolitan Perspectives*. New York: Academic Press.

Greenwood, M. J., and G. L. Hunt. 1984. Migration and Interregional Employment Redistribution in the United States. *American Economic Review* 74 (5): 957–69.

Greenwood, M. J., et al. 1986. Migration and Employment Change: Empirical Evidence on the Spatial and Temporal Dimensions of the Linkage. *Journal of Regional Science* 26 (2): 223–34.

———. 1991. Migration, Regional Equilibrium, and the Estimation of Compensating Differentials. *The American Economic Review* 81 (5): 1382–90.

Guzzardi, W. 1982. The Huge Find in Roy Ash's Backyard. Fortune 106 (13): 48–65.

Gyourko, J., and J. Tracy. 1991. The Structure of Local Public Finance and the Quality of Life. *Journal of Political Economy* 99 (4): 774–806.

Halvorson, A. 1988. An Unpretentious Rodent? *Forestry Research West*. Journal of the Rocky Mountain Forest and Range Experiment Station, Fort Collins, Colorado, Forest Service, June, 14–17.

Hannon, B. 1994. Sense of Place: Geographic Discounting by People, Animals, and Plants. *Ecological Economics* 10: 157–74.

Harmston, F. K. 1979. A Study of the Impact of Retired People in a Small Community. Paper presented at the Annual Meeting of the Midcontinent Regional Science Association, Minneapolis, May 31–June 2.

Hatcher, D. 1993. Mill Dies; Town Comes to Life. *High Country News*, April.

Haynes, R. 1992. Owls, Jobs, and Old-Growth. *Forest Watch* 12 (10): 15–17.

Heberlein, Thomas A., et al. 1994. Forest Dependence and Community Well-Being in the Pacific Northwest. Paper presented at the Rural Sociological Society meeting in Portland, Oregon, August 12–14.

Helvarg, D. 1994. *The War against the Greens: The Wise-Use Movement, the New-Right and Anti-Environmental Violence*. San Francisco: Sierra Club Books.

Hirschl, T. A., and G. F. Summers. 1982. Cash Transfers and the Export Base of Small Communities. *Rural Sociology* 47 (2): 295–316.

Hoch, I. 1978. Variations in the Quality of Urban Life among Cities and Regions. In *Public Economics and the Quality of Life*, eds. L. Wingo and A. Evans. Baltimore: Johns Hopkins University Press.

Hoch, I., et al. Ca. 1983. Real Income, Poverty, and Resources. Part 3 of *Rural Development, Poverty, and Natural Resources*. Washington, D.C.: Resources for the Future.

Hodge, G. 1991. The Economic Impact of Retirees on Smaller Communities. *Research on Aging* 13 (1): 39–54.

Hoidal, O. K. 1980. Norsemen and the North American Forests. *Journal of Forest History* 24 (4): 200–203.

Hoover, E. 1948. *The Location of Economic Activity.* New York: McGraw-Hill.

Horrigan, M. W., and S. E. Haugen. 1988. The Declining Middle-Class Thesis: A Sensitivity Analysis. *Monthly Labor Review* 111 (5): 3–13.

Horvath, F. W. 1987. The Pulse of Economic Change: Displaced Workers of 1981–85. *Monthly Labor Review* 110 (6): 3–12.

Howe, C. W., and W. K. Easter. 1971. Interbasin Transfers of Water. *Resources for the Future.* Baltimore: Johns Hopkins University Press.

Howell, D. R. 1994. The Collapse of Low-Skill Male Earnings in the 1980s: Skill Mismatch or Shifting Wage Norms? Working Paper 105, Jerome Levy Economics Institute, Bard College, Annandale-on-Hudson, New York.

Howell, S. E., and S. B. Laska. 1992. The Changing Face of the Environmental Coalition: A Research Note. *Environment and Behavior* 24 (1): 133–44.

Hunt, G. L. 1992. Equilibrium and Disequilibrium in Migration Modelling. Paper presented at the Annual Meeting of the Regional Science Association International, November 13–15, Chicago.

Isard, W. 1956. *Location and Space Economy.* New York: MIT Press/John Wiley.

Jobes, P. C. 1988. Nominalism, Realism and Planning in a Changing Community. *International Journal of Environmental Studies* 31 (4): 279–90.

Johnson, J., and R. Rasker. 1993. The Role of Amenities in Business Attraction and Retention. *Montana Policy Review* 3 (2): 11–19.

Joyce, L. 1989. An Analysis of the Range Forage Situation in the United States, 1989–2040. General Technical Report RM-180, supporting the 1989 USDA Forest Service RPA assessment, Rocky Mountain Forest and Range Experiment Station, Fort Collins, Colorado, October.

Kahne, H. 1985. *Reconceiving Part-Time Work: New Perspectives for Older Workers and Women.* New York: Rowman and Allanheld.

Kassab, C. 1992. *Income and Inequality: The Role of the Service Sector in the Changing Distribution of Income.* In Contributions in Economics and Economic History Series, no. 133, New York: Greenwood Press.

Keeton, G. W. 1966. *The Norman Conquest and the Common Law.* New York: Barnes and Noble.

Kelso, M., et al. 1973. *Water Supplies and Economic Growth in an Arid Environment: An Arizona Case Study.* Tucson: University of Arizona Press.

Kendall, J., and B. W. Pigozzi. 1994. Non-Employment Income and the Economic Base of Michigan Counties, 1959–86. *Growth and Change* 25 (1) 51–74.

Kieschnick, M. 1981. *Taxes and Growth: Business Incentives and Economic Development.* Washington, D.C.: Council of State Planning Agencies.

Klosterman, R. E., et al. 1993. *Spreadsheet Models for Urban and Regional Analysis.* New Brunswick, N.J.: Center for Urban Policy Research, Rutgers University.

Kosters, M. H., ed. 1991. *Workers and Their Wages: Changing Patterns in the United States.* Washington, D.C.: The American Enterprise Institute.

Krannich, R. S., and A. E. Luloff. 1991. Problems of Resource Dependency in U.S. Rural Communities. *Progress in Rural Policy and Planning* 1 (1): 5–18.

Krause, D. 1993. Environmental Consciousness: An Empirical Study. *Environment and Behavior* 25 (1): 126–42.

Krikelas, A. C. 1992. Why Regions Grow: A Review of Research on the Economic Base Model. Federal Reserve Bank of Atlanta *Economic Review* 77 (4): 16–29.

Krutilla, J. V. 1967. Conservation Reconsidered. *American Economic Review* 57 (4): 777–86.

Krutilla, J. V., and A. C. Fisher. 1975. *The Economics of Natural Environments: Studies in the Valuation of Commodity and Amenity Resources.* Resources for the Future. Baltimore: The Johns Hopkins University Press.

Lane, R. E. 1993. Does Money Buy Happiness? *The Public Interest* 113 (Fall): 56–65.

Longino, C. F., and W. H. Crown. 1990. Retirement Migration and Interstate Income Transfers. *The Gerontologist* 30 (6): 784–89.

Lovins, A. B., et al. 1982. Least-Cost Energy: Solving the CO_2 Problem. Andover, Ma.: Brick House.

Maguire, S. R. 1991. Employer and Occupational Tenure: 1991 Update. U.S. Department of Labor *Monthly Labor Review* 116 (6): 45.

———. 1993. Research Summaries: Employer and Occupational Tenure, 1993 Update. U.S. Department of Labor *Monthly Labor Review* 116 (6): 45–56.

Manning, R. 1992. Mountain Passages. *Wilderness* 56 (198): 23–31.

Martin, W. E. 1988. Back to the Future: A Willingness to Play Reexamined. *Western Journal of Agricultural Economics* 13 (1): 112–20.

Martin, W. E., et al. 1982. A Willingness to Play: Analysis of Water Resources Development. *Western Journal of Agricultural Economics* 7 (1): 133–39.

Mathieson, A., and G. Wall. 1982. *Tourism: Economic, Physical and Social Impacts.* New York: Longman.

Matthews, A. 1993. Slow Death Beyond the 98th Meridian. *Outside Magazine.*

McKibben, B. 1995. An Explosion of Green. *Atlantic Monthly* 275 (4): 61–83.

McMahon, P. J., and J. H. Tschetter. 1986. The Declining Middle Class: A Further Analysis. *Monthly Labor Review* 109 (9): 22–27.

McMahon, W. W. 1988. Geographic Cost of Living Differences: An Update. Faculty Working Paper 1491, College of Commerce and Business Administration, University of Illinois, Urbana.

McNulty, J. E. 1977. A Test of Time Dimensions in Economic Base Analysis. *Land Economics* 53 (3): 359–68.

Meyer, S. M. 1992. Environmentalism and Economic Prosperity: Testing the Environmental Impact Hypothesis. Project on Environmental Politics and Policy, Department of Political Science, Massachusetts Institute of Technology, Boston.

———. 1993. Environmentalism and Economic Prosperity: An Update. Project on Environmental Politics and Policy, Department of Political Science, Massachusetts Institute of Technology, Boston.

Meyers, D. 1989. The Ecology of "Quality of Life" and Urban Growth. In *Growth Management: Critical Issues and a Research Agenda,* ed. D. Brower. Washington, D.C.: Urban Land Institute.

Mills, E. S., and G. Chodes. 1988. Non-Extractive Employment Outside Metropolitan Areas. In *Proceedings of the National Rural Studies Committee, Hood River, Oregon.* Edited by Emery Castle and Barara Baldwin. Corvallis: Western Rural Development Center, Oregon State University.

Mineral Policy Center. 1993. *Burden of Gilt.* Washington, D.C.: Mineral Policy Center.

Moore, C. L., and M. Jacobsen. 1984. Minimum Requirements and Regional Economics, 1980. *Economic Geography* 60 (3): 215–24.

Montana Department of Health and Environmental Sciences. 1992. Stillwater Mine Expansion Draft Environmental Impact Statement, Helena, Montana.

Morison, S. E. 1942. *Admiral of the Ocean Sea: A Life of Christopher Columbus.* Boston: Little Brown.

Mulligan, G. F. 1987. Employment Multipliers and Functional Types of Communities: Effects of Public Transfer Payments. *Growth and Change* 18 (3): 1–11.

Mulligan, G. F., and L. J. Gibson. 1984. Regression Estimates of Economic Base Multipliers for Small Communities. *Economic Geography* 60 (3): 225–37.

Murdock, J. 1991. A Survey of the Economy of Dubois, Wyoming. Paper prepared for the Dubois 2000 League, Dubois, Wyoming.

Muth, R. F. 1971. Migration: Chicken or Egg? *Southern Economic Journal* 37 (3): 295–306.

New Mexico State University College of Agriculture 1992. The Importance of Public Lands to Livestock Production in the United States. Range Improvement Task Force, Agricultural Experiment Station, Cooperative Extension Service. RITF Report 32, June.

Niemi, E., and E. Whitelaw. 1995. The Economic Consequences of Protecting Salmon Habitat in Idaho, ECO Northwest, Eugene, Oregon. A report prepared for the Pacific Rivers Council, Portland, Oregon, March.

Norris, R. 1994. Ecotourism in the National Parks of Latin America. *National Parks* 68 (1-2): 32–38.

North, D. C. 1956. Location Theory and Regional Economic Growth. *Journal of Political Economy* 64 (2): 165–68.

———. 1966. *The Economic Growth of the United States, 1790–1860.* New York: Norton.

———. 1993. Lies, Damned Lies, and Statistics. *Forest Watch* 13 (9): center supplement following p. 30, April/May, 1993.

Oregon, State of. 1989. *Oregon Shines: An Economic Strategy for the Pacific Century.* Salem: Oregon Economic Development Department.

———. 1990. *Oregon Benchmarks: Setting Measurable Standards for Progress.* Salem: Oregon Progress Board.

Otis, T. P. 1977. Ambient Sulfur Dioxide Pollution in Montana: An Economic Analysis of Alternative Standards. Master's thesis, Economics Department, University of Montana, Missoula.

O'Toole, R. 1988. *Reforming the Forest Service.* Washington, D.C.: Island Press.

Park, C. S. 1993. *Contemporary Engineering Economics.* New York: Addison-Wesley.

Paulozzi, L. J. 1987. Fatal Logging Injuries in Washington State, 1977–83. *Journal of Occupational Medicine* 29 (2): 103–8.

Pendleton, T. H. 1975. The High Cost of Injuries. Bulletin No. 86, *Northeastern Forest Experiment Station Report.* School of Forestry, Yale University, New Haven.

Peoples, D. 1989. The Butte–Silver Bow Experience: A Local Government's Active Role in Economic Development. In *Community Stability in Forest-Based Economies,* eds. D. C. LeMaster and J. H. Beuter. Portland, Ore.: Timber Press.

Perlman, M. 1978. Review of Hutchison's *Knowledge and Ignorance in Economics.* In *The Journal of Economic Literature* 16 (June): 582–85.

Persky, J., et al. 1993. Import Substitution and Local Economic Development. *Economic Development Quarterly* 7 (1): 18–29.

Persky, J., and W. Wiewel. 1992. Local Economic Sovereignty. Paper presented at the Annual Meeting of the Regional Science Association International, November 13–15, Chicago.

Peters, T. 1992. *Liberation Management: Necessary Disorganization for the Nanosecond Nineties.* New York: Alfred A. Knopf.

Polzin, P. E. 1976. Local Service Employment and City Size. *Land Economics* 52 (4): 435–51.

Pope, C. 1992. Alive and Kicking. *Sierra* 77 (4): 16.

Popper, D., and F. Popper. The Fate of the Great Plains. *High Country News,* September 26, 1988.

Power, T. M. 1978. *An Economic Analysis of the Central Arizona Project.* Phoenix: CAP Publications.

———. 1978. Alternative W and the RARE II Process in Montana. Unpublished report to the Montana Wilderness Coalition and U.S. Forest Service, Region 1 Forester.

————. 1981. Urban Size (Dis)amenities Revisited. *Journal of Urban Economics* 9: 85–89.

————. 1985. The Aggregate Economic Impact on Cattle Raisers of Eliminating Strychnine As a Control Agent for Prairie Dogs. A report prepared for the U.S. Environmental Protection Agency, EPA/OPTS/OPP/BUD/EAB, TX-768-C.

————. 1987. To Be or Not to Be: The Economics of Natural Gas Development along the Rocky Mountain Front. *Western Wildlands* 13 (3): 20–25.

————. 1988. *The Economic Pursuit of Quality*. New York: M. E. Sharpe.

————. 1988. Testimony before the Alberta Energy Resource Conservation Board, Shell Canada Waterton 6-30-4-1 Gas Well, August 1988, Pincher Creek, Alberta.

————. 1990. Comparing Wilderness Values to Oil and Gas Values along the Rocky Mountain Front: A Net Economic Value Approach. In *Forestry on the Frontier*. American Society of Foresters.

————. 1992. *The Timber Employment Impact of the Northern Rockies Ecosystem Protection Action in Idaho, Montana, Oregon, Washington, and Wyoming*. 5 vols. and an executive summary. Missoula, Mont.: Alliance for the Wild Rockies.

————. 1994. *Not All That Glitters: An Evaluation of the Impact of Reform on the 1872 Mining Law on the Economy of the American West*. Washington, D.C.: Mineral Policy Center.

————. 1994. Measuring Local Economic Well-Being: Per Capita Income and Local Economic Health. In *The Green National Product: A Proposed Index of Sustainable Economic Welfare*, eds. C. W. Cobb and J. B. Cobb. New York: University Press of America.

————. 1995. The Economic Importance of Public Lands Grazing in the West. Southern Utah Wilderness Alliance: Newsletter 12 (1):1-8. Salt Lake City, Utah.

Pulver, G. C., et al. 1984. The Impact of a Major Economic Development Event on Community Income Distribution. In *Resource Communities: A Decade of Disruption*, eds. D. D. Detomasi and J. W. Gartrell. Boulder, Colo.: Westview Press.

Randall, A. 1981. *Resource Economics*. Columbus, Ohio: Grid.

Richardson, H. W. 1985. Input-Output and Economic Base Multipliers. *Journal of Regional Science* 3 (1): 1–48.

Roback, J. 1982. Wages, Rents, and the Quality of Life. *Journal of Political Economy* 90 (6): 1257–78.

————. 1988. Wages, Rents and Amenities: Differences among Workers and Regions. *Economic Inquiry* 261 (1): 23–41.

Robbins, J. 1991. Tourism Trap: The Californication of the American West.

Originally published in *Northern Lights Magazine*. Reprinted in *Utne Reader* 46 (July/August): 88–93.

Robertson, J. 1985. *Future Work: Jobs, Self-Employment and Leisure after the Industrial Age*. New York: Universe Books.

Rogers, G., and C. Carlson. 1992. *The Last Free Lunch on the Old Frontier: Hard Rock Mining and Reform of the 1872 Mining Law*. Washington, D.C.: National Wildlife Federation.

Rosen, S. 1979. Wage-Based Indexes of Urban Quality of Live. In *Current Issues in Urban Economics*, eds. P. Mieszkowski and M. Straszheim. Baltimore: Johns Hopkins University Press.

Ross, D. P., and P. J. Usher. 1986. *From the Roots Up: Economic Development As if Community Mattered*. Croton-on-Hudson, N. Y.: Bootstrap Press.

Rufolo, A. M., J. G. Strathman, and L. M. Bronfman. 1988. Employment Decline in Timber Dependent Regions. Center for Urban Studies, Portland State University. Portland, Oregon.

Sahling, L. G., and S. P. Smith. 1983. Regional Wage Differentials: Has the South Risen Again? *Review of Economics and Statistics* 65 (1): 131–35.

Sample, V. A., and D. C. Le Master. 1992. Assessing the Employment Impacts of Proposed Measure to Protect the Northern Spotted Owl. Forest Policy Center, American Forestry Association, Washington, D.C.

Sastry, M. L. 1992. Estimating the Economic Impacts of Elderly Migration: An Input-Output Analysis. *Growth and Change* 23 (1): 54–79.

Schachter, J., and P. G. Althaus. 1989. An Equilibrium Model of Gross Migration. *Journal of Regional Science* 29 (2): 143–59.

Schechter, J. 1990. The Economy of Teton County, Wyoming. Study commissioned by the Main Street Association, Summit Management Consulting, Jackson, Wyoming.

Schenck, G. H. K. 1984. *Handbook of State and Local Taxation of Solid Minerals*. University Park: Pennsylvania State University.

Schmenner, R. 1982. *Making Business Location Decisions*. Englewood Cliffs, N.J.: Prentice-Hall.

Scholz, A., et al. 1985. Compilation of Information on Salmon and Steelhead Total Run Size, Catch, and Hydropower-Related Losses in the Upper Columbia River Basin, above Grand Coulee Dam. Fisheries Technical Report 2, Upper Columbia United Tribes Fisheries Center, Eastern Washington University, Department of Biology, Cheney, Washington.

Shaffer, R., and E. Vatne. 1984. Changes in Economic Structure and Employment Alternatives Arising from a Major Economic Development Event. In *Resource Communities: A Decade of Disruption*, eds. D. D. Detomasi and J. W. Gartrell. Boulder, Colo.: Westview Press.

Shands, W. E., and R. G. Healy. 1977. *The Lands Nobody Wanted: Policy for National Forests in the Eastern United States*. Washington, D.C.: The Conservation Foundation.

Shankland, G. 1988. *Wanted Work: A Guide to the Informal Economy.* Croton-on-Hudson, N.Y.: Bootstrap Press.

Shepard, J. C., et al. 1992. *Measuring Distress: Economic Indicators and the Great Plains.* Denver: Center for the New West.

Smilor, R., D. V. Gibson, and G. Kozmetsky. 1988. *Creating the Technopolis: Linking Technology Commercialization and Economic Development.* Cambridge, Mass.: Ballinger.

Smith, C. 1979. *Salmon Fishers of the Columbia.* Corvallis: Oregon State University Press.

Smith, E., et al. 1982. A Modified Regression Base Multiplier Model. *Growth and Change* 12 (1): 17–22.

Smith, G. 1986. Transfer Payments and Investment Incomes: Sources of Growth and Cyclical Stability for Nonmetro Counties of Oregon and Washington. *Agricultural Research Center Bulletin* 0981, College of Agriculture, Washington State University, Pullman.

Smith, M. 1989. *Beyond the Glitter.* Lexington, Ky.: Southeast Women's Employment Coalition.

Snyder, D. L., and W. C. Lewis. 1989. The Size and Role of Agriculture in Utah. Research Report 129, Utah Agricultural Experiment Station, Utah State University, Logan, Utah.

Sowell, T. 1980. *Knowledge and Decisions.* New York: Basic Books.

Stabler, J. C., and M. R. Olfert. 1994. Saskatchewan's Rural Communities in an Urbanizing World. *Rural Development Perspectives* 9 (2): 21–27.

Steinnes, D. N. 1978. Causality and Migration: A Statistical Resolution of the Chicken or Egg Fowl-Up. *Southern Economic Journal* 38 (2): 218–24.

———. 1982. Do People Follow Jobs or Do Jobs Follow People? A Causality Issue in Urban Economics. *Urban Studies* 19 (2): 187–92.

Summers, G., and T. Hirschl. 1985. Retirees As a Growth Industry. *Rural Development Perspectives* 1 (2): 13–16.

Tarlow, P. E., and M. J. Muehsam. 1992. Wide Horizons: Travel and Tourism in the Coming Decade. *The Futurist* 26 (5): 28–33.

Templet, P. H., and S. Farber. 1994. The Complementarity between Environmental and Economic Risk: An Empirical Analysis. *Ecological Economics* 9 (2): 153–65.

Thurow, L. 1989. *Toward a High-Wage, High-Productivity Service Sector.* Washington, D.C.: Economic Policy Institute.

Tiebout, C. 1956. Exports and Regional Economic Growth. *Journal of Political Economy* 64 (2): 160–64.

———. 1956. A Pure Theory of Local Expenditures. *Journal of Political Economy* 64 (4): 416–24.

———. 1962. *The Community Economic Base Study.* New York: Committee for Economic Development.

Torell, L., et al. 1992. The Importance of Public Lands to Livestock Production in the U.S. Range Improvement Task Force Report 32, Agricultural Experiment Station, Cooperative Extension Service, College of Agriculture, New Mexico State University, Las Cruces.

Ullman, E. 1954. Amenities As a Factor in Regional Growth. *Geographical Review* 44 (1): 119–32.

Uresk, D. W. 1985. Effects of Controlling Black-Tailed Prairie Dogs on Plant Production. *Journal of Range Management* 38 (5): 466–68.

Uresk, D. W., and A. J. Bjugstad. 1981. Effects of Prairie Dogs and Cattle on Vegetation of the Northern High Plains. *South Dakota Stockgrower* (May): 10–27.

U.S. Bureau of Labor Statistics. 1988. Labor Force Statistics Derived from the Current Population Survey. Bulletin No. 2307, p. 1470.

———. 1993. Productivity Measures for Selected Industries and Government Services. Bulletin No. 2421.

U.S. Bureau of Mines. Annual. *Mineral Commodity Summaries.*

U.S. Bureau of Reclamation. 1977. Preliminary Information and Data Sheets for CAP. Central Arizona Project Office, Phoenix, Arizona.

U.S. Bureau of the Census. Various years. *Statistical Abstract of the United States.* Washington, D.C.

U.S. Congressional Budget Office. 1993. Displaced Workers: Trends in the 1980s and Implications for the Future. A CBO Study.

U.S. Department of Agriculture, Economic Research Service. 1987. Measuring the Size of the U.S. Food and Fiber System. Agriculture Economic Report No. 566.

———. 1993. *Rural Conditions and Trends* 4 (4): 12–15.

———. 1994. Nonmetro Population Growth Widespread in Early 1990s, Countering 1980s Trend. *Rural Conditions and Trends* 5 (1): 14–17.

U.S. Department of Agriculture, Forest Service, and Department of the Interior, Bureau of Land Management. 1992. Grazing Fee Review and Evaluation Update of the 1986 Final Report. Report of the Secretaries of Agriculture and the Interior, April 30, 1992.

U.S. Department of Commerce, Bureau of Domestic Commerce. 1976. Study of the Expected Impact on the Forest Products Industries of Assumed Nationwide Application of the Monongahela-Tongass Court Decisions.

U.S. Forest Service. 1963. Timber Trends in Western Oregon and Western Washington. Research Paper PNW-5, Pacific Northwest Forest and Range Experiment Station, Portland, Oregon.

———. 1969. Douglas-Fir Supply Study. Pacific Northwest Range and Experiment Station, Portland, Oregon.

———. 1990. Economic Diversity and Dependency Assessment, draft. Rocky Mountain Region, Denver.

U.S. General Accounting Office. 1992. Mineral Resources: Value of Hardrock

Minerals Extracted from and Remaining on Federal Lands. GAO/ RCED-92-192, August.

U.S. Water Resource Council. 1979. Manual of Procedures for Evaluating Benefits and Costs of Federal Water Resources Projects. 44 Fed. Reg. 30194, May 24.

———. 1982. Guidelines for Economic and Social Analysis. 47 Federal Regulations 17942, April 26, 1982.

Walsh, N. 1984. Impact of Copper Smelter Emissions on Subalpine Vegetation in the Anaconda-Pintlar Range. Master's thesis, Environmental Studies, University of Montana, Missoula.

Walsh, R. G., et al. 1988. Review of Outdoor Recreation Economic Demand: Studies with Nonmarket Benefit Estimates, 1968–88. Colorado Water Resources Research Institute Technical Report 54. Colorado State University, Fort Collins.

Weber, A. 1929 [1909]. *Theory of the Location of Industries*. Trans. C. Friedrich. Chicago: University of Chicago Press.

Whitelaw, E. 1992. Testimony before the U.S. Senate Subcommittee on Environmental Protection, Committee on Environment and Public Works, May 13, 1992. 102d Cong., 2d sess., May 13.

Wilkinson, C. F. 1992. *Crossing the Next Meridian: Land, Water, and the Future of the West*. Washington, D.C.: Island Press.

Wilson, P. N. 1992. An Economic Assessment of Central Arizona Project Agriculture: A Report to the Office of the Governor and the Arizona Department of Water Resources. College of Agriculture, University of Arizona, Tucson.

Winterbottom, B. 1991. Tourism. *Economic Development Commentary* 15 (3): 9–16.

Wiseman, R. F. 1980. Why Older People Move: Theoretical Issues. *Research on Aging* 2 (2): 141–54.

World Future Society. 1994. Tourism Tomorrow. *The Futurist* 28 (1): 49–50.

World Resources Institute. 1994. Food and Agriculture. In *World Resources: A Guide to the Global Environment, 1994–95*. New York: Oxford University Press.

Worldwatch Institute. 1994. *State of the World, 1994*. New York: Norton.

Wuerthner, G. 1994. Subdivisions versus Agriculture. *Conservation Biology* 8 (3): 904–8.

Yaffee, S. L. 1994. *The Wisdom of the Spotted Owl: Policy Lessons for a New Century*. Washington, D.C.: Island Press.

Young, R. A., and W. E. Martin. 1967. The Economics of Arizona's Water Problem. *Arizona Review* 16 (3): 9–18. Division of Economic and Business Research, University of Arizona, Tucson.

Index

Rental values and tourism, 219
Resettlement of nonmetropolitan
    areas, 4
Residential/commercial sprawl, 244–46
Resort towns, 218–19, 220
Retail trade, 64
Retirees, 12, 39, 47, 48
Royalties collected on mineral
    extraction, 121–28
Rural areas, 89, 135
    see also specific topic areas

Salmon, 1–2
Scarcity of raw materials, 116, 192–93
Scientific reality vs. appearance, 207–8
Self-employed business people, 190
Self-reinforcing stimulation of local
    economy, 40
Self-sufficiency, rise of local, 48–50
A sense of place, 237–38
Service-producing industries, 64, 79
Services sector, 37–38
    see also Shift in employment/income
        from goods to services
Sheep, 183, 202–6
Shift in employment/income from goods
    to services, 57
    advantages of, 240–41
    demonizing service jobs, 65–75
    local economic well-being influenced
        by, 78–88
    negative feelings about service sector,
        61–63
    problems associated with, 75–78
    quality of service jobs, 63–65
    wages, depressed, 58–61
Skill level of service jobs, 73–75
Slavery, 189
Socioeconomic analysis by resort devel-
    opers, 223–28
Socioeconomic perspective on agricul-
    ture, 188–90
Sodium monofluoroacetate, 201, 206
Software design, 65
Sources of local economic vitality,
    31–33
Southwest, desert, 14
Specialization, 4, 12, 43

Sprawl, residential/commercial, 244–46
Squeezed middle phenomenon, 70
Strychnine and prairie dogs, 206–11
Subsidies for agriculture, 171, 199
Suburbanization of U.S. metropolitan
    areas, 14
Summitville Consolidated Mining
    Company (Colorado), 128–29
Supply and demand interactions,
    154–55, 174, 196
Sustained yield, 136

Temporary work forces, 109
Tenure, job, 26
Texas Department of Agriculture, 206
Timber industry, 1
    community stability and social
        forestry, 134–36, 146–48
    impact of federal supplies on local
        economy, 158–59
    income stability, 138–40
    job stability, 140–42
    mills, local, 157–58
    policy through the century, 131–33
    shifting frontiers, 136–38
    wages, 142–43
    as a way of life, 144–46
    see also Forest management
Tokyo, 174
Total economy, 19, 21, 27–28
Tourism, 162, 213
    advantages/disadvantages, 215–21
    alternative, 231–33
    Canmore (Canada), 221–30
    as economic development, 233–34
    Native Americans, 230–31
    travel industry statistics, 214–15
Toxics, 22, 119, 120, 128–29
Trade, global, 58–59, 60
Transients in resort towns, 220
Travel industry statistics, 214–15
Traveling and retirement income, 47

Unemployment, 27, 164
Unions, 58, 59
Utah, 183
Utah State University, 178–81